Faith in the Future

Faith in the Future

*Healthcare, Aging,
and the Role of Religion*

Harold G. Koenig, M.D.
Douglas M. Lawson, Ph.D.

with Malcolm McConnell

TEMPLETON FOUNDATION PRESS
Philadelphia and London

Templeton Foundation Press
Five Radnor Corporate Center, Suite 120
100 Matsonford Road
Radnor, Pennsylvania 19087
www.templetonpress.org

Templeton Foundation Press helps intellectual leaders and others learn about science research on aspects of realities, invisible and intangible. Spiritual realities include unlimited love, accelerating creativity, worship, and the benefits of purpose in persons and in the cosmos.

Designed and typeset by Gopa and Ted2, Inc.
Printed by Sheridan Books in the United States of America

Library of Congress Cataloging-in-Publication Data
Koenig, Harold George.
   Faith in the future : healthcare, aging, and the role of religion / Harold G. Koenig and Douglas M. Lawson, with Malcolm McConnell.
      p.   cm.
Includes bibliographical references and index.
   ISBN 1-932031-35-9 (hc : alk. paper)
   1. Aged—Medical care—United States—Religious aspects.
2. Religious health facilities—United States. 3. Aging—United States—Religious aspects. 4. Pastoral medicine—United States.
5. Medicine—United States—Religious aspects. 6. Public health—United States—Forecasting. 7. Population—Health aspects—United States. I. Lawson, Douglas M., 1936- II. McConnell, Malcolm P., 1962- III. Title.
   RA564.8 .K625 2004
   362.198'97'00973—dc22

                                                        2003016626

04 05 06 07 08   10 9 8 7 6 5 4 3 2 1

To All Those Who Give of Themselves
Because of Their Faith

Contents

Faith in the Future

Introduction

IN MARCH 2001, a historic conference, "Faith in the Future, Religion, Aging, and Healthcare in the 21st Century," was held at Duke University. Sponsored by the Gerontological Society of America, Duke University School of Medicine Office of Continuing Medical Education, Duke Center for the Study of Aging & Human Development, Duke Department of Psychiatry & Behavioral Sciences, and the John Templeton Foundation, this conference brought together internationally renowned leaders in medicine, healthcare policy, religion, government, the media, and hundreds of healthcare and religious professionals, as well as lay members of diverse religious communities.

They examined one of the most serious issues in today's society: What are the challenges facing healthcare in America, and will the members of America's 350,000 religious congregations be able to help prevent or lessen the looming healthcare crisis unleashed by relentless demographic pressures and rising costs? *Faith in the Future* presents a synthesis of the March 2001 Duke University conference and expands on the themes raised there, citing the most recent available research findings and offering many more compelling human examples to provide readers with empathetic role models they can emulate.

Over the next several decades, our elderly population will swell inexorably, and there will be an equally dramatic increase of older people with chronic health problems and disabilities needing long-term healthcare. At the same time, the costs of providing that care, which are already soaring despite all efforts by government and managed-care organizations to limit expenditures, will continue to rise.

Soon these demographic and health-economic trends will clash in what could well prove to be the most serious societal problem in modern history: widespread shortages of increasingly costly healthcare for the growing elderly population.

But it is not inevitable that the looming crisis ends in catastrophe. The situation is full of opportunities for individuals and institutions to make important contributions unique in our country's history. Seniors will have the opportunity to derive true meaning and purpose in their lives by investing their energies and skills in the care and well-being of other members of their religious congregations and wider communities. Within innovative networks of community support, older adults will have the opportunity to live with dignity in their own homes, rather than being automatically shunted off to anonymous, dispiriting institutions to spend their remaining days. Religious institutions ranging in size from a small alliance of congregations to an entire denomination can lead a critical effort to help alleviate a potentially major social disaster by sponsoring effective volunteer programs that reach out to those in need. While making this contribution, religious institutions will also have the opportunity to make a real difference in society at a time when the perceived role of religion in contemporary culture is losing its importance in the face of the juggernaut of scientific and medical progress. Finally, the pending crisis offers healthcare institutions themselves the opportunity to reorient their approach toward providing whole-person care that is cost effective and satisfying for patients and health professionals alike.

But before examining these opportunities, we must take an honest look at the extent of the problems we face. One of the most pressing current problems concerns Health Maintenance Organizations (HMOs) for senior citizens. Many HMOs no longer accept Medicare patients who cannot afford private insurance, and these indigent elderly are shunted aside to somehow fend for themselves. Those who might believe that even discussing these issues is needlessly alarmist need only reflect on the story of the late Robert DeGray.

The last two years of Robert DeGray's life were haunted by disease and anxiety. In his mid-eighties in 1999, the retired Clearwater, Florida, security guard was afflicted by emphysema, throat cancer, and prostate cancer, which were kept in check through the treatment and affordable prescription drugs he received from his Medicare-funded HMO, Prudential Health Care. Like millions of other older Americans, DeGray lived frugally on his Social Security benefits of about $1200 a month. Medicare provided his sole health insurance.

DeGray had been satisfied with his HMO until October 1999, when Prudential suddenly announced that, because of rising costs not matched by government reimbursements, the organization would begin charging its members a monthly premium of $65, an additional fee for clinic visits, raise the patient co-payment for prescription drugs, and also place a drastic cost cap on annual prescription coverage, which would drop from $2000 a year to only $750.

One afternoon in December 1999, DeGray's son, Jim, 57, was shocked and saddened to find his father sitting at the kitchen table of the mobile home they shared. The older man was methodically cutting his medication tablets in half, desperately hoping to stretch the supply a little longer.

"Dad," Jim DeGray said, "you can't do that. The medicine won't do you any good at half strength."

His father nodded stoically. "I just can't afford my prescriptions anymore, Jim. They cost around five hundred dollars a month. If I can't spend more than seven-fifty a *year*, I'll be out of pocket for the whole thing by the middle of February. Then there are the new premiums and charges. You know how much my Social Security check is."

Jim DeGray took a part-time job at a drycleaners to help his father pay for the prescription drugs. But that solution did not solve the problem of paying for the older DeGray's most expensive medication. Once every three months, he received a shot of the hormone Lupron to keep his metastatic prostate cancer from spreading. The medication was very effective, but also very expensive: $2,500 per treatment for an annual total of $10,000. For the moment, the HMO covered the cost of Lupron, but announced it was reconsidering that coverage. Robert DeGray was tormented by images of the cancer taking root across his body.

While his HMO continued to pay for this costly treatment, he and Jim struggled to meet the steadily rising costs of the older man's care. But in July 2000, Prudential announced it would be shutting down its Medicare HMOs in the area. Like so many other companies nationwide, Prudential was forced to confront mounting expenses and low government reimbursements that did not match these costs.

Feeling abandoned by the Medicare system he had trusted for so many years, Robert DeGray told his son, "I might as well just die. There's no way I can afford a regular doctor."

Jim DeGray was upset by his father's words, but understood the elderly man's pessimism.

Although low-cost managed care was the best option for his multiple afflictions and small pension, health insurance companies all around his region were now closing Medicare HMOs.

Luckily, Jim DeGray was able to quickly enroll his father in a Blue Cross and Blue Shield program that looked like it would provide good care at low costs.

Then that HMO also raised its monthly premium, while imposing a ceiling on prescription drug coverage of $250 every six months for an annual maximum of $500. Robert DeGray's primary care physicians were also changed twice in nine months as the company fought to contain costs.

But the true hammer blow to DeGray's morale came in late summer 2001, when he learned that this new HMO would also go out of business the next January 1. Certain he would never receive adequate care, he died in a hospice that October.

——————

Although Robert DeGray had anticipated the pain and discomfort of his failing health, he had never expected the unending complications and frustrations of securing adequate, reliable care just when he needed it so badly.

Originally, he had been well satisfied with his Prudential Medicare HMO, where he had his own regular doctor who also referred him to the specialists working within the system. This sense of stability, as well as the prescription drug coverage that the HMO provided free under DeGray's Medicare coverage, gave him great emotional comfort. Robert DeGray recognized the serious nature of his illnesses, but he also felt he was benefiting from high-quality care paid for by Medicare, which, like his Social Security pension, he would never lose.

But when the security of his healthcare began to crumble, anxiety took grip of DeGray and did not release him. Like millions of other elderly people across the country who faced the problem of their Medicare HMOs suddenly and unexpectedly closing, he was frightened and confused. Would he find an HMO that provided the same coverage he had enjoyed at Prudential? If not, how would he ever cope with the inevitable deterioration of his health while he and his son searched for a practice that would accept Medicare as his sole health insurance and also provide him prescription drugs he could not afford to buy?

This question haunted him up to the time of his death.

——————

How typical was Robert DeGray's troubling experience? Is his unfortunate story representative of his own or future generations of very elderly Americans? According to AARP (known as the American Association of Retired Persons until 2000), the organization has received "countless" letters of complaint from members who—like DeGray—have been abandoned by their Medicare HMOs and have had to scramble to find some form of coverage, which is invariably much less generous and flexible than their earlier managed care. There are almost always higher premiums, no free prescription drugs, and drastic annual caps on prescription reimbursement, one of the benefits the ill elderly can least afford to lose.

And Medicare-funded HMO coverage is simply disappearing in many states. In December 2000, for example, after aggressively marketing its Medi-CareFirst HMO coverage in the mid-1990s, Blue Cross Blue Shield of Maryland shut down—citing inadequate federal reimbursement for services in the face of rising costs—leaving thousands of elderly patients to search for affordable coverage. Senior citizens in neighboring Delaware faced the same problem in 2000, as Medicare HMOs closed for the second consecutive year. Across the country, a similar healthcare crisis prevailed. By federal regulation, Medicare HMOs can arbitrarily cancel coverage on December 31, and none has an obligation toward its patients beyond a year-by-year contract.

Delaware's insurance commissioner, Donna Lee H. Williams, has severely criticized this policy. "The purpose of the Medicare Program is to give our seniors a sense of security regarding their healthcare needs," she observed. "Under its current structure, however, the Medicare HMO option provides no such security."

But the situation is not likely to improve unless we begin to reconsider our traditional concepts of professional healthcare, as well as personal and community responsibility toward prevention and wellness promotion.

The harsh projections of demographics make it clear that the relentless expansion of our elderly population will overpower the limited resources of our public and privately funded healthcare much sooner than most of us care to contemplate.

In 1999, Edward L. Schneider, dean of the Leonard Davis School of Gerontology, Ethel Percy Andrus Gerontology Center at the University of California, Los Angeles, published a provocative policy article in the journal *Science*, "Aging in the Third Millennium." Citing conservative and widely accepted demographic projections, Schneider showed that the number of Americans 65 and older will most likely increase from 35 million in 2000 to at least 78 million by 2050. His 1999 estimate for 2050 is no doubt on the low side, as the current Administration on Aging of the U.S. Department of Health and Human Services projects the increase in people 65 and older to 77 million as early as 2040.

Further, Census Bureau middle series estimates foresee a population of 80 million Americans over 65 by 2050. But the actual number could be closer to 100 million if advances in stem cell and genetics research continue steadily. According to health scientists, most of the improved longevity in the past two decades has been due to medical advances that have expanded lifespan after the age of 65. These increases in longevity will continue. Ed Schneider has no doubt of this. In the near future, "most Americans will live into their 80s," he wrote in *Science.*

The projected increase in the population of Americans aged 85 and above will clearly be dramatic. Some demographers envision a jump in this group from about 4 million in 2000 to at least 18 million by 2050. Indeed, Schneider points out that the Census Bureau projects the actual number of these "very old Americans" at over 30 million by 2050, based on high series estimates.

These projections concern numbers, not the relative health or disability of older people.

As one considers these dry estimates, it is essential to remember the lessons of Robert DeGray's final years. The steady growth of our older population poses a serious threat to the Medicare system itself, not just to Medicare-funded HMOs, which are now collapsing nationwide. If we are struggling even now to meet the needs of 35 million persons over age 65 in this country, how will Medicare, the principal form of health insurance for most elderly, meet the needs of between 18 and 30 million people over 85 — many with multiple disabilities similar to DeGray's that require expensive treatment — in 2050?

We do not have to look so far into the future to pose that question. Department of Health and Human Services research shows that the cost of Medicare will quickly rise as the population ages. The projected yearly Medicare budget for 2011 is $450.1 billion (compared to $224 billion in 2000). But that estimate avoids the fact that the 80 million members of the Baby Boom generation will not reach age 65 until just *after* 2011. No federal agency will make healthcare budget estimates for beyond 2011. That is a sobering reality.

In his article, Schneider has set out two scenarios that address the "major uncertainty" of healthcare and the aging population. Under Scenario 1, the public and private sectors increase their funding to engage in "appropriate levels" of aging research, disease prevention, and breakthroughs in treatment. Dramatic progress is made toward conquering the present-day primary causes of disability among the elderly: cardiovascular disease, cancer, diabetes and its complications, and so on. As a result of such intervention today, Schneider predicts, "the average health of a future 85-year-old in the year 2040 resembles that of a current 70-year-old with relatively modest needs for acute [hospital] and long-term care."

But in Schneider's Scenario 2, the current low levels of spending and relative neglect of health research, disease prevention, and breakthroughs in treatment extend into the future. This results in only small improvements in the average health of the elderly in the future. However, there will be many more members of the over-85 age group. If they are just as infirm as Robert DeGray, they will place an unsupportable strain on the healthcare system.

Medicare-funded HMOs will no doubt have become a distant memory by 2040. Under Schneider's Scenario 2, securing long-term care (in nursing homes and rehabilitation hospitals) for the large numbers of very elderly will be a major challenge. And Schneider indicates that treating these people in their homes or in skilled-care nursing facilities is almost nine times more expensive than similar treatment for people aged 69 and 70.

In the future, the federal government will probably subsidize some form of prescription drug coverage for Medicare beneficiaries. But it is doubtful that this coverage will meet the needs of the huge population bulge of the very old unless they reach this age in relatively good health, even if the stock market turns around, the economy expands steadily, and projected budget excesses are realized. Since Medicare is a universally accepted entitlement, it is not likely that our political leadership will willingly cut benefits until the system is truly facing ruin. To prevent this collapse, Schneider and others foresee senior citizens forced to cover an increasing share of their own healthcare expenses through rising premiums and co-payments and harshly curtailed treatment. Rather than being an entitlement for all older citizens, Medicare may become a "needs-based" program, limited to the poorest elderly, with related healthcare rationing reserved for the oldest and sickest Americans.

Many elderly people, however, will be healthy enough and have the means to live independently, either in their own homes or in retirement communities, locations ranging from traditional neighborhoods to mobile-home parks to resort-like centers featuring their own clinics, recreational facilities, dining, and food catering. These people will have a relatively light impact on healthcare costs.

But for millions of older people in coming decades, even a dilapidated trailer home or camper may be financially inaccessible. It will be this poorest and sickest segment of the swollen elderly population that will present the largest problem. Schneider predicts that assisted-living and acute-care facilities will feel the greatest impact of their numbers. Those who have been paralyzed by stroke, lost feet or legs to diabetes, or are debilitated by emphysema will need specialized long-term care or the help of an assisted-living facility. But it is probable there will not be enough nursing homes to care for these people.

Under Schneider's optimistic Scenario 1, the growing elderly population will reach old age in relative good health. Therefore, the anticipated modest expansion of nursing homes and assisted-living facilities will meet the needs of future generations of seniors.

But under Scenario 2, tens of millions of older Americans enter the final decades of life in failing health, many with multiple disabilities. These "frail elderly" would require greatly increased home care, admissions to acute-care hospitals, or long-term care in nursing homes, which will have become "semi-acute hospitals with long waiting lists."

In the worst-case view of this scenario, the poorest and sickest will simply find no place in affordable government-funded long-term care. "If they do not have relatives, significant others, or friends to take care of them, we may face the gruesome prospect of poor, disabled, homeless older Americans living out the end of their lives on city streets and in parks," Schneider predicts.

Is there any way to prevent this grim view of the future from becoming reality? The simple answer is yes. And one source of this optimism lies in what will be for many an unexpected direction: religious faith and practice and the compassion of America's 350,000 faith communities and congregations.

There is a steadily growing body of scientific evidence that religious involvement is associated with better physical health, a greater sense of well-being, less depression, and a reduced need for health services, including hospital stays. Hundreds of research studies conducted at our leading institutions seem to indicate that religious beliefs and practices help people of all ages cope better with stress, increase their contact with helpful social-support networks, and discourage activity that has a negative impact on their health: drug and alcohol abuse, smoking, and high-risk sexual behavior, which all contribute to disease and disability. Further, the stress reduction and amelioration of depression that are associated with religious involvement have been demonstrated to be key components in the prevention of serious illness such as cardiovascular disease. Religious faith and involvement have also been shown to foster an overall positive mental attitude, assist in positive decision making, and may reduce the likelihood of acquiring preventable illness at all ages.

This "religiosity" also encourages responsibility, commitment, and concern and generosity toward others. The improved health across the lifespan among religious people, from adolescence through old age, may lower their need for expensive healthcare services. Equally important, religious faith and practice enhance the willingness and ability of elders to provide nonprofessional "healthcare" and sustain their emotional support of others on a volunteer basis.

It is quite possible that these religiously motivated volunteers will emerge as a pivotal factor preventing the complete degradation of our healthcare system in coming decades. And, by stepping forward to meet the needs of their congregations and broader communities, these volunteers will personally derive unexpected and unique health benefits.

Even sick and disabled elderly can often assume meaningful roles within their caring faith communities: telephoning to check on other homebound elders, praying with them or bringing them into prayer chains within the faith community, simply listening to them to promote a positive outlook and relieve their painful isolation, and organizing get-well card mailings (cards are now available free over the Internet). If they are physically able, the elderly with lesser disabilities can assist at child-care centers and mentor young people in vocational or academic subjects. Such interaction will enhance the meaning of the elders' life-long experiences and foster in the young a sense of respect for people with whom they normally would not have much contact.

When the disabled elderly are still physically capable of volunteering for such activities as speaking over the telephone, folding and addressing get-well cards, or mentoring children, they invariably enjoy a personal shift toward more hopeful, optimistic attitudes, which may also translate into better physical health and less need for health services. Even if the improvement in physical health is not significant in traditional clinical terms, these optimistic seniors are often less of a burden on others and on the healthcare system.

For centuries, religious organizations have reached out to the poor, the elderly and afflicted, and all those in need of care—the very people Edward Schneider suggested might live out their final years in lonely misery on our city streets. Assisting the downtrodden is a theological mandate as well as a central concern for all the monotheistic faith traditions. Therefore, among the potential solutions to the pending healthcare crisis, there is a major role for the faith community.

One of the most important questions we as a nation—indeed, all the industrialized nations of the world—now face is how we will address the lurking societal crisis of our expanding elderly population and steeply rising healthcare costs. How can we encourage disease prevention and healthy living on an unprecedented scale in our population today in order to minimize health problems that will require increasingly expensive care tomorrow?

How should we raise our children so that they will be prepared for the future burdens—as well as for the future opportunities—they will confront when the traditional demographic pyramid with a broad base of youth and a small apex of the very elderly is turned upside down? This is a crucial question: What can we do now to prepare young people for a society in which they might view such a large proportion of the elderly population as weak, dependent, and simply worthless? Today's children and youth must learn that all people, no matter how physically frail, have spiritual value and are worthy of respect. If this lesson is not instilled today through greater contact between the very young and the very old—perhaps within the nurturing atmosphere of a faith community—the gap between the young and the old will no doubt widen. The disabled elderly will be seen as expendable, obvious candidates for euthanasia or physician-assisted suicide.

Is this prospect overly extreme? Not if you examine the inroads these two practices have already made. The State of Oregon and the European nations of Belgium and the Netherlands (both of which have a high proportion of older elderly) now permit euthanasia or physician-assisted suicide. Experts predict that the practice of assisting the terminally ill (or simply the frail elderly) into death will spread across the industrialized world if the inherent human value of all individuals is not recognized.

—⸻—

How will we provide quality healthcare to older adults who will need it during the next thirty to fifty years? Who will provide this care? How will it be funded? And how can we now establish systems of care in place as demographic and health-related economic pressures mount?

It is essential that we study the actual nature of aging now so that we can nurture *successful* aging and purpose-filled retirement to enhance the quality of the last third of life.

While the monumental policy issues that will affect trillions of dollars in state healthcare expenditures, Medicare, and Social Security budgets over the coming decades are being debated in Congress and in the news media, the nation's religious congregations and faith-based communities are quietly working to build effective practical models of care that bring together the elderly in need with millions of volunteers willing to meet those needs.

How well are they fulfilling that mission? Success requires traditional preaching from the pulpit on the need to care for one another, for the faithful to give of their time and finances, and to train their children to do the same. This approach is not very popular in many congregations that are accustomed to being entertained once a week, not to having new responsibilities thrust on them. But this entertainment expectation is exactly why many churches are dying: They haven't sufficiently involved members of their congregations in the vision and role of the church, and some clergy and lay leaders do not even understand that vision — particularly with regard to addressing the health needs of their present and future congregations. But there is hope.

———

Four years ago, Natalie Romine, a retired Kansas City, Missouri, county court social worker in her mid-eighties, suffered severely from advanced osteoporosis. The mineral loss in the bones of her spine had advanced to the point that she was bent over almost 90 degrees from the waist. Her prospects were grim. Because she lived alone, it was almost certain that she would no longer be able to care for herself as the disability steadily worsened. Although she was still able to drive her car during the day, that independence would soon be lost to Natalie as her condition deteriorated. Her worst fear was falling and breaking a hip, which she knew would result in a long — perhaps permanent — stay in a rehabilitation hospital or nursing home.

A life-long devout Protestant, she found comfort in prayer, but did not expect any miraculous improvement in her osteoporosis. Then, one day in 1999, a friend suggested, "Natalie, do go to the Shepherd's Center. They have a wonderful exercise program that just may help you."

The first Shepherd's Center — a reference to "The LORD is my shepherd" of the Twenty-Third Psalm — had been created by the Reverend Elbert C. Cole, pastor of a Kansas City United Methodist church, in 1972. The purpose of the program was to offer senior citizen participants the chance to enrich and fulfill their lives through volunteer work and ongoing study, as well as to provide health-enhancement instruction — screening and monitoring, nutritional advice, and weight management. Shepherd's Centers were based on the premise that the religious elderly were prepared to serve as volunteers, putting their faith into action and working with community partners for the common good. Centered on religious congregations, seventy-nine Shepherd's Centers are active thirty years after Rev. Cole started the original program.

The "exercise" classes Natalie Romine found at the Shepherd's Center involved T'ai Chi Chih, a relatively recent variant of ancient Chinese meditation-and-exercise disciplines adapted for Western practitioners by American Asian expert Justin Stone in 1974. T'ai Chi Chih entails twenty slow, rhythmic, circular arm, torso, and leg movements meant to improve emotional harmony while increasing physical strength and restoring a sense of balance in people like Natalie, whose strength and balance are failing.

Her first Shepherd's Center T'ai Chi Chih instructor was Jean Smith, an elderly woman who led a small group of people ranging in age from their late sixties to almost ninety. Natalie learned all the basics from Jean Smith, and when Jean withdrew because of illness, Lucy Ann Fleischman, a T'ai Chi Chih instructor and avid enthusiast, took over the group.

After eleven months of ongoing instruction and practice with Lucy Ann, Natalie's legs were dramatically stronger, her balance greatly improved. She no longer felt that the osteoporosis had seized her in a cruel vise and was bending her in half. Then, one afternoon a year after beginning T'ai Chi Chih instruction, she was combing her hair before the bathroom mirror. It had been several years since she had been able to straighten her shoulders high enough to see her face in the mirror. But suddenly her head and smiling face appeared.

She was overcome with tearful gratitude. Lucy Ann Fleischman and all the others at the Shepherd's Center had devoted so much time to her. Now that devotion had borne fruit.

To repay some of the generosity she had received, Natalie accompanied Lucy Ann to demonstrate T'ai Chi Chih to the elderly residents of a retirement home. Natalie avidly described the dramatic improvements in balance, flexibility, and leg strength she now enjoyed.

Since then, Natalie Romine has undergone open-heart surgery and, during her recuperation, lost much of the strength she had gained through practicing T'ai Chi Chih. But now that she has recovered, she plans to resume the program, practicing at home and with a new Shepherd's Center group.

Her experience with T'ai Chi Chih introduced her to the many opportunities available at the Shepherd's Center, which she enthusiastically describes as "a wonderful place." Beyond continuing her exercises, she looks forward to taking part in the center's oral history program. All her professional life she was involved with the careful record keeping of the court system. Now, with the project, she can bring to new elderly friends many of the skills she acquired in her lifetime.

Through the Shepherd's Center, Natalie Romine has overcome the potential disabilities of crippling osteoporosis and heart disease. She still lives independently in her own home. Instead of being a burden on her community, Natalie is able to make a valid and fulfilling contribution.

Faith in the Future does not flinch in its assessment of the challenge our country faces. America confronts a social and economic threat of unprecedented complexity and severity as the healthcare crisis approaches. Further, the book presents a succinct lesson on the demographics of our aging population, their spiraling healthcare costs, and the potentially crippling pressures those soaring costs place on our acute and long-term care institutions and systems of privately and publicly funded health insurance.

From a more optimistic perspective, *Faith in the Future* reviews the impressive and growing body of scientific research linking disease prevention with healthy living, which is in turn associated with religious faith and practice. Studies suggest that devout members of religious congregations might be particularly shielded from such chronic debilitating afflictions as heart disease and certain cancers—perhaps due to the reduced stress and lower depression levels they enjoy and their mutual concern for fellow congregants, which in turn follows the millennia-old religious tradition of caring for the ill.

This ancient caring tradition has led to thousands of religious communities nationwide that fill a need similar to that of the Shepherd's Centers by providing support networks for the elderly. All of the most effective religious social-support communities rely on dedicated volunteers of all ages, who likely derive both emotional and more tangible physical health benefits. For the elderly, spending their mature years in purpose-filled retirement has proven especially beneficial.

As it becomes increasingly clear that "caring" for the frail elderly involves more than medical intervention, we hope that millions of Americans will step forward to help their religious congregations form practical partnerships with healthcare systems, government, and philanthropic efforts to empower faith-based communities to meet the challenge ahead.

This is a book for adults of all ages, of all educational and socioeconomic backgrounds, of all health conditions, and of all faiths. It is of particular relevance for the post–World War II Baby Boom generation and their children, the group that soon will be entering the healthcare foray. The authors also have much to say to the clergy who lead the country's 350,000 congregations; they have taken sacred vows to help care for aging members and their families who increasingly will have nowhere else to go.

Those among the 7 million healthcare and social-service professionals, desperately searching for resources to provide care for aging patients, will find practical direction and guidance on how to prepare to meet this need by drawing on the resources of volunteers and religious congregations. The general reader will find that the book's ultimate message is positive, inspiring, and hopeful, one that speaks of the great opportunity for every person to find personal fulfillment by making a true and lasting difference in our society at this critical time in history.

Part I

The Dilemma and Challenge

Our Aging Population:
The Dilemma and Challenge

1

THE MOST RECENT census data confirm that our elderly population is growing at an unprecedented pace. During the twentieth century, the percentage of the American population 65 and older more than tripled from 4.1 to 12.4 percent. Comparing the 1900 and 2000 census data is revealing in other ways: In 2000, there were eight times (18.4 million) more people in the 65–74 age group, sixteen times (12.4 million) more people 75–84, and thirty-four times (4.2 million) more people over age 85 than there were in 1900. That trend is accelerating: In the thirty years between 1965 and 1995, America's population age 65 and older grew by 82 percent.

The looming population explosion among older Americans is due in large part to those aged 45–64 today — who will reach 65 in the next twenty years — a "cohort" that swelled 34 percent in the 1990s. They are the 76 million members of the Baby Boom generation born between 1946 and 1964, whose sheer numbers have jolted the American social landscape and economy for over fifty years. As they age, the impact of their generation's size will continue to send shock waves through the country. The Social Security pension system and Medicare will be particularly challenged by the financial and health-care needs of the Baby Boomers.

We need only to observe the current state of healthcare for the relatively smaller number of elderly today — compared to the huge post–World War II generation rapidly approaching retirement — to understand the dimensions of the problems that lie ahead. Advances in medicine now allow people with chronic conditions such as cardiovascular disease, cancer, diabetes, kidney failure, and Alzheimer's to live longer, but often with disabilities that require ongoing costly healthcare. This care typically includes repeated hospitalization or residential treatment, eventually in nursing homes funded privately or through state Medicaid. (Medicare does not fund nursing home stays except for the first one hundred days following a qualifying acute hospitalization. Overall, such care makes up less than 10 percent of nursing home costs; the remaining 90 percent of costs comes from the 25 percent that the patient funds out-of-pocket and the 65 percent that Medicaid pays after a person's assets have been exhausted.)

While medical advances in recent years have helped to decrease health problems among older persons, the relative number of people growing older with chronic disabling conditions has largely neutralized these improvements. Further, it is particularly disturbing that the disability rate among younger persons today is increasing even more rapidly than in older adults.

According to the U.S. Department of Health and Human Services, in 1998, 28.8 percent of people aged 65–74 reported at least one "limitation" in their life caused by a chronic health condition such as heart disease or diabetes. That figure almost doubled to 50.6 percent among those 75 and older. Over a third of all those reporting chronic conditions suffered "severe" disability, with many experiencing difficulty carrying out activities of daily living such as bathing, dressing, eating, and moving about their homes. These people needed help. They got it as best they could from family, friends, and public and private caregivers. But we have to bear in mind that this population group was both proportionally and numerically smaller than the Baby Boom cohort moving relentlessly along behind them on the demographic track.

We must also consider an important factor that has been neglected until quite recently. Today's predictable levels of mortality are not immutable: Projections of the future number of elderly are likely to be gross underestimates due to astounding breakthroughs in clinical treatment, including the emerging revolution in stem cell research that will allow the production of immunologically compatible organs almost at will. Also, the application of new techniques that alter genes and thus make the dream of practical, widespread genetic therapies for such chronic conditions as cancer, cardiovascular disease, diabetes, and kidney failure may easily extend the lifespan of many to well over 80 or possibly even 90 years within two or three decades. A biologic lifespan of about 125 years may even become possible for a significant number of people by mid-century if advances in these areas of medical research fulfill their complete potential. But will the quality of this extended life also advance, or will these "mega-elderly" spend their later decades in frail disability, putting even greater pressure on the overburdened healthcare system?

The issue of independent living will become increasingly important as the giant Baby Boomer cohort begins to reach age 75 in 2021. In 1960, 30 percent of older Americans lived with their children, who met their parents' daily care needs. By 1990, that figure had fallen to 15 percent, and it is still dropping today. In addition, the traditional pool of unpaid care providers for the elderly—

married adult daughters—is fast shrinking as more women work outside the home. If the exploding elderly population cannot be cared for within private homes, growing numbers of older disabled people will need the support of institutions, both public and private. But, as Edward Schneider indicated, it is exactly such institutionalized care, including acute hospital stays, nursing homes, and assisted-living facilities, which is likely to become increasingly expensive and scarce in the coming decades.

It is obvious that securing adequate healthcare for the elderly will remain one of the greatest challenges our country will face in coming years. The United States, however, is not alone in its struggle to meet the health needs of a fast-graying population. In fact, America is ranked thirty-third among developed countries in terms of the proportion of older adult citizens. Around 2050, over 40 percent of the population in many European countries will be over 60 years of age. Even more troubling, due to declining birth rates, within fifty years the ratio of people aged 65 or over (retired) to those age 18–64 (working) will drop from the current level of approximately one-to-five to one-to-two in many developed countries.

Thus, the impact that aging populations will have on societies worldwide will be enormous, placing incredible pressure on young workers and on young families trying both to raise children and care for elderly parents. And whatever the sense of personal obligation younger people feel toward their parents, the governments of countries that have built welfare states to solve social problems (e.g., the European Union) will, no doubt, resort to imposing an increasingly heavy tax burden on younger citizens to meet the growing needs of their older populations.

The world's leading economists and demographers agree that the unprecedented population shift from young to old is now spreading from the developed world to the more affluent developing countries. The United Nations designated 1999 the "Year of the Older Person," reaffirming a recognition that the confluence of lowered fertility and improved health and longevity has generated growing numbers and proportions of elderly throughout the world. In the short term, the older population in developing countries will continue to depend heavily on the traditional support of the extended family to meet their financial, housing, and medical needs—even when there is an adequate healthcare system in place.

To explore the extent of this global challenge, the United Nations convened the Second World Assembly on Aging in Madrid in April 2002. The assembly's findings were predictable, but still sobering: By 2050, the number of people 60 and older worldwide will triple to total 2 billion, or one-in-five of the world's projected global population. Most will be living in rural poverty. United Nations demographer Mohammed Nizamuddin compared the situation in the developed and developing worlds. "In Europe," he said, "countries became rich before they became old. But in the developing world, countries are growing old before they become rich."

Although accurate, his view fails to consider the fact that the United States, Japan, and the European Union do not possess limitless wealth to meet the social and healthcare needs of their expanding elderly populations. And, ironically, it is in the most affluent countries of the developed world that older citizens perhaps face the greatest jeopardy—because they do not have the human safety net of a large traditional family to care for them as they age.

———

This social separation between generations is usually caused by two factors: Adult children who once might have remained in hometowns follow their professions from one location to another, leaving their parents behind. And even if these elderly parents settle in retirement communities—most of which are in the Sunbelt—they often do not forge the human bonds they enjoyed when they were raising their families. A sense of painful isolation, what social psychologists call "anomie," can grow, potentially leading to depression, substance abuse, and loss of purpose and meaning among the aging. This problem is especially acute among the inner-city minority who are already cut off from mainstream society. But religious communities can fill the role of the missing family among the psychologically isolated and physically infirm elderly.

The caring congregation of a church, synagogue, or mosque makes the newly arrived older member welcome and eases the transition to the new community. Congregational programs such as parish nurses and Meals on Wheels sustain the older member, body and spirit.

In the case of retired older people who remain in their hometowns, the comforting presence of a close and loving congregation with its familiar ritual and liturgy provides invaluable emotional support. Many of these religious elderly are themselves caregivers for an even older generation, afflicted by stroke or Alzheimer's. Increasingly, as the older population grows with the aging of Baby Boomers, congregations will have potential volunteers to provide needed respite for caregivers such as these.

What should motivate healthy religious elders to take on the volunteer role? Among Christians, there is a biblical imperative to do so: "The Church should

take loving care of women whose husbands have died, if they don't have anyone else to help them" (1 Timothy 5:3, LIVING BIBLE) is just one of several scriptural references that urges such action by the religious community.

❦

For the millions of older Americans well enough to live independently, finding
or retaining affordable housing will also become an increasing challenge. The
mathematics involved are starkly inflexible: Whether homeowners or renters,
39 percent of today's elderly spend more than a quarter of their income on
housing, compared to 36 percent of homeowners of all ages. But the number
of elderly living on a small fixed income is growing. As out-of-pocket healthcare costs absorb a greater proportion of older people's Social Security and
private pensions, the need for subsidized low-income housing — a national
infrastructure investment that has not kept pace with elderly population
growth — will only increase.

According to the 2000 census, in 1999, there were about 22 million households headed by older persons. Eighty percent owned their homes, and 20 percent rented. Most of the elderly renters aspired to home ownership — or at
least to being able to afford a better class of rental property. Among elderly
homeowners — including the chronically ill and disabled — the desire to
remain living independently in their houses, condominiums, or mobile homes
as long as possible was virtually universal. But the median annual family
income for both older homeowners and renters, $22,500 and $12,500 respectively, hovered at or below the official poverty level.

Unfortunately, the recent collapse of the U.S. stock market has seriously
eroded the private retirement savings on which millions of older Americans
planned to supplement their small Social Security income (on which 44 percent of retirees in 2002 said they depended as their sole source of income,
according to the Employee Benefits Research Institute). Economists point out
that the "younger elderly" (aged 50 to 65) may be able to weather the current
economic storm, remain in the work force a few years longer than planned,
absorb their losses, and wait for the market to rebound. But for untold millions
in the traditional elderly age group, 65 and older, the stock market upheaval was
tantamount to financial disaster. According to the Social Security Administration in 1999, 62 percent of retirees supplemented their Social Security pensions
with investment earnings, generally private stock portfolios in 401(K) plans or
traditional bank savings. Those who have invested heavily in equities face the
greatest financial insecurity.

And now, with the burden of healthcare costs steadily growing heavier, the elderly must increasingly make the difficult decision of spending their limited resources on health or on housing expenses such as rent, mortgage payments, or property taxes. Unless older people have younger family members willing and financially able to help maintain their property, their housing conditions can rapidly deteriorate, especially when they suffer a chronic illness or disability.

However, all this does not mean that the senior housing picture is totally without hope. Indeed, there has been a phenomenal and rising groundswell of faith-based volunteer efforts nationwide to assist older people in need so that they can live independently with dignity in decent, affordable housing.

Habitat for Humanity is probably the best known of these programs. Founded in 1976 by Millard and Linda Fuller, Habitat for Humanity had its roots in the small, interracial, Christian community of Koinonia Farm, near Americus, Georgia. One of the leaders of the community was Clarence Jordan, a farmer and biblical scholar who believed in living the teachings of the Gospel in all aspects of daily life. The Fullers were at a personal crossroads when they met Jordan, having sold their successful business in Montgomery, Alabama, and turned their backs on an affluent lifestyle to embrace a life of simple Christian service to those in need.

Millard Fuller and Jordan jointly developed the concept of "partnership housing," in which the poor would join volunteers to build simple but decent homes. The person receiving the house—who normally would not qualify for a commercial mortgage—would be expected to contribute "sweat equity" by laboring side-by-side with the volunteer builders. Material costs were covered by a revolving Fund for Humanity, which was replenished by new homeowners' small, interest-free house payments, charitable donations, and community fundraising. With these resources, the Fund for Humanity has been able to finance more than 100,000 houses.

Although the majority of people who benefit from Habitat for Humanity are younger than 65, the houses the organization funds and the owner-partners help build are the homes they will occupy for the rest of their lives. Thus, Habitat for Humanity literally provides a solid foundation on which the future elderly can live independently as long as they are physically able to do so.

Karen Williams, 62, of Eudora, Kansas, was typical of this group approaching retirement age with only the hope of a minimal Social Security pension. In itself, this prospect would not have been so grim: She could have continued living in her rented two-bedroom mobile home until she qualified for low-income housing for the elderly. But in 1999, her three grandchildren, Amanda, now 12; Adam, 9; and Kelly, 7, moved into her cramped quarters. During the day, while the children were in school, Karen used one of the small bedrooms as an improvised day-care center for several neighbors' children. At night, she and Amanda shared one bunk bed, the two boys the other. The situation was far from ideal. Then Karen received permanent custody of her grandchildren in October 2000. Although happy to have become their legal guardian, she had to face the fact that their living arrangements were clearly inadequate.

"We were literally stepping on each other," she recalls.

A devout Baptist, for whom religion had long been a "top priority," Karen asked the family to pray with her for a better house. "We were not asking God for anything fancy," she says, "just a place with a little more room."

When she heard of Habitat for Humanity, Karen initially thought she would not qualify because of her age. But then she met a local Habitat coordinator, Marilyn Laws Porter, a retired stockbroker from nearby Lawrence, who encouraged Karen to apply for the program.

"The day I got word that our house had been approved," Karen remembers, "I knew that our prayers had been answered."

The foundation of the three-bedroom house was poured in spring 2002, and the home was completed later that year.

Reflecting on her experience, Karen calls her family's new Habitat house "a miracle."

Karen Williams can now look forward to her later years, confident that she can provide a decent, comfortable home for the grandchildren she loves so much.

•══════╗

While Habitat for Humanity concentrates on building new houses, another large national volunteer group, Rebuilding Together—originally called Christmas in April—focuses exclusively on refurbishing and repairing existing homes, many owned by the elderly, the chronically ill, and the disabled.

In 1973, concerned citizens of Midland, Texas—many members of religious congregations—banded together to help solve the desperate housing problems of their low- or fixed-income neighbors. These people, who included many elderly and disabled, were homeowners, but the homes they owned were in terrible condition, often lacking indoor plumbing or electricity. Roofs and floors had caved in; windows had been broken and were boarded up.

The activists in Midland were stunned to discover that there were no government programs available to help these people repair their homes so that they could continue to live independently. The only alternative most faced was accepting often-dangerous squalor or being shunted off to bleak, Medicaid-funded nursing homes.

Out of this situation, a unique effort was born, receiving its name when one of the first beneficiaries described the joy of seeing thirty-odd volunteers descending on her small, dilapidated home on the last Saturday of the month — armed with paint, wallboard, carpentry tools, and even plants for the long-neglected garden — as being like "Christmas in April." The number of Midland volunteers increased rapidly as the concept of updating the traditional barn-raising, in which farmers banded together to help neighbors in need, spread.

By 1988, Christmas in April had become a national organization, with branches in thirteen cities. At first, volunteers only assembled on the last Saturday in April. But that changed when the group expanded to include a Jewish affiliate, "Sukkot in April" — named for the festival commemorating the Israelites' life in the desert wilderness after the Exodus — which completed the home renovations on the following Sunday. In the years since Patty Johnson, the group's dedicated and tireless president and CEO, took charge, the program has exploded to 245 chapters in more than 770 towns and cities. In 2001, the organization became Rebuilding Together to better reflect the ecumenical nature of the volunteer force and the fact that they work throughout the year, not just on National Rebuilding Days on the last weekend in April.

Hundreds of thousands of volunteers dedicate their skill, labor, and leisure time rehabilitating the homes of the needy, as well as repairing run-down public facilities such as homeless and adult day-care shelters. In 2002, over 250,000 volunteers joined the effort, repairing almost 8,000 homes and nonprofit facilities. Sponsors ranging from large corporations, to family businesses, to labor unions, to religious congregations donated tens of millions of dollars in contributions, building supplies, and household appliances. The skilled volunteer workforce repaired over 1,700 roofs and fixed 3,000 electrical problems, 3,400 plumbing problems, and almost 1,000 heating problems. The group installed thousands of doors and windows and hundreds of new, donated stoves and water heaters, as well as 6,000 smoke detectors.

Among those whom Rebuilding Together helped in 2002 were almost 11,000 elderly — aged 65 to over 90 — and more than 6,200 people with disabilities. Many of the disabled received wheelchair ramps so they could enter and leave their homes independently.

This work is known as "home modification" and is one of the organization's priorities. Rebuilding Together recognized early the importance of finding means to facilitate long-term, practical, private-home residency among today's millions of elderly and disabled Americans — and to prepare programs to meet the needs of the millions of Baby Boomers who will soon join the ranks of the elderly. Through this pioneering effort, the group is training its armies of volunteers in the specific techniques of home modification—ramp building, adapting bathing and toilet facilities for wheelchair use, and so on—so that the disabled and low-income elderly can continue to live safely with dignity in their own homes.

Modifying a disabled person's home often alleviates his or her sense of painful isolation and helps bring the person back in contact with the community. These people have seen firsthand that they have human value, that there are volunteer carpenters, lawyers, students, suburban mothers, church and synagogue members, and clergy who are willing to climb ladders to repair their roofs, rip up and replace dangerous old flooring, install water heaters, or hang new windows. And when they slide from their wheelchairs onto the seats mounted in their new shower stalls for the first time and feel the luxury of hot water from the new heater, the homeowners understand that there is love in the world that they thought had disappeared from their lives.

In April 2002, an older couple in Skokie, Illinois (who prefer to remain anonymous), called the local Council for Jewish Elderly to inquire if they might qualify for Christmas/Sukkot in April work on their dilapidated home, which badly needed painting, carpentry work, and plumbing repairs. Having just suffered a heart attack and undergone triple bypass surgery, the husband was a semi-invalid, unable to work. He and his wife had exhausted their savings. Their only asset was the house. But they could never afford the needed repairs. And the house was steadily decaying around them.

Rebuilding Together agreed to help. After the group's veteran house captain, J. B. Phillips, a commercial loan officer by profession, inspected the property, he drew up a roster of volunteers and materials needed. Christian and Muslim volunteers would work on the project on Saturday, April 27; Sukkot in April volunteers would work on Sunday the 28th. The team assigned to the elderly couple's house came from the Lakeside Congregation for Reform Judaism, Grace Lutheran Church in Evanston, and from a third congregation, the Islamic Cultural Center of Greater Chicago.

For two days on a chilly Midwestern spring weekend, while Muslims, Christians, and Jews fought on battlefields from Chechnya, to Palestine, to Afghanistan, other men and women from the world's three great monotheistic religions hammered nails, painted, plastered holes in walls, and repaired broken pipes in the home of one frail and timid elderly Jewish couple.

Today, Rebuilding Together has 252 branches that serve 955 towns and cities.

The work of these volunteers is testament to the positive power of faith to help find solutions to the problems posed by our swelling elderly population.

Spiraling Healthcare Costs

2

AFTER HOLDING relatively steady in the 1990s—thanks in large part to rigorous cost cutting by managed care firms—private and public healthcare expenditures began to climb steeply. The Medicare budget alone is projected to double from the 1999 level of $213 billion per year to over $450 billion annually by 2011. During that period, total healthcare outlays in the United States will also more than double from $1.2 trillion to $2.8 trillion per year. It is important to note that the elderly population will increase by only about 8 million during these years: The true population explosion among the elderly will begin after 2011, when 42 million Americans will have reached age 65, a number that will then double over the next few decades.

Dr. Richard Corlin, former president of the American Medical Association, has called the looming healthcare financial crisis a "perfect storm," a reference to the 1991 collision between a hurricane and a Canadian cold front that produced ship-killing winds and seas in the North Atlantic. The collision that Dr. Corlin envisions could be just as severe. For example, in order to restrain the runaway Medicare budget, the federal government imposed a 5.4 percent cut in physicians' reimbursement fees in 2002. This prompted managed care companies to follow suit, further reducing doctors' incomes and services available to patients. Many physicians responded by simply refusing to accept new Medicare patients.

Yet, despite concerted efforts at cost cutting, the U.S. healthcare system is the most expensive in the world. In the ten years between 1991 and 2001, per capita annual expenditure almost doubled from $2966 to $4637. The United States spends 13.2 percent of its gross domestic product on healthcare, almost twice as much as Great Britain. This huge expenditure is partially due to our insatiable demand for healthcare: The U.S. Centers for Disease Control and Prevention has noted that doctors' office visits have been steadily increasing over the past ten years and passed a total of 824 million consultations in

2000. The CDC credits this increase to both overall population growth and the steady increase in the proportion of elderly.

What will America's total healthcare costs be after 2025, when the crest of the huge Baby Boom generation officially reaches old age, eventually swelling the number of elderly persons to more than 80 million?

Much will depend on their health. As we have noted, there are two basic scenarios: In the first, through an appropriate level of public and private aging research, renewed efforts supporting disease prevention and innovative treatment, as well as clinical research breakthroughs, the current immutable link between advancing age and declining health will be broken. The average health of an 85-year-old in 2040 will resemble that of a fit 70-year-old today. And both public and private healthcare costs will remain within manageable limits.

But in the second scenario, we continue to drift with the current low levels of support for research, disease prevention, and innovative treatment. This will result in scant improvement in the health of the burgeoning elderly population. Even small improvements in their health will be offset by the size of their cohort. Unless medical research achieves widespread breakthroughs, future members of the 85-plus age group will be afflicted by multiple health problems and prone to chronic disability.

Based on the most recent research, for example, approximately 33 percent of those over 85 are afflicted with Alzheimer's disease—the average prevalence worldwide for this age group—which requires an annual per-patient care cost of $170,000 in some countries. The Rush Institute for Healthy Aging has estimated that there could be between 11 and 16 million Americans living with Alzheimer's in 2050. This means the disease could cost our country up to $25 billion a year for direct professional patient care and billions more in lost productivity and absenteeism among caregivers. And this projection does not take into account the younger elderly suffering chronic cognitive disability that also requires expensive treatment. (Today as many as 20 percent of people between the ages 75 and 84 are already afflicted with Alzheimer's disease.)

Obviously, care for the chronically disabled such as Alzheimer's patients, but also for those afflicted with stroke, cardiovascular disease, diabetes, and different forms of cancer, will continue to present a major challenge. But the cost of that care is not the only obstacle our institutions must surmount. Caring for the whole person—offering optimistic companionship and spiritual reassurance, which are roles now usually filled by limited numbers of social workers and chaplains—will become increasingly difficult as these resources are stretched thin.

But here is a case that presents exactly the type of opportunity we mentioned earlier, the chance for older religious people to reach out to those in need and, by so doing, enrich both their own and the patients' lives.

Rosetta Belk, in her late fifties, is a former employee of the county schools in Warrenton, North Carolina, who retired on disability several years ago. Rather than become inactive, however, she and her sister, Flora Alston, joined the Warrenton Missionary Prayer Band, whose fifteen members, drawn from five local Baptist Missionary and Holiness churches, have dedicated themselves to providing spiritual care for elderly people who request it or who are recommended to them by members of the local community. At 53, Flora Alston is the youngest member of the group, whose ages range up to 95. Warrenton is a small town near the Virginia border, astride the Bible Belt; the Prayer Band's services are much in demand.

The group's schedule takes them on a regular series of visits to hospitals, nursing homes, and to the homes of elderly shut-ins. The Prayer Band's members socialize and pray with those they visit; they also sing the familiar old hymns the patients find so reassuring. Many of the people to whom they offer spiritual comfort have no surviving family members living locally and would have withdrawn within a shell of isolation if not for the Prayer Band.

"We visited one very elderly lady who had gotten quite senile," Rosetta explained. "She never had any other visitors. But when we came and prayed with her, she held our hands tight and smiled. Maybe she didn't understand everything that we were saying, but she knew we loved her."

The same sense of generous spirituality extends to the shut-in visits. The Prayer Band always takes home-cooked meals that they share with those they visit. Sitting around a kitchen or dining-room table, hands clasped while saying grace, they provide a tangible reminder to disabled people that they are not forgotten, that they are part of a close, larger family of faith.

The members of the Prayer Band derive real meaning and purpose in their lives by devoting their time and energy to helping others. Although she lives on a small disability pension, Rosetta Belk is proud that she can serve as the group's driver, able to offer her own sports utility vehicle to convey the members along their weekly routes.

"We may not have a whole lot ourselves," she says, speaking of the members' worldly goods, "but the Lord has enriched us through the work we do."

It might surprise Rosetta Belk that the Warrenton Missionary Prayer Band probably accomplishes tangible physical good among the elderly patients they visit. Research conducted at many of our leading academic institutions in the past thirty years has revealed a direct connection among people's stress level, their social support network, and their degree of religious belief. All these elements affect the immune system, which in turn plays an important role in the development of or the ability to recover from serious illness such as cardiovascular disease, infection, and possibly cancer.

An August 2002 report in the journal *Cancer* reveals that researchers have discovered another link connecting a person's level of stress, social support, and the progression of cancer. A research team led by Dr. Susan K. Lutgendorf of the University of Iowa studied twenty-four women with ovarian cancer and five others who had nonmalignant pelvic tumors. The researchers measured levels of vascular endothelial growth factor (VEGF), a chemical in the body that promotes the extension of new blood vessels to tumors, allowing them to expand more rapidly. Survival probability can be predicted by measuring a patient's VEGF level.

Dr. Lutgendorf's team made an interesting finding. Patients with a higher level of social well-being as well as close contact and support from friends and neighbors had lower blood levels of VGEF. But the patients who reported feelings of isolation, helplessness, or worthlessness had higher levels of the tumor-growth factor.

"The exciting thing about these findings is that they open up the possibility of a new mechanism by which psychological factors may be related to cancer progression," Dr. Lutgendorf told Reuters Health Service.

Almost by definition, a patient receiving the warm, close comfort of spiritual and social support as provided by the Warrenton Missionary Prayer Band —and thousands of similar congregational volunteer groups nationwide— will not feel abandoned, helpless, or worthless.

Even as we consider the important work of religiously motivated volunteers, we must face important challenges squarely. The growing number of elderly and the soaring cost of treatment are two of the most important factors fueling the "storm" that threatens to destabilize our healthcare system. Until now, we have had little control over either. And they are closely related. In large measure, people are living longer because medical science has made astounding break-throughs in fields such as cancer detection, cardiovascular treatment, digital imagery technology, pharmacology, and a host of other healthcare innovations. The fact that people over age 50 enjoy greater longevity, however, does not mean that they are healthier and require fewer expensive healthcare services (as in our optimistic first scenario). On the contrary, according to AARP, older people today are more likely to be obese, suffer disabilities, and need increasingly expensive prescription medications, just when the financial underpinning of our private and public medical funding has become insecure.

One of the main problems is that today's medical procedures, treatments, and medications are so expensive. Simply stated, as more people have become elderly and have come to expect state-of-the-art treatment, the cost of their care has risen. This is one of the main reasons that the current lamentable trend of HMOs rejecting new patients who only have Medicare coverage with no supplemental insurance is bound to continue. When HMOs were still expanding in the 1990s, they promised to provide quality, affordable care for Medicare patients, as well as for private sector businesses that fund health insurance for 75 million employees and their family members. But even with the most stringent efforts HMOs adopted to control expenses, their costs have mounted inexorably in recent years—due in part to the steady increase in delivering quality state-of-the-art care to an aging population suffering from often preventable illnesses, such as adult-onset (Type 2) diabetes associated with obesity and cardiovascular disease due to poor diet and sedentary lifestyle.

One indication that cost reduction has become an increasingly common priority is the rapid expansion of in-office surgery, which includes invasive or high-risk procedures such as colonoscopies, biopsies, and coronary stress tests. The Medicare system actually encourages this approach and reimburses physicians more for procedures they conduct in their offices than for the same service performed in a hospital. So, by relying on their own employees as assistants and nurse anesthetists rather than on more expensive (but possibly better trained) hospital staff, physicians manage to still make an income from Medicare patients. But this trend is not without risk: Private clinics are generally less able to cope with emergencies such as cardiac arrest and severe pulmonary distress.

As Dr. Charles Coté, a professor at Northwestern University School of Medicine, points out, "In some offices, the only backup they have is dialing 911."

But, with a steady increase in malpractice lawsuits (which nearly doubled between 1995 and 2000), insurance premiums have soared, causing many of these clinics to close. Those that do continue to stay open will probably offer care comparable to that available in larger hospitals.

———

We will probably see a de facto two-tiered healthcare system for the elderly in coming years. A fortunate minority will have adequate private resources to supplement their shrinking Medicare benefits and to meet the steadily increasing co-payments and cost of prescription drugs. Those whose savings have been depleted through economic hard times and long periods of unemployment—downsizing often hits the older workforce hardest—will have to make do with basic Medicare coverage.

This will create a huge backlog of elderly people needing some form of assistance in the community, where most care will have to be delivered. All adult members of society will be affected by this trend, with young workers expected to pay increasing amounts from their paychecks for social programs for the elderly, while simultaneously having to absorb the emotional burden and financial cost of their own aging parents' care.

The hope that Medicare and Medicaid can somehow be "fixed" with a single magic bullet grows less likely each year. Medicaid, which is administered by the states but receives over 50 percent of its budget from the federal government, funds treatment for the poor and long-term nursing home care for millions of elderly lacking adequate private means. The program takes a huge chunk out of states' budgets and governors are begging Washington for more money. But, in the wake of the economic downturn, the war against terrorism, and the war in Iraq, the huge recent federal budget surpluses have disappeared.

So, with the Medicaid pie not growing as fast as in the past, the states will have to slice it into thinner pieces, eliminating non-priority treatment such as dental coverage, requiring cheaper generic drugs rather than brand-name prescriptions, and steadily increasing the beneficiaries' co-payments. Still, the huge, complex Medicaid system will face mounting financial strain. In the near future, for example, Congress could take the unpopular step of freezing payments to nursing homes and home healthcare agencies.

Private health insurance companies such as Blue Cross and Blue Shield are already shifting toward cheaper generic prescription drugs whenever possible. This can result in significant annual per-patient savings. For example, the popular brand-name arthritis drug Celebrex costs over $730 a year, but the Blue Cross system in some states has opted for much cheaper generic versions of other arthritis medications no longer under patent, available for less than $100 for an annual supply. The pharmaceutical industry claims that their brand-name drugs are both safer and more effective than generic substitutes and have launched ambitious advertising campaigns encouraging consumers to "ask your doctor about" the expensive patented products.

It's too early to tell if generic drugs will dominate the prescription market, but that seems likely, at least among increasingly cost-conscious private health insurers and Medicaid administrators who determine prescription coverage for low-income beneficiaries. Prescription drugs account for the fastest-growing increase in rising healthcare costs: In 1990, the average brand-name drug cost around $27, but was over $65 a decade later. A generic prescription cost on average just $10.29 in 1990 and $19.33 in 2000. Congress is under great political pressure to remedy this discrepancy. One practical solution might be a legal reform to prevent pharmaceutical companies from repeatedly obtaining automatic thirty-month extensions of their drugs' expired patents, a ploy that has worked well in the past to prevent rivals from producing less-expensive generic versions of the medication. On the other hand, pharmaceutical companies do tremendous research and development to identify new, more effective drugs, and cutting their profits excessively could also cause them to cut way back on efforts to develop new pharmaceuticals.

But, despite the increasingly heated political debate over prescription drugs, millions of Medicare beneficiaries remain without coverage and — like Robert DeGray, whose prescription costs exceeded his small Social Security pension — are unable to pay for their medications.

———

In the United States, another factor has a major negative impact on the health of our elderly: We have the largest number of people without health insurance of any developed country. According to the Institute of Medicine of the National Academy of Sciences, this lack of insurance prevents serious illness and its related complications from being diagnosed in a timely manner. The institute's recent report, "Care Without Coverage: Too Little, Too Late," indicated that thousands of "premature deaths" annually — from cancer, diabetes, heart disease, hypertension and stroke, as well as HIV/AIDS — can be traced to the inability of the 43.6 million working adult Americans (aged 18 to 65) to afford private coverage. These are the people who fall between the Medicaid program for the poor and younger disabled and Medicare for senior citizens. (There are also 23 million poor non-citizen adult immigrants who do not yet qualify for Medicaid.)

And in 2001 alone, two million workers lost their health insurance due to lay-offs. In 2002, 14 percent of Americans between 50 and 64 (5.6 million people) lacked health insurance. But many were far from healthy; 27 percent of this age group was estimated to be dangerously ("morbidly") obese. As any clinician will tell you, carrying so much body fat dramatically increases your chance of suffering from high blood pressure, diabetes, stroke, and heart disease. The problem is, however, that all too many people do not regularly consult clinicians because they cannot afford health insurance.

———

Recently, *New York Times* reporters Robin Toner and Sheryl Gay Stolberg surveyed people across the country who had either lost their health insurance due to the economic downturn or who had never been able to afford coverage. The *Times* found families living on the brink of catastrophe. Paul McGonnigal, a New England executive, saw his coverage vanish when his high-tech company collapsed. He and his wife hope to make a living as private consultants, but could not afford health insurance when they were interviewed. "We could be financially wiped out if either one of us got seriously ill," he said.

In Richmond, California, Maryanne McMillan, a professional person disabled by the autoimmune disease lupus, has struggled to afford adequate health insurance. "I feel like I'm on a high-wire act," battling both the illness and the mounting cost of healthcare, she said.

For employers facing uncertain economic times, steadily rising health insurance expenses are an ongoing problem. After holding firm for several years, premiums have begun to soar, with annual increases averaging between 11 and 25 percent. Companies have had to pass these costs on to their employees in the form of both higher payroll deductions and co-payments. According to Kate Sullivan, a healthcare expert for the U.S. Chamber of Commerce, employers are seeing their health insurance outlays "explode."

The mounting expense of healthcare has become a volatile political issue. But so far, neither party has managed to convince voters it can offer a practical solution.

Meanwhile, American families are suffering. East Texas poultry farmers David and Nicole Adler, who are in their forties and pay for their own health insurance, watched premiums rise beyond their reach. So they opted for a policy with a harsh $15,000 deductible. David Adler voiced his anxiety to the *New York Times*. If premiums and deductibles continue to mount, health insurance "is going to be unaffordable when I'm 60," years before he qualifies for Medicare.

Bob Patafio, a self-employed Long Island boat mover, and his homemaker wife, Trish, fear being priced out of the health insurance market. Even though their three children qualified for the Children's Health Insurance Program administered by the U.S. Department of Health and Human Services, the Patafios can barely afford their own premium of over $500 a month. Noting that they often already eat pancakes for dinner to reduce expenses, Trish Patafio is worried about what lies ahead. "What are we going to do, sell the house so that we can pay health insurance?"

For millions of working Americans whose employers do not offer health insurance benefits, any coverage is unaffordable. They do not qualify for Medicaid, either because they are not citizens or because their income is above the official poverty line, and usually turn to subsidized low-income clinics for care. Although an American citizen, Dolores Stanfield, 50, a waitress in Columbia,

South Carolina, has not been able to afford health insurance for over fifteen years. When the local clinic open to low-income patients cannot provide the care she needs, she turns to a hospital emergency room, where her debt for treatment is steadily climbing past her ability to ever repay. All too often, hospital emergency rooms, which many states legally require to treat all patients, have become the HMO of the uninsured. This places a financial burden on the hospital that most, in turn, pass on to insured patients.

Another major but generally overlooked consequence of the lack of health insurance coverage is that millions of people reach their mid-sixties and qualify for Medicare each year already afflicted with needlessly advanced chronic illnesses that could have been diagnosed and treated earlier, had they been able to afford insurance. But most of the uninsured only seek medical advice when they have Medicare coverage. By then it is often too late to repair the damage to the vascular/nervous systems and the retinas in diabetics who have gone for years without diagnosis or treatment because they could not afford checkups or co-payments. This same situation prevails among all those with high blood pressure and elevated cholesterol who discover their condition for the first time after age 65.

But, as we will relate in greater detail in a later chapter, this problem can be at least partially addressed if religious congregations begin considering both the spiritual and the physical health needs of their members. The rapidly expanding parish nurse program is the best known of these programs. Today thousands of "parishes" (a term that includes both Christian and Jewish congregations, and which is now often called "congregational nursing") provide a professional nurse as a volunteer or in a salaried staff position. Among the nurse's responsibilities are to coordinate regular health screenings—for high blood pressure, cholesterol levels, skin, breast, and colon cancer, and diabetes—and offer education on weight management, proper nutrition, and the risks of smoking. The nurse offers this service free.

In the mid-1980s, the Baltimore Church High Blood Pressure Research Project determined that it could draw on the trust women members of inner-city congregations traditionally felt toward their churches to conduct successful hypertension screening and education. These women were in heightened danger for high blood pressure and associated cardiovascular disease, as well as for obesity and diabetes. And few had been regularly screened, treated, or educated about the importance of proper nutrition, exercise, and other healthy lifestyle choices.

Fifteen years later, Dr. Iris Keys, a University of Maryland Medical Center internist and an ordained minister in the AME Church, continues the work begun in the 1980s in both her university clinic and from the pulpits of the Baltimore churches she visits. Many of her patients are older African American women on Medicaid or Medicare who follow her guidance as much for Dr. Key's serene and confident manner as for the respect they feel for her as a member of the clergy.

Once she has established a bond of trust with her clinic patients, Dr. Keys convinces them that the changes they must make in their lives are not complicated and do not require expensive treatment. Reducing caloric intake—especially from high-fat soul food—and regular exercise, even a daily pattern of walking for fifteen minutes (as well as a regimen of medication) can bring down blood pressure and reduce the risk of stroke, heart attack, and diabetes.

Dr. Keys carries this same advice to Baltimore's black church congregations. "The people listen to me," she says. "I can mix sound medical advice with 'church talk.'"

Beyond the question of personal tragedies, there are important policy issues involved in weighing the impact that the widespread lack of health insurance will have on the future needs of the elderly. Obviously, if millions of people reach retirement age already afflicted with disabling chronic conditions, Medicare will be placed under enormous strain to fund their treatment. A huge, chronically ill elderly population advancing into extreme old age is exactly the type of nightmare situation Edward Schneider described in his pessimistic Scenario 2.

For example, if current cancer screening levels and treatment techniques do not improve dramatically, the disease will become more difficult to manage as our population ages. The American Cancer Society, the National Cancer Institute, the Centers for Disease Control and Prevention, and the North American Association of Central Cancer Registries recently released a study indicating that the number of Americans diagnosed with cancer each year will double by 2050. Today, about 1.3 million people annually hear the dreaded words, "You have cancer." By mid-century, the number of new patients will have soared to 2.6 million. This projected increase is largely due to the predicted greater overall longevity of our population: Almost half (1.1 million) of the new cancer patients in 2050 will be 75 and older.

Community-based healthcare can meet some of the need. And the "community" that those in need will call upon will most likely include religious congregations that have the structural organization, the volition, and the dedication to meet this responsibility.

The Mercy Health Clinic in Germantown, Maryland, northwest of Washington, D.C., is a good example of just such a program. The clinic, organized by Our Lady of Mercy Catholic Church in Potomac, Maryland, provides free care to hundreds of uninsured local residents each week—most in minimum-wage jobs such as construction day laborers, motel maids, and restaurant workers. Twenty primary care and specialist physicians, forty-five professional nurses, as well as interpreters and social workers staff Mercy Clinic. Aside from two administrators, they are all volunteers who offer their services three afternoons a week. Most are members of the Our Lady of Mercy congregation. The Montgomery County Department of Human Services underwrites part of the clinic's funding, but the most expensive item in the budget—personnel costs —is provided free by the volunteers themselves. This is their way of responding to the "opportunity" provided by the healthcare crisis looming over their community.

Having completed a major fundraising drive for a new church and renovations to its school in 1988, the congregation of Our Lady of Mercy felt they should also meet non-spiritual community needs and decided to fund and staff a free clinic. After consulting closely with Lynn Frank, chief of public health services for Montgomery County Department of Human Services, the congregation selected Germantown and a building provided by the county government. As some volunteers renovated the interior spaces, others worked with two county hospitals that donated badly needed equipment and supplies. Another area hospital signed an agreement to provide free laboratory testing, which is an essential part of modern medical practice that the poor often are obliged to forego because they cannot afford laboratory fees. One of the congregation's nurses organized local doctors to donate sample medications from drug salespersons to stock the clinic's pharmacy. Another member of the congregation, an experienced radiologist, convinced colleagues to offer their services at the clinic gratis.

Thanks to a $30,000 grant from the county, a $10,000 donation from the Our Lady of Mercy congregation itself, and hundreds of donations from other churches and family members, the Mercy Clinic opened its doors to patients on October 3, 2000. One of the most important contributions from Montgomery County was malpractice insurance for the volunteer doctors.

The clinic's medical director is Dr. James A. Ronan, a cardiologist. After thirty-five years in that specialty and about to retire, he learned that the clinic was due to open and volunteered his services. "I've always wanted to do this kind of work," he later told the *Washington Post*. "I just wanted to give something back."

Many of the patients whom Dr. Ronan and his volunteer colleagues at the clinic treat are recently arrived immigrants, some who have never received modern medical care. An Iranian patient consulted Dr. Ronan for what he thought was a routine problem related to diabetes. But Ronan discovered the man had life-threatening arteriosclerosis with several heart arteries completely blocked. Ronan arranged for his colleagues to perform open-heart surgery on him during two hospital stays, treatment that normally would have cost a minimum of $100,000, but which the volunteer physicians and their affiliated hospitals provided pro bono.

Since opening in October 2000, the Mercy Health Clinic has seen its patient load steadily increase. Although most of the patients are uninsured recent immigrants, a growing number are low-income American citizens. "We really have met a big need here," remarks the clinic's executive director, Alvina E. Long.

Mercy Health Clinic is just one of many similar faith-based healthcare programs in the area and one of thousands nationwide. Not far from Mercy Clinic, the Spanish Catholic Center in Gaithersburg provides similar services, as does the People's Community Baptist Church in Silver Spring, which has opened a permanent wellness center that focuses on offering primary healthcare for uninsured African Americans.

Echoing Dr. Iris Keys, Montgomery County healthcare professional Lynn Frank comments on the clinics' success: "People have trust in their churches."

Indeed, she stresses that patients are confident they will receive quality care because they have faith in the ethical integrity of the volunteer healthcare professionals and the religious communities that stand behind them.

In the future, as private and publicly funded traditional facilities such as HMOs, acute-care hospitals, rehabilitation hospitals, and nursing homes strain to deliver quality healthcare, clinics staffed by volunteers drawn from religious congregations—working in partnership with local governments—might provide the highest quality and most cost-effective alternative.

Healthcare Institutions: Financial Pressures, Innovative Opportunities

3

I N THE LATE 1990S, Diana Aviv, vice president for public policy of the United Jewish Communities in Washington, D.C., and legislative director Stephan Klein received reports of growing discontent at Jewish not-for-profit assisted-living facilities and nursing homes funded by Medicaid. And they also learned that the problem affected nursing homes nationwide affiliated with other faiths.

The issue involved rigid policies concerning elderly residents who needed temporary hospital treatment. Medicare-funded HMOs provided this acute care. On release from the hospital—and almost always because of financial pressure—these patients were transferred to HMO-owned convalescent facilities, often located far from their original assisted-living or nursing homes. They were uprooted from an emotionally comforting and spiritually nurturing milieu and thrust alone into a culturally alien environment, among strangers with whom they had little in common. But budget considerations had convinced the healthcare management firms that they could not afford to provide convalescent care separately for their Jewish, Protestant, or Roman Catholic clients. The HMOs found it convenient to neglect the spiritual and emotional aspects of these patients' healing and to concentrate instead on the bottom line.

This situation was especially troubling for religiously observant Jewish clients who ate kosher food; celebrated the Sabbath, which begins at sunset each Friday and lasts until nightfall on Saturday; and for whom the annual cycle of High Holidays had deep spiritual significance. Many of these people had arrived in America as refugees after the World War II Holocaust and still spoke Yiddish among themselves. Others had come from the former Soviet Union after the collapse of Communism and spoke Russian. Jewish culture and religion were the underpinnings of their lives. The facilities in which they planned to spend their later years had in fact become their "homes."

"It didn't matter if they came from Eastern Europe or the Lower East Side," Stephan Klein notes. "They were still Jewish, and they wanted to stay with their own people, in their own community."

The tragic pattern was often manifest among elderly immigrants from the former Soviet Union who had suffered deprivation as young people during World War II and later under the repressive, anti-Semitic Moscow regimes. After the collapse of Communism, they managed to immigrate to the United States and took comfort in both the spiritual and cultural shelter of our established Jewish communities. When the time came to enter a Jewish assisted-care facility or nursing home, they found the familiar atmosphere very satisfying. It was as if they had transplanted the nurturing neighborhood into the institution. Their fellow residents were friendly and welcoming. The kitchen was kosher. Each Friday at sunset, a member of the congregation initiated Sabbath services that would continue for most of the next day. The immigrants felt they had finally found security after decades of upheaval.

But when an elderly resident was hospitalized for treatment and then was arbitrarily transferred to another facility for what was ostensibly more cost-effective care, the other member of a married couple and their circle of friends were truly bereaved. In the past in Eastern Europe, when authorities took someone away, they often did not return. Husbands or wives were often gripped by anxiety, unable to sleep, and slid into crippling depression.

The pain and spiritual isolation were especially severe for the individuals uprooted from the emotional comfort of nursing homes where they had often lived for years and abruptly relocated to the alien world of the nondenominational rehabilitation hospital where no one spoke a familiar language. The level of medical care per se was not lacking, but the patients—whether they were native-born Americans or immigrants—almost always found themselves gripped by an agonizing sense of isolation, of spiritual separation. It was virtually impossible to concentrate on rehabilitation without friends and loved ones nearby. Again, patients' recovery was haunted by the specter of depression.

This was understandable.

Over the past two decades, as societal isolation in general has increased, diagnosed cases of depression have been steadily rising among the American population. They have now almost doubled to over 20 million annual consultations with healthcare providers. New anti-depressant medications—Prozac being among the best known—are now some of our most commonly prescribed drugs. This epidemic of depression has certainly not spared the elderly, including nursing home residents.

Among the symptoms of serious depression is the conviction that life will never improve, that the depressed person has reached a dead end. Other psychological symptoms include sleeping problems and difficulties concentrating. Personal withdrawal occurs frequently. Many depressed elderly people are seized by the irrational conviction that their life has been totally worthless.

Because depression is often triggered by the sudden stress of the loss of a loved one through death or separation, the inflexible managed care policies of uprooting nursing home residents after temporary hospitalization was especially problematic. For an elderly religious person arbitrarily shunted from a faith-based nursing home to a secular facility, this feeling of social isolation and the depression that ensues can trigger changes that make physical recovery very difficult.

Researchers at Duke University and elsewhere have closely studied the link between depression, feelings of social isolation, and poor physical health. Such serious depression unleashes a cascade of the stress hormones cortisol, epinephrine, and norepinephrine—all produced in the adrenal glands—which overstimulate the autonomic nervous system. Blood pressure and heart function can be adversely affected, exacerbating any existing cardiovascular disease. This is hardly an ideal situation for an elderly person trying to recover from a stroke or heart attack.

The overproduction of the stress hormone cortisol, associated with serious depression, also weakens the immune system. When the immune system is debased, an already frail elderly person can become vulnerable to chronic post-surgical infections, to atherosclerotic plaque in arteries and veins that can trigger strokes and heart attacks, and eventually perhaps to some types of cancer.

＊━━━━◦

But Diana Aviv and her colleagues seized this dilemma and turned it into an opportunity, a chance to act decisively to correct the root problem, not just for the Jewish elderly, but also for all of the elderly people of other faiths in similar circumstances who desperately wanted to return to the comfortable communities they had been forced to leave after hospitalization.

"United Jewish Communities, acting on behalf of the North American Jewish Federation, made remedying this problem one of its top legislative priorities in 2000," she says. "We galvanized efforts in Congress to pass needed 'Return to Home' legislation that guarantees elderly Jews the right to return to Jewish nursing homes after temporary hospitalization."

She adds that the Return to Home legislation corrects a gap in public policy under which HMOs could arbitrarily transfer elderly patients to live in convalescent facilities outside their community even when there were Jewish or church-affiliated nursing homes available to them.

To exploit the opportunity for sweeping change, the United Jewish Communities helped organize a large interfaith coalition of religious-based healthcare providers to work toward winning Congressional support. In March 2000, thousands of young Jewish volunteer leaders from around the country came to Washington and met with virtually every member of Congress to present the case for Return to Home legislation.

A strong bipartisan base of support was quickly established. House Speaker Dennis Hastert took a personal interest, which proved crucial to the legislative success. He was joined by one hundred Republican and Democratic representatives and senators who sponsored the bill that became law as part of larger budget legislation. President Bill Clinton signed this law in his final days in the White House.

Diana Aviv explains the significance of the pioneering bill. "Under this legislation, most elderly patients of all faiths living in senior facilities and who are temporarily hospitalized will not be prohibited by their HMOs from returning to their local communities for post-hospitalization recovery and rehabilitation." She adds: "The result for Jewish patients is that they will be able to heal in community skilled nursing facilities that comply with Jewish dietary laws, holiday observances, and other essential religious or cultural practices that are central to their mental and spiritual well-being."

The passage of the Return to Home legislation had a positive effect on more than the nursing home residents' emotional and spiritual lives. Once a patient had come back to the comforting atmosphere of a Jewish home, the cloud of depression often began to lift and physical healing progressed.

There is growing evidence that spiritual well-being is associated with less depression among older adults with serious medical illness. The importance of this finding is that patients whose spiritual needs are met in an emotional-spiritual nurturing environment are much more likely to experience spiritual well-being and therefore be shielded from depression during their recovery process. For Jewish patients recuperating from surgery or other medical illness, the warm, sustaining milieu of their nursing home and the reassuring pastoral care they receive is an intangible form of "treatment" they could not expect from a nonsectarian rehabilitation facility.

The Return to Home legislation also permits elderly people of all faiths to return to their religiously affiliated nursing homes, where spiritual concerns and pastoral care always receive greater emphasis than in nondenominational facilities. Regular Bible classes and hymn services are held in Baptist and Methodist homes, and the sacraments of the church are prominent in the spiritual life at Roman Catholic nursing homes.

The United Jewish Communities and their interfaith coworkers addressed a crisis in which elderly patients' emotional health and faith had become secondary to the financial concerns of HMOs and transformed the situation into an occasion to continue delivering cost-effective care that also specifically addressed the cultural and religious needs of the elderly.

"Today, when you enter a Jewish nursing home near sunset on *Shabbat*," Stephan Klein says, "and see the women lighting the candles and smell the rich aroma from the kitchen, and then look into the radiant, expectant faces of the elderly residents, you will understand that you really are in a *home*, not just an institution."

Stephan Klein also points out that many HMOs have come to recognize the Return to Home legislation represents a "zero-sum" transaction, costing Medicaid- and Medicare-funded HMOs no more in the long run to offer recuperative care in the original assisted-living facility or nursing home than providing that same care in a company-owned rehabilitation facility. And the spiritual aspect of patients' healing was far better addressed when they were allowed to return "home."

Resolving the wider problem of the steadily increasing—and increasingly expensive—healthcare needs of our growing elderly population, which are expanding faster than available resources, will no doubt require solutions every bit as innovative as the Return to Home legislation. As we have noted, Medicare, which provides the basic health insurance for the great majority of elderly Americans, has already been badly stretched. Today there is a disturbing trend among physicians nationwide to refuse to accept new Medicare patients because the government reimbursement for that care does not cover the cost to deliver it.

Under budget pressure from Congress, the government will cut Medicare reimbursement fees a total of 17 percent between 2002 and 2005. (In 2002, Medicare cut its healthcare payments by 5.4 percent; the 2003 cuts were 4.4 percent.) Private insurers that peg their fee coverage to Medicare scales have also reduced reimbursement, putting doctors and Medicare HMOs under increasing strain to make ends meet.

Many HMOs have already followed the trend of dropping coverage in areas that produce less revenue, raising premiums for routine office visits, and introducing sharply increased fees for hospital stays and specialized care such as kidney dialysis and chemotherapy.

Whether the elderly population opts for a Medicare HMO or conventional Medicare coverage, Congressional efforts to control runaway spending have already had an impact on older people and will continue to do so as their numbers steadily increase. With the Medicare budget rising inexorably to match the total number of elderly beneficiaries, the services that can be offered to them free of charge are declining. Those who feel the pinch most drastically are retired people whose only income is Social Security and whose only health insurance is Medicare. Hundreds of thousands of the near-indigent chronically ill, including widows struggling to live on Social Security survivor's benefits of less than $600 a month, have seen the cost of their Medicare HMO rise beyond their reach. In theory, Medicare coverage should meet their needs. In practice, the surcharges the HMOs have felt obliged to impose — all the while cutting programs such as free or nominal-cost prescription drug coverage — have often made adequate treatment an unaffordable luxury.

This state of affairs will only worsen as federal budget deficits following in the wake of the economic slowdown and the war on terrorism accumulate until at least 2006.

Dr. Mark Krotowski, a family physician who practices in a blue-collar Brooklyn neighborhood, told *New York Times* reporter Robert Pear that his current relationship with Medicare is "an insult." Medicare reimbursement, he points out, has fallen far behind the inflation in the cost of treatment for beneficiaries.

"I love my elderly patients," he says. "But they are very sick. They need a lot of attention, a lot of medication, and a lot of time."

His words echo the sentiments of thousands of practitioners across the country who are losing money trying to provide adequate healthcare for the expanding elderly population. Depending on location and service performed, Medicare might reimburse a doctor about $60 for an office visit. But in many cities and suburbs that same consultation can cost physicians — or their clinics — as much as $100. This includes malpractice insurance, staff salaries and benefits, rent and utilities, leaving little or nothing for the physician fee. And as every doctor treating Medicare patients knows, reimbursement has been shrinking in recent years. Obviously, there is little incentive for doctors to accept new Medicare patients if each office call results in a net loss of $40.

As with Dr. Mark Krotowski, physicians nationwide have also made the painful decision to limit or even eliminate new Medicare patients from their practices. Dr. Baretta R. Casey, a family physician in rural Kentucky, told the *New York Times* that it was no longer possible to meet earlier government goals of establishing practices in areas short of medical care. Dr. Casey watched income steadily decreasing and expenses rising. When the government chopped physicians' reimbursement rates in January 2002, Dr. Casey also decided not to take any more new Medicare patients.

One result of this disturbing trend is that elderly people who do not have an established physician—including those who move to popular Sunbelt retirement communities—have great difficulty finding doctors who accept Medicare. Lee Goldberg, who works on legislative matters for the National Committee to Preserve Social Security and Medicare, an advocacy group, observes that the "growing reluctance" of physicians to accept new Medicare patients will become a major healthcare problem in coming years.

Another serious issue looming on the healthcare horizon is that of adequate qualified geriatric care. Traditionally, the medical specialty of geriatrics—which focuses on the elderly—has not been popular among young American physicians-in-training, who have preferred more prestigious specialties such as cardiology, dermatology, and surgery.

This has left a shortfall in physicians qualified to treat the diseases of aging, including bone and skeletal afflictions, pulmonary illness, failing vision, and dementia. Louisiana Senator John Breaux, who has shown a keen interest in healthcare for the elderly, notes that only a small number of America's 125 medical schools train physicians to be gerontologists, qualified to treat the fastest growing cohort of our population. Senator Breaux told CBS News correspondent Bobbi Harley that this situation "cannot continue. We're headed for a real cliff."

Despite the fact that the elderly already comprise half of all patients in the healthcare system, there are only a relative handful of specialists trained to treat them. "There's no incentive," Dr. Bernard Roos of the University of Miami Medical School told CBS. Again, Dr. Roos cites budget pressure in Medicare as the major disincentive to training gerontologists. "The reimbursement for those patients is so low," he says, "you will actually lose money."

Yet, there is a growing consensus among healthcare experts that improved geriatric care could result in savings to the Medicare budget of $50 billion per year. This stems from two fundamentals in medicine: Prevention is preferable to treatment, and intervention conducted early in an illness is preferable to more expensive later treatment of a chronic condition. In this regard, gerontologists are better qualified than their colleagues in other specialties to diagnose illness and treat older patients.

Yet prevention and timely treatment of potentially chronic illness such as diabetes, emphysema, and cardiovascular disease remain an elusive goal.

But is the picture totally bleak? Or are there untapped resources among America's thousands of religious communities and medical professionals whose deep-seated faith might impel them to come forward to meet the emerging needs of the elderly?

Central Dallas Ministries (CDM) and Project Access, the innovative community healthcare system with which it cooperates, offers a model for providing treatment, health education, and preventive care for the millions of America's working poor unable to afford private insurance.

CDM began modestly in 1988, when the congregation of the Preston Road Church of Christ and other Dallas congregations decided to create a storefront food pantry to serve the inner-city poor. Jim Sowell, a Dallas business and civic leader and a dynamic member of the Preston Road congregation, sparked the effort to expand the food pantry beyond a traditional charity institution into a vibrant, multi-function alliance of churches and individual and business supporters that created initiatives meant to attack the root problems of poverty. The key to the program's success lay in its relationship with the members of the community it served. The original food pantry grew to include a thrift store and became a Resource Center, managed and operated by neighborhood volunteers who had made their initial contact with CDM as recipients. They now have the opportunity to reinvest in the community, not merely receive impersonal charity.

Using the Resource Center as a template, CDM has steadily expanded its services under the tireless leadership of Reverend Larry M. James, a Church of Christ minister who became executive director in 1994. Today, forty permanent staff and a volunteer base of three hundred serve over fifty thousand CDM clients annually. This growing urban ministry is now located in several locations and provides a variety of services:

- The Community Health Ministries' medical/dental clinic — offering free or low-cost care, a pharmacy, and health-services coordination to more advanced care, as well as wellness education — to the uninsured. The clinic emphasizes preventive care and teaching patients measures to take control of chronic conditions such as diabetes and hypertension.

- Central Dallas Urban Justice Center — offering free or low-cost legal services.

- CDM's Job Readiness and Employment Program, structured to break the cycle of missing or low skills, chronic unemployment, and welfare dependence.

■ The After-School Program, providing tutorial and mentoring services to children.

The entire effort also identifies and builds leadership within the central Dallas community. Its goals are to help promote physical healing, support families, foster educational and vocational growth, and strengthen the community's spiritual foundation.

"Our mission drives us deep into these challenging areas," Reverend James says. "We work hand-in-hand with our neighbors to change, shape, build and in many cases 'reinvent' community."

And, he adds, "we make no apology for the fact that a living and active faith fuels our work."

Wealthy individuals of many denominations, as well as foundation and corporate contributors, have recognized CDM's success and have been generous in their support.

———

Reverend James recognized early that healthcare programs were an important aspect of CDM's work. In a community gripped by poverty, people struggling to survive on low wages were often caught in the familiar vise: They were employed and did not qualify for Medicaid, but their employers did not offer health insurance and they could not afford to buy it. Inevitably, they neglected healthcare.

After two years of careful study and preliminary organization with the Dallas medical community, Project Access was inaugurated in February 2002. The goal of the program is to provide the working poor with access to medical care when they cannot afford health insurance and to offer the otherwise unavailable services of private physicians, including highly qualified specialists. Project Access has at its base a private practice network of volunteer physicians and other healthcare providers, including dentists, nurses, therapists, and community care coordinators. The volunteer-led community effort is managed by the Dallas County Medical Society and funded through the Society's foundation and the Dallas Academy of Medicine. Several key participants support Project Access: Central Dallas Ministry, which provides patient referrals, case management, interpreter services, and transportation; the Health Texas Provider Network, which has 325 physicians and has actively supported CDM through its Volunteers in Medicine; the Dallas–Fort Worth Hospital Council; and a host of metropolitan Dallas–Fort Worth medical and community clinic organizations.

Dr. Jim Walton, director of community health at Baylor Hospital, worked hard throughout the development phase, organizing and "shaking the kinks" out of Project Access. By the time Project Access began treating patients in February 2002, a practical system had been established. Volunteer primary care physicians each agreed to accept up to ten patients per year free of charge and to manage their care for a maximum of twelve months. Specialist volunteers who only see a patient once or twice each agreed to accept up to twenty-five patients per year. In this manner, no individual physician was given an unfair burden.

Project Access in Dallas followed the model of a very similar program that began in 1996 in Asheville, North Carolina, under the sponsorship of the Buncombe County Medical Society. Since the North Carolina program began, about 11,000 individuals have received specialty healthcare from 520 volunteer physicians who represent an amazing 85 percent of the Medical Society membership. Emergency room visits — previously the only access the uninsured had to healthcare — have declined 28 percent. When surveyed, 80 percent of the Project Access users reported a marked improvement in their health since enrolling in the program.

One of the goals of Project Access is to provide a transition for patients from uninsured status to acquiring health insurance. In Asheville, that goal is being met; half of those who previously depended on Project Access now have healthcare insurance. This change is probably due to several factors, including counseling and encouragement from physicians, guidance from social workers, and awareness among the former Project Access patients that they, themselves, must take responsibility for their individual and family healthcare needs. The progress in metropolitan Dallas is running parallel to the experience in Asheville.

While helping organize Project Access in Dallas, Dr. Jim Walton noticed an interesting phenomenon: There were approximately six thousand doctors in the metropolitan area ready to participate, due in large part to their personal religious faith and the long medical tradition of helping the indigent. This group of medical professionals was literally the untapped resource needed to fuel the program. And religious faith was the spark needed to start the process.

"Many doctors consider their volunteer work in Project Access as a form of 'tithing,'" Walton observes. "They derive both personal and spiritual satisfaction from participating."

It must be also pointed out that participation in Project Access is not limited to Christian physicians. Jewish, Muslim, and Hindu doctors also join the effort.

In addition, Dr. Walton comments, treating patients in Project Access gives the volunteer physician the opportunity to overcome the daily frustrations of dealing with the government and insurance company healthcare bureaucracy and increasingly annoying Medicaid and Medicare reimbursement cuts. By abolishing the question of fee altogether, the physician is freed to practice medicine in its purist form. And by joining a program such as Project Access, healthcare professionals are able to spread the burden of providing this pro bono care, so that no individuals are forced to carry too heavy a load.

One of the great advantages of Project Access is that it provides the middle-aged working poor person with medical care that can diagnose and treat chronic conditions before they become too far advanced by the time the person qualifies for Medicare.

A cardiologist referred "Frank S.," a 54-year-old Hispanic resident of central Dallas, to Project Access for evaluation. He had undergone heart surgery after suffering a heart attack, had experienced complications, and had received extensive treatment and follow-up care, all of which were covered by health insurance from his employer. But follow-up care not related to the surgery and primary care for his other serious health problems, such as high blood pressure, high cholesterol, and high blood sugar, were not. Through Project Access, Frank was assigned a primary care doctor to follow his general health, and was also able to consult a cardiologist for follow-up evaluation on his heart. Unfortunately, Frank was the sole breadwinner for his family at the time of his heart surgery. Although his wife has since found employment, they can no longer afford the high cost of health insurance and must rely instead on Project Access. Frank will not qualify for Medicare for eleven years. If he did not receive the regular healthcare from the program, Frank's health would no doubt be precarious by age 65. But thanks to the volunteers of Project Access, he receives regular, high-quality medical care from caregivers who are deeply concerned about his health.

"I feel that these doctors stepped in and rescued me just in time," he says.

"Rose M.," a 63-year-old white woman, came to Project Access for a follow-up mammogram, which discovered a "round mass with obscured margins" in her right breast. Such a mammographic image might indicate a dangerous breast tumor. The news left her almost crippled with anxiety. Rose needed an experienced radiologist to complete her diagnosis, but could never afford the services of such a specialist. Then Project Access referred her to a volunteer radiologist for a diagnostic mammogram that indicated the mass was simply a lump of liquid-filled tissue. Rose works full time as caregiver to her grandchildren and lives with her daughter, who also works full time. They must rely on indigent programs like Project Access for healthcare. Without access to diagnosis from the well-qualified volunteer specialist, Rose would be still living with the gnawing knowledge that she had a possibly cancerous lump in her breast that might never be treated in time to save her life. And it would be another two years before she qualified for Medicare and would learn for certain.

"But now I can say my prayers as I go to sleep at night," she says. "And thank God for Project Access."

Many other faith based programs similar to Project Access and Central Dallas Ministries are springing up around the country. In Nashville, Tennessee, one such group is Faith Family Medical Clinic. The mission of Faith Family Medical Clinic is to follow the biblical and historical commitment of people of faith to care for those in need who are sick. The Clinic provides quality, affordable healthcare to uninsured working families in the greater Nashville area. Healthcare professionals and other concerned individuals join together at the Clinic to meet this need.

Bess is a beautician who came to the Clinic recently. She realized she needed to have a physical but had not done so because she was unable to find a physician who would perform a complete physical for what she could pay. At Faith Family Medical Clinic she received a physical examination, lab work, mammogram, and pap smear for $33.00.

Although Project Access has treated a relative handful of hardworking, low-paid American families who cannot yet afford private health insurance, the program promises to serve as a nationwide model. Religiously motivated healthcare providers — physicians, dentists, nurses, and physical therapists, for example — could offer their services free to patients whose numbers are kept limited so as not to overburden the provider's regular practice.

Presently, patients qualifying for Project Access are the working poor who cannot afford private health insurance. But if budget-cutting trends in Medicare continue as our elderly population cohort maintains its expected growth, this principal form of government-sponsored health insurance may become so inadequate in meeting the needs of the elderly that some form of free supplemental care must be found to support the system.

Within a few years, millions of Americans who long expected that Social Security pensions and Medicare would meet all their requirements of later life may face a rude awakening. The pensions could be shrunk by inflation, and standard Medicare might no longer be adequate to secure the treatment they need.

If this crisis arrives, as many believe it inevitably will, we hope that practical systems of faith-based medical volunteers such as those in Project Access will be ready to step in to fill the gap.

Part II

Some Solutions to Our Healthcare Crisis

Prevention, Healthy Living, and Wellness

A GROWING NUMBER of America's 350,000 religious congregations are developing and supporting health programs, most aimed at screening, detection, and prevention of disease. These efforts vary in degree of formality and scope, ranging from occasional health fairs and periodic wellness seminars to highly organized health ministries run by full-time congregational nurses. Such programs represent opportunities for congregations to channel their faith toward prevention, fitness, health education, and patient advocacy among members and the local community. Indeed, their services are in great need now and the need will become more urgent in the years ahead. Consider the following.

A century ago, infectious diseases were the leading causes of premature death and disability in America. The medical community was virtually powerless to prevent or effectively treat these illnesses. Overall longevity was curtailed: In 1900, life expectancy at birth for men and women averaged 47 years (with women typically living 51 years). But the incidence of life-threatening afflictions such as cardiovascular disease or colon, breast, or prostate cancer was also relatively low.

Today, the situation has changed dramatically. Our combined average life expectancy for men and women is now 77.2 years, with an increasing number of women living into their late eighties. This improved longevity stands on the firm foundation that medical science and public health created during the first half of the twentieth century. In 1900, the three leading causes of death in America were pneumonia, tuberculosis, and diarrhea, which together accounted for 31 percent of all mortality. Now, the greatest health threat we face is from cardiovascular disease and cancer, with the incidence of diabetes growing at an alarming rate.

Although influenza and pneumonia continue to threaten the frail elderly, most infectious diseases have been dramatically reduced through a combination of better sanitation and personal hygiene, immunization, and public education on safe food storage and preparation. And, while AIDS and malaria continue to ravage much of the developing world, the latest alarming epidemic of Severe Acute Respiratory Syndrome (SARS) has been contained to a few countries.

By the 1960s, almost everyone in America had been vaccinated against the major infectious diseases, and even the scourge of polio had been defeated through inoculation. Moreover, the discovery of penicillin, which ushered in the antibiotic revolution of the 1940s, led to innovative treatment of potentially deadly infections such as septicemia (blood poisoning). The availability of antibiotics also allowed surgeons to undertake highly invasive procedures with much less risk of complications than previously possible.

The result of the public health and treatment revolution was that overall average longevity continued to rise.

But in the 1920s, mortality from cardiovascular disease had also begun to rise. The relative risk of heart disease increased slowly but steadily and eventually replaced infectious diseases as the leading cause of death as improved sanitation and widespread inoculation had their full impact. By 1950, heart disease and cancer had become the leading adult health threats in America and the industrialized world. In recent decades, we had to also confront widespread adult-onset (or Type 2) diabetes. And this surge in noninfectious disease was accompanied by rising rates of disability, especially among the elderly, an unfortunate trend that has continued.

◦━━━◦

In the 1970s, another major public health issue became apparent. Americans were beginning to eat a lot more high-calorie, high-fat fast food than ever before. With two-income households more common, families spent an increasing proportion of their incomes eating out, usually at fast-food franchises.

What had once been a monthly treat has become an almost daily habit. Originally, parents saw driving to a McDonalds, Burger King, or Kentucky Fried Chicken as an easy solution to the kids' age-old question, "Hey, Mom, what's for dinner?" But piling in the mini-van to head off for a fast-food meal night after night raises serious public health concerns.

The problem is that a dinner consisting of a double cheeseburger, large

French fries, and a milkshake—while certainly tasting good—exceeds more than half an adult's recommended *total* daily caloric intake in only one meal, and many of those fast-food calories are from unhealthy, artery-clogging saturated fat. The *New York Times* recently reported that University of Minnesota researchers have found that restaurant food now averages about 22 percent more fat than the food we eat at home. This type of meal also offers virtually none of the dietary fiber that nutritionists urge us to consume each day, while being seasoned with unhealthy amounts of salt that contribute to high blood pressure.

The situation has become so serious that U.S. Health and Human Services secretary Tommy Thompson has appealed to the fast-food industry to make more fruits and vegetables available, reduce fatty food, and eliminate "supersized" portions. The industry responded by noting that 70 percent of customers preferred the current menu choices.

Further, one unfortunate offshoot of the fast-food revolution is that frozen variants of these unhealthy meals—miniature pizza rolls, precooked burgers, and so on—which are easy to prepare in the home microwave, have become a new staple in the American kitchen. On many days when a family does not eat out, dinner at home might consist of high-calorie, highly salted frozen macaroni and cheese, an iceberg lettuce salad (with very little nutritional value) drenched in high-fat dressing, with ice cream or cake for dessert—again jamming more than half the recommended daily caloric intake into a single meal that provides almost no fiber.

As American nutritional patterns shifted away from a well-balanced diet that included plenty of fresh fruits and vegetables to the unhealthy food so many of us eat today, our traditional levels of physical activity have also decreased drastically. For decades, children walked to and from schools; but then sprawling suburbs replaced compact neighborhoods, and school children now have to be bused or driven. And many school districts have replaced energetic playground games with computer classes or indoor clubs. After the transformation from an agricultural and manufacturing economy (where rigorous daily physical labor was commonplace) to a service industry, moving a computer mouse or strolling to the coffee machine now represents the greatest expenditure of physical energy for many.

And the automobile continues to dominate our lives. We commute to work—often in stressful traffic jams—and we drive even short distances from our homes to pick up a forgotten loaf of bread or jug of milk. Whereas Americans once regularly walked several blocks each way to bus or streetcar stops on workdays, public transportation has become the most neglected resource in our urban-suburban infrastructure.

The health implications of our current poor nutrition and lax physical exercise habits are ominous. Growing numbers of Americans suffer from coronary heart disease (CHD), cancer, and Type 2 diabetes (with its host of disabling complications). Most of these afflictions are largely preventable "diseases of affluence."

One of the major causes of these diseases is the epidemic of obesity that has taken hold of the population. Centers for Disease Control and Prevention (CDC) research published in the *Journal of the American Medical Association* in 2002 revealed that the proportion of "overweight adults" (which includes the obese) jumped from 56 percent to 65 percent of our total population between 1999 and 2000. The figures for obesity alone stand at a grim one-third of the adult population. Overweight and obesity can be measured in several ways, but the easiest is to compare height with weight: Depending on gender and body type, a person 5'9" weighing 126 to 168 lbs. is considered normal; between 169 and 202 lbs. is overweight; 203 lbs. or more is obese. A person 6' tall weighing 137 to 183 lbs. is normal; 184 to 220 lbs. is overweight; 221 lbs. or more is obese.

Another definition of obesity is being one-third above ideal body weight, with many of those extra pounds stored as abdominal fat. African American women age 40 and older have the most severe national weight problem, although being overweight and obesity cuts across all lines of gender, social class, and racial or ethnic background.

Although obesity is far more serious than living with an unflattering body image, Harvard and Princeton researchers have released findings that show only a third of Americans view the condition as a major public health issue. To the large majority of people surveyed, AIDS, cancer, heart disease, and diabetes were a "very serious concern." Apparently they are unaware that obesity is the direct cause of death in more people than AIDS, and that obesity is often closely connected to heart disease, diabetes, and cancer.

In 2001, the U.S. Surgeon General Dr. David Satcher, responding to our "obesity epidemic," issued a Call to Action in which he indicated that obesity would soon surpass smoking as a cause of "preventable death." Dr. Satcher warned that about 300,000 Americans would die annually from illnesses stemming from obesity. These included Type 2 diabetes and high blood pressure. Researchers nationwide have identified obesity as the predominant factor in the explosion of new Type 2 diabetes cases in the United States. This connection has become so obvious that many physicians now informally call obesity "diabesity."

But diabetes is not the only risk obese people face. The American Heart Association warns that our leading killer, coronary heart disease, is often directly related to weight. Among the chief heart disease risks associated with being overweight or obese are dangerous increases in blood cholesterol and triglycerides levels. These fatty serum lipids contribute to sticky, artery-blocking plaque that often accompanies heart attack. Being overweight also lowers "good" HDL cholesterol that decreases heart disease and stroke risk. (It must be noted that good HDL can be increased through regular exercise.) People who are overweight or obese almost always have elevated blood pressure, a risk factor in stroke—our third leading cause of death and a leading cause of disability.

Although many Americans are coming to recognize the connection among weight problems, poor nutrition, and lack of exercise with heart disease and diabetes, relatively few people understand that these risk factors are also directly connected to common cancers. In 2002, the American Cancer Society (ACS) published the five-year update to its periodic Guidelines on Nutrition and Physical Activity for Cancer Prevention. One of the most startling findings was that "one-third of the more than 500,000 cancer deaths that occur in the United States each year can be attributed to diet and physical activity habits." (Another third of these cancer deaths are due to cigarette smoking.)

Dr. Anne McTiernan, director of the Prevention Studies Clinic at the Fred Hutchinson Cancer Research Center in Seattle, estimates that as many as 175,000 Americans die each year of cancers related to diet and lack of exercise. "Obesity and inactivity are like our version of the infectious diseases of one hundred years ago," she observes.

The 2002 ACS report discusses specific components of diet—fat, protein, whole grains, fresh vegetables, and so on—with relative risk for or protection against common cancers. In general, the higher proportion of fresh fruits, vegetables, and whole-grain foods we consume, the lower the incidence of cancer. The ACS dietary guidelines recommend we eat five or more servings of various fruits and vegetables each day. Fruit and small portions of nuts should replace potato chips, French fries, and other deep-fried vegetable snacks. Substitute 100 percent juice for soda. Increase daily consumption of whole-grain cereals, including bread and pasta. Fish, poultry, or beans are a healthy alternative to red meat. But if you do eat meat, choose small, lean portions and avoid pan- or deep-frying and charbroiling.

Regular consumption of dietary fiber (found only in fruits and vegetables) is an important and easy means of aiding digestion. Fiber speeds food through the digestive track and helps protect the colon from carcinogens. High-fiber fruits and vegetables are often also rich in phytochemicals, which have shown cancer-fighting qualities during experiments. Among the most promising foods are members of the cabbage family (cruciferous vegetables), including broccoli, brussels sprouts, and kale.

The research also compares opportunities to be physically active with cancer risk and sounds the alarm against reduced leisure time (connected with increased stress), greater reliance on automobiles, and a generally rising shift toward a sedentary lifestyle that emphasizes electronic entertainment rather than vigorous exercise.

The American Cancer Society also recommends that adults engage in at least thirty minutes or more of moderate physical activity on five or more days a week, and more vigorous activity to optimize the reduction of risk of breast and colon cancer.

By and large, the dietary and exercise recommendations of the American Cancer Society match those of the American Heart Association. Hypertension (high blood pressure) is a major and growing American health problem. It has been called a ticking national time bomb. "It's the major risk factor for heart disease," says hypertension expert Dr. Thomas Pickering, "which is one of the number one killers in the country and also for stroke, which is one of the causes of disability." Like other conditions, high blood pressure is much easier to prevent before its onset than it is to control.

If people understood that they could control their risk of cancer, heart disease, diabetes, and high blood pressure through modifying their diet and level of physical activity, undoubtedly millions would change their habits. But effecting these changes will not be easy: Research indicates Americans practice widespread denial when it comes to describing their eating and exercise patterns. They simply prefer not to recognize the worst, and seem willing to face the possible health consequences.

Yet these consequences continue to become more evident as cardiovascular disease, cancer, and diabetes rates grow inexorably. Unless Americans as individuals and collectively as a nation take responsibility to prevent these largely preventable afflictions, the country faces a tragedy as its population ages.

Either we gain control and reverse the grim trends in unhealthy nutrition and declining physical exercise, or the national health consequences for the future are disturbing: An unprecedented number of Americans will enter middle age and their elderly years already chronically ill or disabled. As UCLA gerontologist Dean Edward Schneider warns, this scenario could overwhelm our healthcare system.

Once more, is America facing an unavoidably grim future in which there will be too many elderly, chronically ill people for us to treat effectively and with compassion? Not necessarily. But bringing change will require what we now call a "paradigm shift." As Ralph Snyderman, M.D., chancellor for health affairs and dean of the School of Medicine at Duke University, has indicated, the clinical model or paradigm underlying American medicine is almost solely dependent on scientific and technological treatment intervention. But Dr. Snyderman is outspoken in his belief that the American healthcare system is "dysfunctional" specifically because of that dependence. "The current system reimburses healthcare providers for therapeutic procedures," he says, "but does not reimburse for those interventions that prevent disease and maintain good health and well-being."

This situation is reflected in the steadily increasing number of visits to and overnight stays in acute-care hospitals. Spending on hospital care in 2001 alone jumped 12 percent, accounting for more than half the total increase in healthcare costs. Unfortunately, these soaring costs—which must be absorbed by public or private health insurance—reveal the generally mediocre health of our aging population.

Indeed, it is unfortunate that—despite the now indisputable evidence on the power of prevention to reduce disease incidence (and the mounting cost of treatment), which organizations such as the American Heart Association and the American Cancer Society have assembled—practical prevention programs have not gained hold nationwide.

Ironically, health maintenance organizations, where so many million Americans now receive their clinical care, actually do very little to "maintain" the patient's health through properly guided prevention programs. Hard-pressed HMO doctors can spend approximately twelve or fifteen minutes for each patient consultation. It is difficult for the patient and doctor to exchange much clinical information or for the physician to impart useful advice on prevention during such truncated encounters.

The net result is often that the patient, still confused and often anxious, leaves the office clutching several brochures on weight loss and the risk of high blood pressure, and a handful of hastily scrawled prescriptions. Depending on patients' financial position and insurance coverage, most (so far) will be able to fill the prescriptions. But relatively few will do more than glance at the educational material their doctor has provided. As Dr. Snyderman indicates, people have become so dependent on their physicians' direct intervention to treat existing illness that they rarely consider prevention as a preferable alternative.

These patients need education and consistent counseling from a healthcare professional in whom they have confidence. But for many, this has proved to be an unattainable goal. (Stories such as Robert DeGray's, whose HMO shunted him from one physician to another, are becoming increasingly common.) Many people are aware that better nutrition, practical weight-reduction and management programs, and early disease detection are better than waiting until a condition has become chronic. But most need consistent, practical counseling to achieve these goals.

<hr />

When positive attitudes toward wellness and disease prevention are combined with spirituality, the resulting synergy is often mutually reinforcing.

For example, one entire Christian denomination, the Seventh-Day Adventists, places great doctrinal emphasis on wellness and disease prevention through promotion of a healthy diet and avoidance of tobacco, caffeine, and alcohol. The Seventh-Day Adventists (SDA) chose this path to preventive health in the mid-1800s on the premise that consumption of food and drink should honor and glorify God and preserve the health of the body, mind, and spirit. This was one of the first modern, codified approaches to what we now call holistic health.

Today, SDA nutritional guidelines are quite specific, and their impact on health and longevity has been the subject of considerable scientific research. The SDA diet is formally known as lacto-ovo-vegetarian and emphasizes whole-grain breads, cereals, and pastas, a liberal use of fresh vegetables and fruits, moderate consumption of beans and other legumes, seeds, nuts and low-fat or nonfat dairy products, including milk, cheese, and yogurt. SDA guidelines recommend limited consumption of whole eggs—three or fewer a week. The diet also recommends avoiding foods high in saturated fat and cholesterol such as meat and seafood. Coffee, tea, and alcoholic drinks should be avoided because they provide little nutritional value and are thought to interfere with absorption of essential nutrients. Fats and high-calorie food, oils, and sweets should be consumed only in small amounts.

From these components, which many Americans would find Spartan, members of the SDA have fashioned a diet that is both appetizing and healthful. But, because the SDA nutritional patterns were so different than those of the mainstream, the health impact of the diet and overall church lifestyle has been the subject of scientific interest for decades. And this pioneering research provided much of the foundation of what we have subsequently learned about the connection between nutrition and health.

In general, research on adult members of the SDA community has revealed significantly less chronic illness—such as cardiovascular disease and certain cancers—and greater longevity than the general population.

For example, several large, multi-year studies begun in the 1950s and 1960s revealed that SDA men died of respiratory disease at between 25 and 50 percent the rate of their peers in the general population. This health advantage was generally attributed to the widespread avoidance of tobacco among church members.

A study of over thirty-four thousand SDA from the 1960s showed their life expectancy advantage at age 35 substantially exceeded their mainstream counterparts. Once more, researchers credited this relative better health and longevity to diet and lifestyle.

Researchers found that the SDA diet was associated with colon cancer mortality rates of between 50 and 70 percent of the general population. "This strongly suggests," the researchers concluded in *Cancer Research* in 1975, "that the [SDA] lacto-ovo-vegetarian diet may protect against colon cancer."

Study after study published in our leading cancer, cardiovascular disease, and epidemiological journals since then have reached similar conclusions about the preventive health advantages of the SDA diet and lifestyle. What this research did not consider, however, was the faith and the congregational-support aspect of this healthful living. It's only common sense that members of the Seventh-Day Adventists find it relatively easy to follow the natural path toward preventive health when this is the doctrine of their faith and they receive such strong peer encouragement to do so.

Another model program is exemplified by the nondenominational Free Sacred Trinity Church, a California-based Christian spiritual movement that also operates an active mission in Austin, Texas. The church combined with the Hippocrates Institute of San Diego in 1977, emerging as the Optimum Health Institute. The movement's doctrine includes: "Putting biblical truths in action by placing equal stress on the blending of three individual duties to include development of the soul, the hygienic care of the temple of that soul—the body, and the purification of the mind through positive thinking." The church emphasizes "the harmonious blending of the physical, mental, and spiritual (holistic) that eliminates harmful habits and negative impulses, enabling the individual, at all times, to merit the ever-present help of the Almighty." The movement also stresses carrying its beliefs into practice as part of a life-long "24/7" commitment.

To achieve this harmonious balance of mind, body, and spirit, the church emphasizes prayer and meditation, as well as physical healing through detoxification and cleansing of the body. Following the teachings and lifestyle of the pre-Christian Essene sect, initiates in the church pass through a detoxification period that may last up to six months, during which they eat a raw vegetarian diet. After this, a more traditional vegetarian diet is usually adopted. Church members often worship individually rather than collectively, and rely heavily on monastic-style prayer and meditative discipline. But collective worship is also a regular feature in which congregants and guests participate.

Initiates and those simply curious about the spiritual and health advantages of the movement register as "guests" at the Optimum Health Institute centers in San Diego and Austin. Many become converts. Others learn healthful nutrition and develop meditative methods to relieve chronic stress. Once more, it is the linking of specific health techniques with spirituality that has brought this growing movement its success.

———

Can the doctrine and disciplines of movements such as the Seventh-Day Adventists and the Free Sacred Trinity Church be modified to apply to the preventive health needs of our general aging population? With the existing healthcare system — including Medicaid, Medicare, private health insurance, and pro bono care from hospitals — becoming badly stressed, where will we find the resources needed for a national program of effective health counseling? The answer to both these questions may well lie no farther away than your church or synagogue.

Seventy percent (approximately 197 million) of Americans consider themselves members of religious denominations. Forty percent of our population attends weekly services at America's many places of worship. When examined on a monthly basis, the percentage of those attending religious services increases to almost 60 percent. Obviously, members of these congregations worship regularly because they derive spiritual peace and emotional satisfaction from the practice. They also feel comfortable as members of their congregations, which many call their "home" church.

It is this level of trust and psychological comfort that has helped the country to initiate a quiet revolution in preventive healthcare: the parish or congregational nurse movement.

———

The late Reverend Granger E. Westberg, a Lutheran pastor in the Chicago area, became a full-time hospital chaplain in the 1940s. In this capacity, he concluded that most physicians were focused on treatment and cure of physical afflictions and ignored the patient's emotional and spiritual health. With rapid advances in scientific medicine, doctors had begun to view the people they treated not as whole individuals, but rather as a collection of symptoms. It was not unusual to hear physicians speak of "the colon cancer in room four-eighty" instead of "Mrs. Jones in room four-eighty."

But from his work as the pastor of St. John's Lutheran Church in Bloomington, Illinois, and especially from his experience as a hospital chaplain during which he devoted himself to intense counseling sessions, Westberg knew that any effective treatment had to involve the whole person, body, mind, and spirit. His revelations, however, came at the height of the treatment revolution, when antibiotics and advanced surgical techniques seemed to promise the ultimate victory of science over disease. And, increasingly, doctors saw themselves as scientists, not as healers in the traditional sense.

Westberg, however, had become firmly convinced from his in-depth counseling sessions with hospital patients that their physical afflictions could not be separated from their emotional state or spiritual health. He saw people as whole individuals who needed "wholistic" care. It was from this concept that Granger Westberg established several pioneering clinics in the Chicago area that treated people wholistically, recognizing that their mind, body, and spirit were inseparable. The patients who came to the clinics responded enthusiastically. Many were poor and needed free care; others gladly paid standard fees for this innovative approach.

The clinics' care teams consisted of salaried physicians and nurses and volunteer pastors and seminarians who served as counselors. But operating these clinics was expensive. Westberg was forced to examine the practicality of such wholistic care. What he found was surprising: Although people trusted the physicians who treated them, nurses showed the patients the most compassion, and patients took great comfort from this. Westberg realized that the nurse was the key member of the clinics' professional teams.

He saw that the nurses' sensitivity, what he called "peripheral vision," allowed them to look beyond symptoms and verbal statements to hear the underlying truth that had often been unsaid during preliminary consultations. Nurses might not have the refined diagnostic skills of physicians, but they usually shared great empathy with the patient. Years later, Westberg summarized his unexpected finding:

> Nurses seem to have one foot in the sciences and one in the humanities, one foot in the spiritual world and one in the physical world. The nurses I've had the privilege to work with have been very perceptive, they have great insight into the human condition.

So many nurses I work with have a deep spiritual desire to help people. They don't view the hospital as a warehouse for sick bodies. They see people as sacred in God's eyes. Consequently, they look at the whole person, not just the ailment.

When it was not practical to expand his clinic program, Westberg drew on the untapped resource the nurse represented. He helped place nurses as half-time staff members at local churches. With the backing of Lutheran General Hospital in Park Ridge, Illinois, a trial project was established at six greater-Chicago churches, four Protestant and two Catholic. The nurses' primary responsibilities would include, among other duties, health education, individual counseling, patient referral, and a variety of programs focused on preventive medicine. Lutheran General Hospital underwrote the nurses' salaries for the first four years, beginning at a 75 percent rate (the church contributed 25 percent) and decreasing each year until the church assumed the full cost.

This was the beginning of the parish nurse movement. What started as a small, pioneering effort in one city has spread across the country and has also taken root abroad. Today there are more than seven thousand parish nurses in America who have received formal training and are serving as paid or volunteer staff members in congregations in all fifty states. There are also thousands more who have not undergone structured parish nurse training, but who have honed their skills through reading professional literature and attending periodic conferences and workshops. It may be that the parish nurse movement is among the fastest growing branches of healthcare in America.

(A mounting number of synagogues also offer nurses to their congregations. But, purely for convenience, we will generally refer to "parish" nurses and to the leader of the congregation as the "pastor.")

What began in the mid-1980s as an experiment born of necessity has flourished beyond Granger Westberg's most enthusiastic vision.

Each year, parish nurses help arrange preventive care for hundreds of thousands of members of their congregations — many of whom might never benefit from techniques such as serum cholesterol, blood sugar, and cancer screening. Parish nurses lead seminars on nutrition and exercise, weight management, stress management, overcoming tobacco addiction, and safe sexual practices.

The key to the success of these preventive health programs is that the parish nurse and the congregation members share a bond of faith. The message that the parish nurse delivers is offered within a religious context, the most important of which is stewardship of God's priceless gift of health.

To reinforce this message, some parish nurses working with their clients on more healthful nutrition and weight management distribute refrigerator magnets with the verse from 1 Corinthians 10, "Whatever you do, whether you eat or drink, do all for the glory of God." When a person tries to sneak that gallon of fudge ripple ice cream from the freezer for a little midnight snack, he or she must first read these words.

The fact that tens of thousands of additional people each year are turning to parish nurses when much of our population seems to ignore the importance of prevention underscores the success of the program.

Today, the seven main responsibilities of a parish or congregational nurse include serving as:

- Integrator of faith and health

- Health educator

- Personal health counselor

- Referral agent

- Coordinator of volunteers

- Developer of support groups

- Health advocate

Although these duties might initially appear to be separate functions, parish nurses understand that they usually overlap. For example, because the nurse and her client belong to the same congregation, they already have a spiritual connection—similar to that Dr. Iris Keys enjoys with the inner-city African American church members she advises in Baltimore. People listen to the advice parish nurses give because they know it is rooted in loving concern.

As health educators and personal health counselors, parish nurses teach members of the congregation about such important issues as proper nutrition and developing healthful exercise habits.

In the role of health counselor, parish nurses also help clients negotiate the often-confusing web of rules surrounding Medicaid, Medicare, or HMO treatment.

Parish nurses often help develop and coordinate the work of volunteers from the congregation—people willing to visit shut-ins, drive them to doctors' appointments or to and from church.

If there is an interest in developing support groups, ranging from smoking cessation to stress reduction to weight reduction and management, the parish nurse is often the member of the congregation who initiates the program and makes sure it is conducted in a professional manner.

Health advocacy is another responsibility of parish nurses; they are often called on to help organize congregational health fairs at which other clinicians draw blood for cholesterol and PSA tests. (Parish nurses are prevented by state Parish Nurse Acts from conducting any invasive procedures, such as drawing blood or dispensing medication.) As clients' health advocates, parish nurses can make sure their clients benefit to the maximum degree possible from prevention programs, such learning how to use the free home occult blood-stool testing kits to check for possible colon cancer distributed at these health fairs.

Although parish nurses cannot take blood for laboratory tests, they perform regular blood pressure screening, usually seeing clients one-on-one twice a month. Prayer is often part of these private consultations, which helps deepen bonds linking both parties. Frequently during these confidential meetings, clients will reveal important health information such as their struggles with stress, marital tensions, or depression. The parish nurse can then counsel the client and guide him or her into the healthcare system to seek professional help.

How difficult is it to establish a successful parish nurse program? The recent accomplishments of clergy, a healthcare system, a local university, and committed nurses in Birmingham, Alabama, provide an example of what can be done.

Reverend D. Randal Walton, a Baptist minister and hospital chaplain with fifteen years' experience, had long noted a sad and disquieting phenomenon as he counseled seriously ill patients in the Baptist Health System (BHS) hospitals in Birmingham where he worked.

"Almost every time we talked of the person's illness," Walton recalls, "they would say the same thing, 'I wish I would have taken better care of my health.'"

Typically, these were people afflicted with cardiovascular disease, diabetes and its complications, and the types of cancer related to known risks, such as smoking, poor nutrition, and sedentary lifestyle. Walton was frustrated. He understood these men and women had strong religious faith, but few had ever been taught the concept of personal stewardship for their own health. For many of the very ill—those suffering from kidney failure or advanced heart disease—it was too late to begin that stewardship. But for others, Walton recognized that their home churches represented fertile ground to promote health education, individual counseling, support groups, and early detection screening—

if parish nurse programs could be established. Reverend Walton also recognized, however, that many of these congregations were small and lacked the ability to fund a parish nurse.

Perhaps Baptist Health System, which was well established in the community, would support the effort. Randal Walton approached the new president of the BHS Foundation, who expressed interest in helping. By 1998, Walton had BHS backing to proceed. But he soon realized the process was not going to be simple or straightforward. In Walton's initial, informal contact with local ministers, almost all reported that the health of their congregations was "good" or "excellent." When Walton visited these churches, however, he recognized that obesity alone was a serious problem for many members.

If the pastors of these congregations were unable to recognize existing or potential health problems, how could someone like himself, coming from outside the church, better determine the true nature of the members' health?

Walton turned to BHS health-assessment expert Lou Cohen for assistance. "Lou," he said, "can you help me write some type of survey that will capture an accurate picture of a congregation's health?"

Cohen was intrigued and motivated to meet the challenge. Soon Kelly Preston, a BHS nurse coordinator who was a devout Christian serving as a volunteer health ministry coordinator at the Brook Hills Southern Baptist Church, joined the project. Walton, Cohen, and Preston worked hard to develop the first survey. They based the questions on the Healthy People 2000 goals of the U.S. Department of Health and Human Services, as well as on standard measures of emotional health and spirituality.

The purpose of the initial survey was to determine if BHS could acquire a precise picture of congregation members' physical, emotional, and spiritual health. This questionnaire was approximately eight pages of multiple-choice questions; for example, "In general, would you say your health is: Excellent, Very Good, Good, Fair, Poor?"

But before the BHS team could administer the first surveys to a small test group of churches, Rev. Walton and Kelly Preston discovered there was confusion among many congregation members who did not understand the purpose of the questionnaire. The team found they had to conduct considerable groundwork explaining the function of the survey and its importance in building a practical prevention program. But once congregation members did understand the need for the survey and were confident that their privacy would be guaranteed, many were willing to participate.

In the section on spiritual health, people answered questions on the importance of prayer and spiritual well-being in their lives. They described on a range of "strongly agree" to "strongly disagree" questions about meaning and purpose in their lives, as well as overall life satisfaction, their capacity for forgiveness, and their general acceptance of their lives.

The personal health profile revealed a person's age, gender, height, and weight, and whether they were caregivers for an elderly person (a recognized stress factor). This section also asked people to describe what they considered the leading health problem in their communities.

To assess their general health, participants were asked to describe any problems they encountered during regular daily activities such as housework or climbing several flights of stairs, which might limit the kind of other physical activities they wished to perform.

Questions assessed people's emotional condition and whether depression or anxiety were problems that caused them to accomplish less than they wanted or made them perform work or other activities less carefully than normal.

A series of follow-up questions, such as, "Do you feel downhearted and blue?" and verifying the number of visits to a doctor's office or emergency room, supplemented the earlier answers to help substantiate their accuracy.

Another section of the survey asked if a doctor had ever told the person that he or she had high blood pressure, heart disease, diabetes, or cancer. People were asked to list the date of their last visit to a doctor for a routine checkup.

The survey tried to determine people's smoking habits, and whether a health professional had given them personal advice about losing weight and modifying their alcohol use. Again, there were supplemental questions designed to verify the accuracy of the earlier answers.

One of the most important sections of the survey dealt directly with prevention. It sought an estimate of people's health consciousness and habits: whether they kept up their flu and pneumonia shots; their patterns of seatbelt use; their exact levels of alcohol consumption; and their participation in physical activities or exercise. The survey also asked if a healthcare professional had talked with the person about diet or eating habits, blood cholesterol levels, and blood pressure patterns.

In separate sections for men and women, the survey tried to determine awareness of the mammogram as a breast cancer-detection technique, and how regularly the woman had undergone the procedure. Men were introduced to the prostate-specific antigen blood test to check for prostate cancer, as well as the digital rectal exam, and asked how frequently, if ever, they had taken the tests.

Once the results of the initial trial surveys were collected from the representative churches, Rev. Walton and his team produced their edited Congregational Health Survey. There were fifty-three questions on the final version. This was designed as a tool to enable each congregation to get a "snapshot" of the health of its church members. The completed surveys also provided the

BHS team with insights into the overall health status of the congregations individually and as a group.

To Rev. Walton, the most obvious conclusion was that the predominantly white, middle-class-to-affluent congregations enjoyed overall satisfactory physical health — especially those with many younger members. But their mental health — levels of stress, anxiety, ability to forgive and seek forgiveness, and depression — was much worse than expected. Members of white churches also derived much less satisfaction from their spiritual faith and practices, such as prayer, than Walton had anticipated.

A different situation prevailed among the predominantly black congregations. Their spiritual and emotional health was robust. But, although many of their pastors' original estimates describing members' physical health as satisfactory were accurate, the Congregational Health Survey found high levels of obesity and high blood pressure in too many churches. An unacceptable number of members had never had their cholesterol checked or been screened for cancer.

After Walton carefully reviewed the results of the survey, he consulted pastors individually. They now agreed that they had to look at the health of their congregations in a "wholistic" manner that integrated mind, body, and spirit and helped empower people to take responsibility for the stewardship of their own physical health, emotional well-being, and spiritual formation.

The next step was to begin establishing congregational health programs led by parish nurses at each church that requested them. Depending on the size of the congregation, the position would be paid, full-time or part-time, or volunteer. By the summer of 2002, the first five parish nurses — all experienced RNs — had completed the basic BHS preparation course, as well as specialized training at Samford University's Ida V. Moffett School of Nursing, and more were preparing to follow them to congregations in the Birmingham area. Each of them has acknowledged a strong calling by God to pursue the ministry of parish nursing. In doing so, they have entered a demanding but rewarding professional specialty, one that they share with thousands of dedicated colleagues nationwide.

(Currently, Rev. Walton is employed by CentraHealth in Lynchburg, Virginia, where he plans to establish the same type of parish nurse program he helped develop in Birmingham.)

———

As the five BHS parish nurses assumed their new responsibilities, they encountered challenges and found unusual opportunities to serve.

Debbie Duke became parish nurse of the ClearBranch United Methodist Church in Trussville near Birmingham. This was one of the area's fastest growing congregations, predominantly white, well educated, with an average age in the forties. The Congregational Health Survey had revealed that church members were especially interested in smoking-cessation classes, support groups for stress management, and disaster/emergency planning (possibly a psychological echo from the 9/11 terrorist attacks in 2001). Indeed, like so many other Americans, diffuse anxiety triggered by terrorism probably exacerbated some congregation members' ongoing stress problems and unhealthy habits such as smoking.

Many were also interested in the protective aspects of childcare, dealing with grief, and—among the older members—the medical concerns of the elderly, such as negotiating the Medicare system and dealing with HMOs. All expressed interest in health fairs that offered blood pressure and blood sugar screening.

Debbie Duke did not think obesity was a pressing problem, but some members wanted to start an aerobics program to maintain a healthy weight and cardiovascular fitness.

During the first Wednesday night blood pressure checks she helped organize, Debbie examined a 34-year-old male member of the congregation who was an emergency medical technician and appeared to be in good physical condition. But, perhaps due to diet combined with lack of exercise and an extremely stressful occupation, the man's blood pressure was at a life-threatening level.

"It's essential that you see a doctor as soon as possible," she told him, as she held his hand, speaking with obvious concern. "This is serious."

Then Debbie turned to the man's girlfriend to emphasize the point. "He really *does* need to see a doctor."

The next day at her hospital, Debbie encountered the man in the corridor. He had consulted a physician during an emergency appointment, received medication, and was scheduled to take a stress test to check for damage to his heart. Debbie was very pleased that he had accepted her advice and acted so quickly.

"I've had my blood pressure taken before," the man said, "but I just never did anything about it."

Debbie smiled. She had no doubt that, within the church setting, the man had trusted her and had been motivated by their common faith. Even though he worked with doctors and nurses every day, he had never been prodded into action before. But the message of stewardship of his own God-given health that she had tried to deliver had obviously been received.

Stella Ervin is another of the BHS parish nurses who assumed her duties in 2002. The Green Liberty Mission Baptist Church where she works has a congregation of around three hundred, predominantly African Americans. She did not need the Congregational Health Survey to show her what the people's principal concerns and needs were.

Obesity associated with poor nutrition and lack of exercise was an obvious problem. One of Stella's early priorities was to organize a nutritional fair that would become a regular event on the church calendar. This program would feature guest speakers and dieticians who would offer practical advice and provide healthful alternative meals and cooking methods to the fatty, high-salt traditional Southern cooking to which people were accustomed.

Stella was pleased and surprised that people came forward asking her to help organize an exercise program at the church. Obviously, members knew there were healthy alternatives to the lifestyles they had been leading. But they needed the catalyst of a skilled organizer such as Stella to channel their concern and religious faith into practical action.

For the first time, the people of the congregation were seriously addressing prevention and accepting stewardship of their own health.

In her role as a health counselor and advocate, Stella worked closely with individual members. One of her clients was a woman in her fifties who suffered from emotional problems and was confused about the prescription drugs she received through Medicaid. Despite her condition, this woman was a devout member of the church and never missed a service. This gave Stella the opportunity to cement the bond of trust between them. Soon, Stella was able to untangle the bewildering web of prescriptions and conflicting medical appointments, and work with the woman's doctors to better meet her physical and emotional needs.

Once more, it was the common bond of religious faith and the trust generated within the congregation that permitted Stella Ervin to reach a person in obvious need who had previously been shrouded by confusion.

The parish nurse and health ministry programs elsewhere in Alabama have also made impressive strides among congregations where the concept of preventive health based on stewardship was unknown. One such congregation was at the Living Light Church of God in Walker County. This area has some of the highest rates of cancer, obesity, and diabetes in the state. Yet the Congregational Health Survey showed parish nurse Reitha Cabaniss that church members—like so many other Americans—did not connect diet with health.

Working with the church pastor, Rev. James Newton, Reitha arranged for a team of student dieticians from Samford University to substitute a more healthful meal for the traditional dinner accompanying the regular Wednesday night service. Baked and poached fish replaced deep-fried chicken; steamed vegetables were served instead of collards stewed with fatty ham hocks. To their delight and surprise, Reitha and the dieticians saw that the congregation loved the food and were eager to learn the recipes and cooking techniques.

This was a single, but decidedly positive, step toward better health. Once more, prevention had been fostered within the context of faith.

Multiply the accomplishments of the parish nurses in Alabama across fifty states and thousands of congregations and the enormous potential of the movement becomes obvious. The Lutheran Hospital in inner-city Cleveland has trained fifty parish nurses to serve sixty congregations. Sinai-Grace Hospital in Detroit is active in congregational health, as is the Parish Nurse Program of the Trinity Regional Health System in Iowa. In some rural areas, congregational health ministries such as the parish nurse at St. Leo's Catholic Church in Lewistown, Montana, are among the most energetic healthcare providers. Nationwide, from the Bible Belt of the Southeast, all the way to the Pacific Northwest, parish nurses are spreading the gospel of preventive healthcare, educating members of their congregations, and serving as their health advocates.

To summarize in a graphic manner the contribution and potential of congregational health, a schematic model has been created that shows the relationship between prevention and disease management.

In this model, a congregation is part of a larger community, and, as such, is subject to all of its potential health problems, including stress, poor nutritional habits, and lack of exercise.

Under the guidance of the pastor, parish nurses or lay leaders can educate and motivate members of the congregation to adopt better patterns of preventive health. For example, individual members can be directed to examine honestly their own nutritional and exercise habits. Lay ministers and other individual members of the congregation — after receiving training and motivation coaching from parish nurses — can manage support groups and exercise programs. The parish nurse can also teach these lay congregational members

PREVENTION AND MANAGEMENT OF DISEASE

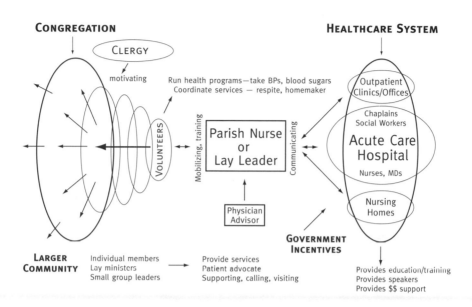

to provide other services, including telephoning and visiting homebound members, and serving as their advocates with the healthcare system. This last function is especially important for the elderly. If lay leaders in the congregation can assume much of this burden (under the supervision of a parish nurse), the parish nurse will have more time to devote to other members of the congregation.

One of the important responsibilities of the parish nurse is to train, motivate, and organize volunteers to run health programs such as blood pressure and blood sugar screenings, and to offer respite and homemaking assistance to caregivers of elderly disabled loved ones.

The parish nurse or lay person leading a congregational health ministry also has the responsibility of keeping lines of communication open with the local healthcare system. The leaders of the congregation's health program, whether parish nurses or lay people, should be familiar with the staff of their community's outpatient clinics and offices, as well as with the clinicians, social workers, and chaplains at acute-care and rehabilitation hospitals. With the patient's permission, they may need to communicate with nurses in these offices to clarify the medical plan, benefits and risks of treatment, or how to take medications and what their side effects are.

Finally, a congregation's parish nurse or health ministry lay leader should be in regular contact with nursing homes where members reside. This last responsibility is especially important to the elderly, who need close and nurturing human contact to prevent the onset of depression with all the physical afflictions that can follow.

———

Congregational nurses and health ministries led by lay volunteers now comprise a rapidly growing facet of our immense healthcare system. And it is crucial to recognize that these programs—which cost the Medicaid, Medicare, and health insurance systems virtually nothing—have the potential to provide huge savings in both financial outlay and physical suffering. No other national effort can compete with this potential as we face the healthcare challenges of the twenty-first century.

And, as our population steadily ages, congregational health programs—with their emphasis on prevention—can rise to fill the gap when other methods have failed.

———

Two recent books provide a more detailed examination of the parish nurse movement and the role of health in the faith community. They are: *Parish Nursing: Stories of Service and Care* by Verna Benner Carson, Ph.D., and Harold G. Koenig, M.D. (Philadelphia: Templeton Foundation Press, 2002), which offers a practical guide to individual nurses and congregations interested in starting programs; and *Healing Bodies, Minds and Souls: The Church's Role in Health Ministries* by W. Daniel Hale, Ph.D., and Harold G. Koenig, M.D. (Minneapolis, Minn.: Fortress Press, 2003), which is written specifically for the faith community to try to inform and excite religious leaders and lay members to develop health programs in congregations, with a focus on the role of trained lay leaders.

Religion, Aging, and Health

5

AN ELDERLY African American woman lay in a dim San Diego hospital room in 1998, tormented by anguish. Early the next morning, she would undergo kidney surgery, an invasive procedure she did not fully understand, but which she was certain was life threatening. Ellen Beck, M.D., who led the team that would operate, found the woman so gripped with anxiety that her limbs were rigid.

Dr. Beck took her patient's hand, seeking a way to comfort the woman. As an experienced and compassionate physician, Ellen Beck's heart went out to this gentle old person. And, from a purely medical standpoint, Dr. Beck also recognized that the stronger the woman's emotional state, the better her chances of survival during surgery, and the lower the risk of postsurgical complications.

"What are your sources of strength?" Dr. Beck asked.

The woman cited her faith and practice of reading the Bible. "But what I really love is church music," she said. "'Amazing Grace' is my favorite song."

The church choir could not be there, of course, and visiting hours were long over. Still holding the patient's hand, Dr. Beck, who is Jewish, suggested that they sing the Christian hymn together.

> Amazing grace! How sweet the sound
> That saved a wretch like me!
> I once was lost, but now am found;
> Was blind, but now I see.

As they continued to sing softly, Ellen Beck felt the woman's hand and arm slowly relax. Soon after they finished singing, the patient slipped into a peaceful sleep.

When the woman was prepared for surgery in the morning, her crippling anxiety had disappeared and she was calm.

Describing this encounter to health editor Alice McCracken of *Senior World Online*, Dr. Beck comments, "We brought her source of strength into the hospital setting."

———

Is this simply an inspiring vignette, or does the story of the role faith played in one woman's recovery help illustrate the positive association between religion and health in later life? As a single anecdote, the incident reveals very little. But viewed in a broader perspective, what occurred in that San Diego hospital reflects the vast amount of research findings on this intriguing subject.

Over the past one hundred years, researchers have conducted more than twelve hundred studies on the connection between religion and physical and mental health. Often this association is clearest among the elderly, who, as we have seen, draw on expensive healthcare resources in greater proportion than the younger population. A growing volume of research suggests both young and old religious people enjoy better emotional well-being and optimistic outlook, lower levels of depression (of reduced severity), less need for healthcare, and shorter hospitalizations than those with less robust religious faith. And it is especially noteworthy that the religiously active and privately devout healthy elderly enjoy significantly improved longevity when compared to their less religious peers in some studies.

This is not a matter of opinion, wishful thinking, or anecdotal account, but rather stems from decades of scientific research at many of our leading academic and clinical institutions.

———

Michael E. McCullough, Ph.D., and his colleagues analyzed forty-two studies on the relationship between attendance at religious services (church, synagogue, mosque, or Buddhist monastery), private religious activity, and lifespan. The key variables they examined were public religious involvement and membership in congregations and private religious activity, such as self-perceived degree of faith and devotion and how frequently a person prayed alone, read Scripture, or found comfort in religion as a coping resource. After taking into account factors such as age, education, and race, the research revealed a 29 percent better survival rate among those who are highly involved in religion compared to their less religious peers. This finding may be ascribed to the fact that faith bolsters social contacts and marital stability, tempers health-destructive behaviors such as alcohol and drug use, and also fosters positive attitudes and emotions known to contribute to good physical health. In turn, these benefits strengthen regular religious involvement.

Among the most provocative findings on religion and longevity are the results of the largest national survey on the subject to date. In 1999, Robert Hummer, Ph.D., a sociologist and demographer at the University of Texas, Austin, and colleagues analyzed a random national sample of 21,204 adults followed from 1987 to 1995. During that period, 2,016 deaths occurred among the group. The researchers examined religious attendance as a predictor of survival. Non-attenders lived to an average age of 75.3 years, compared with 81.9 years for those attending religious services once a week, and 82.9 years for those attending more than weekly (an additional seven and eight years, respectively). Life expectancy estimates followed established patterns of sex and race, with women generally living longer than men, and whites living longer than blacks. But among African Americans, frequent church attendance was also a strong predictor of improved longevity: Those attending services more than once a week lived an average of 80.1 years, compared to only 66.4 years for those who never attended services. The investigators took great care to ensure that their findings were not due to poorer health or lower socioeconomic status of non-attenders at the beginning of the survey and also employed rigorous statistical methods as control for limitations to physical activity, self-reported health, and days spent in bed in the year before the study started in 1987. Further, they repeated the analysis, excluding those in the sample who died between 1987 and 1991, reasoning that people who were unhealthy in 1987 and thus unable to attend church might bias the results. After this second analysis, the results were similar to those obtained initially: The association between religious attendance and mortality remained robust, with those who were most active in religion living significantly longer lives.

This study is typical of other research examining the relationship between religion and longevity. Over 70 percent of the research on the connection between attendance at services and other measures of faith reported longer survival associated with this activity.

In 1999, Duke University's Center for the Study of Religion/Spirituality and Health published the results of more research on the relationship between attendance at religious services and improved longevity. This study focused on the elderly: 3,968 people 65 years or older who were followed for six years to determine if psychosocial and behavioral pathways associated with religious community involvement could affect health and ultimate survival. The findings pointed toward a clear, positive association. The risk of dying for frequent attenders was 46 percent lower than for those attending services less often. Even after adjusting for demographic factors such as race and gender, physical and emotional health status, degree of social connections, and better health practices (diet and exercise, etc.), people who attended religious services once a week or more frequently had a significantly better chance of survival than those who did not. The researchers suggested that this improved survival might be due to several factors: Almost by definition, people who attended church frequently had more personal contact and support than those who rarely attended services. Earlier research had indicated that such social support might directly benefit the immune system to help the body defend against heart disease and cancer. Further, frequent attendance at services probably bolsters the concept of stewardship of one's health, so that such persons will see their doctor regularly and follow the medical treatment plan. Frequent attendance has also been shown to decrease rates of depression, responses to daily stress, and anxiety triggered by unfortunate events. Finally, the research indicated that the religiously involved had much lower rates of smoking than the non-attenders, which would certainly influence overall health for the better.

In a related study, Duke University researchers examined the link between private religious activity such as praying, reading Scripture, or spiritual meditation, and longer survival among 3,851 elderly people living in their North Carolina homes between 1986 and 1992. By the end of the 6.3-year study period, 1,137 subjects (29.5 percent) had died. After controlling for physical and emotional health status and stressful events at the beginning of the study, the researchers found that the healthy elderly (people without disability) who reported little to no private religious activity were 63 percent more likely to die during the research period than the frequent participants. Even after controlling for secular social support and health behaviors, the investigators found that lack of private religious activity continued to predict a 47 percent greater risk of dying.

The implication that emerges from this research is that both private devotion and regular congregational worship help form inner reserves of emotional and physical health that promote longevity. One man's story illustrates this point.

○———◦

On a night late in 1944, Second Lieutenant Jim Murry, a young Army Air Force bombardier, was curled up sound asleep in the Plexiglas nose of a B-24 Liberator, droning west, 8,000 feet above the black Pacific. The hulking four-engine bomber was en route from California to the Hawaiian island of Oahu, two thousand miles distant; its ultimate destination was New Guinea and the war zone of the Southwest Pacific. For now, the frenetic final months of training were over. But the airmen had not yet faced the test of combat. Those not actually flying the plane could catch up on their sleep.

Suddenly Murry was jolted awake by three clanging alarm bells: the prepare to bail out signal from the pilot. The normal roar of the motors had become much softer, and Murry realized that they had lost power in at least two engines. His compartment tilted wildly to the left and he felt the plane stall and plunge toward the ocean. Jim Murry remembered his training: snap on his parachute pack and open the nosewheel to serve as an emergency exit.

But, as he fumbled with the snaps of his parachute, Murry heard the pilot's voice in his earphones, radioing the distress call to other Liberators flying ahead and behind their own plane.

"We've lost three engines," the pilot called frantically. "We're going in!"

Three engines, Murry thought. We'll never make it. Even if some of the crew did manage to successfully bail out of the plunging bomber, they would splash down in the cold North Pacific five hundred miles from the California coast, too far for any practical rescue before they died of exposure.

The slipstream rose to a howl, Murry was pinned against a creaking aluminum bulkhead by centrifugal force, and he realized they had to be falling at more than three hundred miles per hour. If the two pilots did not immediately regain control, the tail would snap off and everyone on board would die.

"Please, God," Murry heard himself say, "get us out of this."

He had never been particularly devout. But now he understood with piercing clarity that God quite literally held the lives of all ten crewmen in His hands.

Suddenly, the three dead engines sputtered, coughed, then roared again. The two pilots strained at the controls, leveling the wings and pulling out from the near-fatal dive at an altitude of just three thousand feet.

Murry hunched in his compartment, listening to the four big engines straining at full power. Over the intercom, the pilot explained what had happened: On this long flight they relied on gasoline tanks in the bomb bay. But an airlock had developed, and engines had choked, starved of fuel, before the engineer could shift pumps and overcome the stoppage. Somehow, he had managed to do so before the plane was ripped apart by stresses that far exceeded its design limits. They turned east, and flew back toward California. As the first hint of dawn rose ahead, Murry said a prayer of thanks.

The crew landed at Sacramento, assuming the Air Corps would flight test the bomber and reject it from further service due to the damage it had sustained in the five-thousand-foot plunge. Instead, maintenance officers simply ordered the plane refueled and sent it back on its way to Hawaii. But the airframe had been warped, which drastically increased drag and reduced fuel efficiency. Ten hours into the flight, it was clear they would never make Oahu. The navigator saw they might possibly be able to stretch their dwindling fuel to Hilo on the big island of Hawaii, and the bomber diverted south.

Once more, Murry asked for God's protection. "Lord, we're in your hands."

The plane landed safely late that afternoon. But as it rolled to the end of the runway, first one, then two more engines sputtered and died, again starved of fuel.

Over the coming months, Murry flew many combat missions, some over the Japanese Home Islands themselves. His plane survived antiaircraft fire and fighter attack. Murry came to rely on his intense but quiet faith as a shield against the hazards of war. This allowed him to perform his duty without being preoccupied with fear. He felt confident that God would continue to protect him.

Murry returned from the Pacific in 1946, married, and somehow compressed a four-year course in journalism at the University of Georgia into two years, while also working at the radio station affiliated with the *Atlanta Journal-Constitution.*

He and his young family joined the local United Methodist church, where he became very active, serving as the chairman of the church board. His strong personal faith endured. Once, while driving through heavy traffic during a downpour on I-20, his car skidded across the median into the path of oncoming vehicles.

"God," Murry prayed in the same tones he had first used that night in 1944 as his bomber plunged toward the dark ocean, "if it's Your will, get me out of this."

Cars and trucks fishtailed around him, but there was no collision.

Murry enjoyed good health for most of his life. But he had to undergo emergency gall bladder surgery in his sixties. Just before he slipped under the anesthesia, he again called on God for protection in simple, direct terms: "God, it's up to you."

When Murry's leadership role in his congregation tapered off after he retired, he became active in the Lay Witness Mission, through which lay people formed teams to visit congregations on weekends and share Christian fellowship and worship. Sometimes these encounters involved very personal testimonies of faith as a single congregation member shared experiences with a Lay Witness visitor. "I found these meetings very emotionally and spiritually satisfying," Murry recalls, noting that people were often more willing to open up and share their burdens with strangers than with those in their communities.

For years, Murry was also active on the board of trustees of Candler Hospital in Atlanta, where he oversaw the spiritual care department, responsible for chaplains. This experience led him toward the Institute of Religion and Health, a national resource center on faith, healing, and health. The South Carolina-based institute focuses on a wholistic approach to health and healing, in which wellness is a balance of mind, body, and spirit. Working with institute founders Dr. Don Berry and Dr. Ron Eaker to develop branches of the organization in Georgia, Murry came to understand that much of his own physical and emotional well-being into his seventies could be attributed to that healthy balance of mind, body, and spirit. Even when he was diagnosed with prostate cancer at age 73 in 1996, he opted for a then relatively unproven treatment involving small radioactive seeds implanted directly in the gland, as opposed to more radical surgery.

"I trusted my doctor's advice on this," Murry recalls. "But I also felt confident that God had protected me so far and He wouldn't let me down."

Today, Murry is 80 years old. All tests indicate he is free of cancer and in overall excellent health.

His spiritual health also remains robust. He regularly attends services and practices daily, private, silent prayer, sharing his concerns and aspirations for himself and his family directly with God. He sleeps well and awakes eager to face each day.

Jim Murry's reliance on faith is common among elderly people. Recent Gallup polls (2002) indicate most older Americans are religious. Approximately 96 percent of people over 65 believe in God or a universal spirit; 90 percent pray regularly; and 55 percent attended religious services in the past seven days. They also use religion to cope with difficult changes associated with aging, including declining financial status, bereavement, and worsening health.

It is when older people become sick that religious beliefs and practices become particularly important, at a time in life when they are often dependent on others and personal resources have become exhausted. Religious belief, however, is seldom affected by changes associated with age, and usually becomes stronger as a result of those very changes, which might help promote longevity.

The mechanism linking private religious activity and improved lifespan might be similar to that assumed to connect attendance at services and better survival: a strengthened emotional state, including the ability to deal more effectively with stressful events. If this is the case, those who, like Jim Murry, regularly practice private devotion might have stronger immune and cardiovascular systems than those who do not. In other words, people for whom personal devotion is important might be shielded from the physical damage uncontrolled stress hormones can inflict on their immune and cardiovascular systems. This does not mean to suggest that people who pray, read the Bible, or practice spiritual meditation will not encounter the life stresses we all must address, but rather that they are better able to cope with them.

The importance of religion as a way of coping became evident during research that Duke University conducted. In one study of several hundred hospitalized men over age 70, the subjects were asked what enabled them to cope with health problems and life changes—including declining financial and social resources—that they encountered as they aged. In the research questionnaire and interview, no mention whatsoever was made of religion. Despite this, almost 25 percent of the men spontaneously reported that religion was *the most important factor* that enabled them to cope. The researchers asked the same question of more than three hundred men and women patients admitted to Duke University Medical Center. Among this group, no fewer than 42 percent spontaneously reported that religion was the most important factor enabling them to cope.

What did the patients mean by this? They meant that praying, trusting in God, turning problems over to God, and receiving support from a minister or from members of their congregation provided an important means of shielding them from the stress, pain, grief, and disappointments that so often accompany aging. Although 42 percent gave religion as the most important factor, more than 90 percent of the patients indicated that they had used religion to at least a moderate extent to help them cope with health problems and other stressful circumstances: One only need recall the elderly surgical patient in that San Diego hospital, wracked by fear and anguish the night before her operation, who gained so much comfort from Dr. Ellen Beck praying with her in the form of the beloved hymn, "Amazing Grace," to grasp the power of the religious experience as a coping technique.

○━━━◦

If religious involvement is related to better health and greater well-being, perhaps the need for and use of costly medical services may also be affected. Beginning in August 1993, researchers at Duke University examined the relationship between religious affiliation and religious attendance and use of acute hospital care among 542 older medical patients. These men and women had a mean age of 70 and were consecutively admitted as inpatients to the Duke hospital's general medicine, cardiology, and neurology services. Interviewers first determined the subjects' religious affiliation, including mainline Protestant, Fundamentalist, Jewish, Catholic, or none. All told, the affiliation category was divided into fifty-seven different denominations and sects.

The study was designed to test three hypotheses: If higher attendance at religious services was in fact associated with better relative health, that might be reflected in lower rates of acute hospitalization during the year prior to admission and also with a shorter stay at the Duke University Medical Center during the study period. If this were the case, people not affiliated with a religion, who rarely if ever attended services, might be in relatively worse health, have been hospitalized more frequently, and would require longer stays in the Duke hospital. Finally, the researchers thought that the relative health benefit of religious affiliation and involvement would persist even after they took into account factors likely to affect length of hospitalization, such as age, gender, race, and severity of illness and degree of disability.

Interviewers asked the subjects how often they attended church or other religious services. The patients had six response options ranging from "never" to "more than once a week." The interviewers also determined how frequently and for how many days the patients had been hospitalized during the year prior to their current admission at Duke.

This information was analyzed using statistical models to determine whether number of hospital admissions and lengths of stays were related to religious affiliation and attendance. The effects of age, race, gender, education, physical and emotional health, and levels of social support were also carefully taken into account.

The findings were interesting: The probability of being hospitalized once or more in the previous year was lower for those who attended religious services at least once a week (the "frequent attenders") than for those who attended less frequently. The total number of days hospitalized in the year prior to admission at Duke was also significantly lower among frequent attenders. Patients not affiliated with any religious denomination had significantly more hospital admissions in the previous years and tended to have spent more days in the hospital during the three months prior to their admission at Duke.

The study's main findings were significant:

■ After taking into account all the variables, it was determined that people who attended religious services at least once a week were 44 percent less likely to have been admitted to the hospital in the prior year than the study's less religious subjects.

■ Frequent attenders spent fewer days in the hospital in that year than those less religiously involved.

■ Compared to people affiliated with a religious denomination, subjects with no religious affiliation spent an average of *fourteen more days* at the Duke hospital (24.8 vs. 10.6 days). This meant that the people affiliated with a faith community stayed less than half as long in Duke hospital as people their own age and background suffering similar illnesses, but who lacked a connection with a congregation.

The economic significance of this study, when viewed through the perspective of our looming healthcare crisis, cannot be overstated. Today, acute-care hospitalization can cost as much as $5000 a day at leading teaching hospitals. Although less at smaller hospitals, the daily cost of acute care is rising dramatically in many parts of the country.

In the Duke study, one of the significant factors common among those who were discharged from the hospital unusually early was that their faith either shielded them from depression or reduced its severity. As we have seen, depression has a serious impact on physical health. Depression triggers internal stress that unleashes hormones and other chemicals that are harmful to both immune and cardiovascular systems, which can undercut healing and prolong illness.

The power of religion to shield against stress and depression engendered by illness emerged among many of the participants in the study subjects. Some spoke warmly of their "home" congregations, as if they were discussing a close, supportive family. For others who were depressed facing serious procedures such as open-heart surgery, reliance on their personal faith helped them deal with the stressful anxiety of the ordeal ahead. And frail, very elderly patients with serious conditions such as congestive heart failure and unstable angina found unshakable strength in their faith.

This enduring or renewed inner strength may have been reflected in the higher numbers of the religiously active patients being discharged from the hospital significantly earlier than their less religious peers.

⌕⟶

Currently, our population over 65 whose main hospitalization costs are covered by Medicare is steadily increasing. Within ten years, as millions more Baby Boomers retire, the strain of paying for their hospitalization threatens to cripple the Medicare system.

Yet, if religious faith and practice can foster better health among older people, which may reduce the need for repeated hospitalizations as well as the length of hospital stays, shouldn't the public health community seriously investigate this intriguing phenomenon more closely? Furthermore, shouldn't the public health community welcome congregations and their members as part of the healthcare team?

———

Breast cancer is a disease that every woman fears. Although mortality rates from this most prevalent female malignancy are improving with advances in early detection and treatment, more than 182,000 American women still die each year from breast cancer, many middle-aged and older. And the cost of treatment mounts steadily as our population ages.

Beyond the prevention and early-detection efforts now gaining momentum, as well as the breakthroughs in surgery and chemotherapy, are there any other innovative approaches being investigated? There is intriguing evidence emerging that religious faith and practice might offer a degree of protection for women already diagnosed with the disease.

Previous research has indicated that the progression of breast cancer is related to the patient's immune system. In simplified terms, the stronger a woman's immune function, the more efficiently she can fight malignant cells and thus augment treatment such as chemotherapy and radiation.

Sandra E. Sephton, Ph.D., and colleagues at Stanford University investigated the connection between religious practice, immune function, and endocrine activity in 112 women whose breast cancer had spread beyond the original tumor site. Most of the women were Caucasian with a mean age of 53. Thirty-eight percent were Protestant, 15 percent Roman Catholic, 13 percent Jewish, with other affiliations 18 percent. Sixteen percent had no religious affiliation. The women all answered questions on their frequency of attendance at religious services and the importance of religious or spiritual expression in their lives.

The researchers took two morning blood samples per subject to assess white cell numbers, natural killer (NK) cell activity, and other lymphocytes, which are indicators of general immune system strength. The blood samples were taken about one week apart to determine overall immune status among the women.

The results were interesting. Women who reported that spiritual expression was important in their lives had greater numbers of white blood cells and total lymphocytes, helper T cells, and cytotoxic T cells, indicating a stronger immune system than did less religious subjects. Factoring in social network size did not affect these results, nor did cancer treatments such as chemotherapy, which affect immune cell counts.

"These findings supported our hypothesis that greater spiritual expression would be associated with greater immunity," the study's authors concluded.

Since social network size was statistically controlled for, the findings suggested the possibility that religious expression by itself could help preserve immunity under physically taxing and emotionally stressful circumstances.

———

Ovarian cancer is much less prevalent than breast cancer, with about thirty thousand new cases diagnosed each year in the United States. But, tragically, the disease has a far greater mortality rate, with approximately fifteen thousand victims dying annually. For many who learn they have this "silent killer" (so named because ovarian cancer is often symptom free until its fatal end stages), the news is a virtual death sentence.

This seemed to be the case for western Minnesota grandmother and Lutheran social worker Betty McGuire, now 50.

On a Friday night July 1999, while her husband, John, and son, Bill, were away on a weekend fishing trip, she became desperately ill, stricken by burning pelvic pain. Soon the agony spread up her abdomen, across her torso, and into her left shoulder. Striding endlessly around her kitchen table like a tormented animal, she found no relief from the physical pain. But incessant prayer offered some respite. Although she was alone in their country home near the small town of New London, Betty did not feel isolated. Instead, as she prayed more deeply, the tangible presence of God filled the room, calming her fears. She decided to wait until the morning before seeking medical help.

Early that Saturday at the nearby Willmar Hospital, the physician on call ordered a sonographic image of Betty's pelvis, which revealed an ominous shape. The initial diagnosis: "Complex 11cm left ovarian cystic mass."

Eleven centimeters, Betty thought. *That's four inches.*

She saw from the look on the doctor's face that he was very concerned. "This does not look good at all. I can definitely feel a mass on your ovary, and it's probably hemorrhaging. That's what's causing the pain. You're going to need surgery to take biopsies of the mass and the nearby lymph nodes. Then you'll probably need an oncologist."

"Biopsies?" Betty said, aghast. "Do you mean I might have cancer?"

"I'm sorry, but you certainly have all the symptoms," the doctor said frankly.

Her own physician advised Betty to have the surgery done in Minneapolis as soon as possible.

Betty was the director of the City Life Ministry in Minneapolis, which addressed the needs of women who were destitute, homeless, or substance abusers, as well as victims of domestic abuse. She knew the city healthcare system well and was able to arrange an emergency consultation on Monday with two experienced obstetric specialists at the Larson Clinic, Drs. William Meyer and Paul Jensen.

Still alone in her home that Saturday afternoon, Betty was haunted by the words "oncologist, lymph nodes, large ovarian mass, and emergency surgery." But as she turned to prayer, her fears began to ease, and she thanked God that He was still in control of her life.

Later that afternoon, she picked up the phone and went to work, contacting friends around the country with a simple request: "Pray for me. Ask God to remove this cancer. Spread my appeal in your churches."

Her friends assured her that they would follow her request, and that they would ask their relatives and other "prayer warriors" in churches and Sunday schools from the Gulf Coast, to the Midwest, to the Rockies, so that eventually hundreds or even thousands of people would be praying for her.

As each friend called to report progress on the lengthening prayer chains, Betty felt her confidence build. The Lord was indeed her Shepherd, just as it said in the Twenty-Third Psalm. All that Saturday night and Sunday she meditated on the Psalms and on gospel passages, finding assurance that the Lord did answer prayer.

On Monday, July 12, she met with Drs. Meyer and Jensen in the Minneapolis clinic. They concurred with her hometown physician's tentative diagnosis. She had all the symptoms, and her blood test for the telltale CA 125 cancer marker was "off the chart": Normal CA levels ranged from 0 to 35.0; Betty's was an ominous 50, suggestive of ovarian cancer. Dr. Jensen scheduled her for laparoscopic surgery the next day. In this procedure, he would insert thin, flexible tubes into her pelvis to inspect the ovarian growth and take tissue samples from it, as well as from adjacent lymph nodes, to determine if the probable malignancy had spread. If a pathologist confirmed the presence of cancer, the surgeons would open her pelvis the next week and remove the affected ovary and lymph nodes. Then she would begin chemotherapy in the slim hope the cancer could be stopped before it spread farther.

Betty was again overcome with anxiety. Although her husband, John, was at her side, and her family had rallied to her, she felt deep anguish. *I'm only forty-nine years old*, she thought. *Please, God, help me.*

Then her anguish suddenly abated. *Either way,* she calmly realized, *I'm a winner.* If the cancer claimed her life, God would shepherd her into the next world. If He intervened to cure her of cancer, her life with her loved ones here on Earth would continue. Waiting for the surgery, she once more meditated on Scripture and pictured her family. She had planned to fly to North Carolina to visit her young granddaughter, Megan, in two weeks. Betty did not intend to cancel her airline reservations.

The morning of the procedure, Betty said her prayers and was wheeled into the operating room, her mind serene.

To the profound surprise of the surgeons, the pathologist detected no trace of cancer. When Betty spoke to Dr. Meyer, he was at a loss to explain what the surgeons and pathologists had found.

He showed her a photograph of malignant ovarian cells. "This is what cancer cells looks like," he said, shaking his head. "But the pathologist found no cancer. If it had existed, it's gone now."

He handed her pictures of her own healthy ovaries taken through the laparoscope during the surgery.

"It was the prayer," Betty assured him. "There's no other way to explain this."

Dr. Meyer frankly conceded, "I didn't know God could remove cancer cells."

Since the surgery, Betty has joked while speaking to church groups: "God even saves Lutherans." Then she adds in a more reverent tone, "I don't have great faith. I have faith in a great God."

During a checkup in December 1999, Dr. Paul Jensen and Betty discussed her amazing recovery. Her CA 125 level in the latest blood test had dropped to 15, about midway on the normal range. "It truly is a miracle," he told her. "There is no other way to explain it."

Research suggests that prayer may have a significant impact on immune function. And going beyond the breast cancer study, we have to recognize that regular attendance at religious services includes close and sustained social contact and a sense of religious belonging and emotional support. The deep assurance that Betty McGuire gained from knowing that scores of prayer groups nationwide were focusing their devotions on her cure was also immensely reassuring. In turn, this lowered her anxiety level, which may have strengthened her immune function.

At the interface of medicine and religion today, we should also consider the intangible factor of congregational worship and ritual, including group recitation of familiar, reassuring prayers and participation in liturgical music. Interestingly, all three of the world's monotheistic religions (Judaism, Christianity, and Islam) incorporate these elements to some degree. Whatever the physiological effect of attending a religious service, it is a common observation that those who participate in congregational worship leave the service with positive feelings that might help counteract the stress of illness as well as provide physical health effects that go far beyond simply the prevention of depression or other negative emotions.

Research indicates that religious beliefs and practices may also affect the cardiovascular system of older adults. With heart disease and stroke being the primary cause of death and disability in later life, such a connection is worth exploring. In a study of the relationship between religious attendance, private religious activity, and blood pressure, Duke researchers examined the worship practices among four thousand people in North Carolina age 65 or over. Again, there was an association between these religious activities and better health outcome. Persons who attended religious services weekly and prayed or read religious Scriptures daily were 40 percent less likely to have high diastolic blood pressure (the measure taken when the heart is at rest) than those who attended services less often and prayed less frequently.

As previous research has found, reduction of average diastolic blood pressure of just two to four milliliters in the population as a whole could reduce cardiovascular death rates by up to 20 percent. If religious faith and practices play a significant role, it is time for the traditional medical community to reexamine the importance of religion in healing and wellness among our growing elderly population in whom high blood pressure is a serious health threat.

If the link connecting religious faith, coping with disease, and recovering from illness is present in older people, is this association also evident in younger adults? One man's story offers evidence that it is.

By most principles of medical science, David Montini, now 48, should not be alive. As a student at the University of South Florida in the early 1980s, Montini was struggling to complete a bachelor's degree at age 26. His education had been earlier interrupted by a failed marriage and unsuccessful forays to break into the world of entertainment. When he was stricken with intense lower-abdominal pain, Montini underwent an intestinal examination with an endoscope.

"My God," the infirmary physician said with an involuntary gasp. He explained to Montini that the interior of his colon was virtually covered by polyps. This proved to be Gardner's syndrome, a serious inherited medical condition in which the lining of the intestinal tract and adjacent internal organs become riddled with small tubular tissue growths. Montini's only treatment option was surgical resection of the most badly affected part of the large intestine. Otherwise, the polyps might become malignant and spread to nearby organs.

Montini, who was studying clinical social work and wanted to become a therapist for the handicapped, was not particularly religious or spiritual at the time. He had been raised in a home divided between a Roman Catholic and a Baptist parent and had become an adult without much personal faith. In fact, this spiritual split at home pushed him toward atheism.

When he underwent his first surgery, he felt cold and isolated, almost alone in the uncaring universe. And, when his doctors confirmed that he faced a second major operation, Montini teetered on the brink of another emotional void. If he were to die on the operating table or not recover from the surgery, he wanted to be prepared. "I'm just not spiritually ready," he told his physicians. "I'll let you know when I am."

"Don't wait too long," they warned.

David Montini began to pray and meditate, tentatively at first, and then more intensely. When he underwent the second surgery, he continued his prayer and spiritual meditation discipline. Prayer became a major part of his life as he felt his strength return. For three years, it appeared that the Gardner's syndrome and its complications had been defeated. But his health problems had overwhelmed both his second marriage and his career. Then alarming symptoms, including intense abdominal pain, flared up. He endured the Whipple procedure, during which surgeons made a long, Y-shaped incision in his abdomen. They found hundreds more polyps spreading beyond the intestinal tract and confirmed the suspected presence of a pancreatic tumor. Even though the surgeons removed the obviously involved portions of this organ as well as adjacent parts of the intestine and stomach, they were not optimistic that they had stopped the cancer's spread.

"We can only give you a survival prognosis of two years," they told Montini. He would be lucky to live to age 30.

This grim prediction seemed accurate when life-threatening postsurgical infections broke out and he was confined to the intensive care unit of a hospital for forty-nine days.

When he was finally released, David Montini went to his sister's house to recover. But, while his body was slowly healing, his emotions dropped into a deep depression. He began to drink heavily and could find no comfort in prayer or meditation. What good would it do? Pancreatic cancer was fatal in all too many cases. He wasn't a recovering patient; he was terminal. What was the sense of waiting to die a painful death?

One afternoon when he was alone in the house, Montini choked down half a bottle of Percodan opiate painkillers with three water glasses of whiskey. This was a lethal dose: The combination of so many pills and that much alcohol should have killed him within thirty minutes.

"But God intervened," Montini remembers. Before the opiate and alcohol could completely suppress the respiration center of his brain, he vomited and recovered.

Still, the need for alcohol to ease his anguish was acute. At dusk one winter day, he made his way down the icy sidewalk toward the beckoning neon sign of a liquor store. A lighted cross atop a steeple to his left caught his attention and drew him toward the church. At the altar, he knelt and said one simple sentence: "Jesus, please be the Lord of my life."

As he spoke, Montini felt the grip of his fear and depression loosen.

Later, when he was finally strong enough to attempt chemotherapy, he felt an odd but unshakable conviction that this treatment was not necessary. For the first time in over a year, he was eating well and gaining weight. He had his strength back. His mood was serene. Although he felt it was unnecessary, Montini took his first course of chemotherapy, which made him wretchedly ill. *This will kill me of the cancer doesn't*, he thought.

He stopped the chemotherapy, over his physicians' strong objections. Weeks, then months passed. He continued to eat well and gain weight. His doctors were puzzled. Either the surgical team had somehow managed to remove every malignant cell or Montini had experience a spontaneous remission, which was almost unheard of in pancreatic cancer.

"I think there's a third possibility," Montini told his physicians. "God cured my cancer."

"The Lord works in amazing ways," one of his doctors said, shaking her head.

Montini returned to Florida and began preaching in churches and working toward certification as a clinical therapist, addiction counselor, and pastoral counselor. Following his own experience, he became a strong advocate for the spiritual model of healing that addresses the needs of the mind, body, and spirit.

Despite additional personal turmoil and a serious injury in a car accident, Montini has not been assailed by depression. He copes with the stress in his life through daily spiritual discipline, praying privately morning, afternoon, and night. His prayers are always a positive affirmation of his submission to God's will.

"God is my direction" has become one of his spiritual mainstays.

Although he is partially disabled by the spine injury he suffered in the car accident, he does not feel that this or his long, painful encounter with illness has left him a victim.

David Montini now lives in Augusta, Georgia, and is working to complete his Ph.D. in psychology. He has married a wonderful young woman named Jennifer and they have a two-year-old son, Jonathon.

Montini discounts the possibility that disease will return to haunt his life. "I *know* that God is taking care of me and my family."

Without question, David Montini's life represents one of the best examples of the role faith and devotion can play in successful coping with poor health and depression, and may help to explain why so many elderly people alive today are so religious. It may be that their religious faith has simply enabled them to survive their nonreligious peers.

However, we must emphasize in no uncertain terms that people should use religion to *supplement*, not to *replace* the advice of medical experts. Faith enhances treatment but should not be a substitute for it.

The personal stories of healing you have read in this chapter are modern-day examples of miracles — of people whose physical bodies over the years have been touched through their faith and God's mercy. How does this occur? Does God break through in the created world and change the course of nature in scientifically inexplicable ways? We believe this is so, not because of science, but because of our faith. Does God use the natural world, operating through a person's mind, to ignite the natural healing processes in the body to contain or eliminate a disease? We believe this to be so, not because of faith, but because of science. We know from scientific research that the way our physical bodies are constituted, our beliefs and emotions can and do influence our immune and cardiovascular systems to speed the healing process. In other words, one way that God heals is by using scientifically understandable processes in the body (through our faith and belief in God) to boost those natural healing mechanisms, which are part of the created order, to defeat disease and illness. This kind of healing, we believe, is as great a miracle as the times when God heals through unexplainable ways that are not part of nature as we understand it.

We also think it is important to have a broad understanding of what it means to be healthy, what it means to be healed. Many persons restrict their definition of health and healing to physical health and physical healing. Sometimes prayer and deep spiritual faith does not result in the disappearance of ovarian cancer, the cure of pancreatic cancer, or the restarting of a crashing plane's engines. In the majority of cases, it does not. When prayers for health and healing are not followed by miraculous physical cures, many become frustrated and confused, feeling that God has not answered their prayers or doesn't care or, even worse, is punishing them for past errors or sins. But has God really not answered these prayers for healing? Does God really not care? Is God really ignoring us during our times of apparent greatest need? This raises the question of what exactly is real health and real healing, since we do not want to miss God's answers to our prayers if they are not in the form that we think they should be.

We define healing and health broadly, including not only physical cures and physical health, but also healing in our relationships with others (giving and receiving forgiveness from family members and loved ones), healing in our relationship with ourselves (accepting forgiveness for past failures), healing in the priorities we have established for our lives (realignment of those priorities for the better), and healing in our relationship with God (becoming more concerned with spiritual matters or coming closer to God). Would it really be that surprising if God decided that curing us so that we could live a couple more years on Earth is less important than healing us in these other areas that could end up influencing our well-being for eternity? We don't think so. Therefore, having a broad understanding of health and healing is important in order to recognize many of the real miracles that happen to us when we are sick and we pray.

———

But what do these personal testimonials, research findings, and theological musings tell us about the overall importance of the relationship between religious faith and healthcare?

First, there is ample evidence that people consider faith to be an important aspect of their lives: When undergoing treatment, they want to be seen as whole persons whose being has physical, emotional, and spiritual dimensions. Disregarding any of these aspects of humanity could leave the patient feeling incomplete and may even interfere with healing. As the research indicates, spirituality is an important component of "wholeness," and when addressing the psychological, social, and physical aspects in medicine, that part of a patient's identity cannot be ignored.

Research has also shown that many seriously ill patients rely on religious beliefs to cope with their illnesses. Religious involvement is a widespread practice that predicts successful coping with physical illness. In fact, a high level of faith predicts more rapid remission of depression, especially among patients whose physical function is not improving. More than seven hundred studies have now examined the relationship between religious involvement and mental health. Two-thirds of these studies have found that people experience better mental health and adapt more successfully to stress if they are religious.

An additional 350 studies have examined religious involvement and physical health. The majority of these have determined that religious people are physically healthier, lead healthier lifestyles, and require fewer expensive health services. The possible impact of religious belief and practice on physical health — particularly survival — may approximate that of abstaining from cigarette smoking, or adding seven years to life.

What inferences can clinicians draw from these findings? Although there is no research on the impact of physician-directed religious assessments or interventions, we can make some recommendations based on clinical experience and common sense. Clearly, physicians should *not* "prescribe" religious beliefs or activities to treat their patients. Physicians should not impose their religious beliefs on patients or initiate prayer without knowledge of the patient's religious background and likely appreciation of such activity. Except in rare instances, physicians should leave in-depth religious counseling to the trained clergy: hospital chaplains, pastoral counselors, and so on.

But what role can physicians play? They should acknowledge and respect the spiritual lives of their patients, and always keep interventions in this area "patient-centered" (following what the patient would want). Recognizing and assessing the role of faith in the lives of patients often involves taking a spiritual history. This may not be appropriate for every patient, although for those with chronic or serious illness, it probably is. We suggest five simple questions that doctors might ask seriously ill patients:

1. Do your religious or spiritual beliefs provide comfort and support or do they cause stress?

2. How would these beliefs influence your medical decisions if you became really sick?

3. Do you have any beliefs that might interfere or conflict with your medical care?

4. Are you a member of a religious or spiritual community and is it supportive?

5. Do you have any spiritual needs that someone should address?

Taking a spiritual history is often a powerful intervention in itself, which supports the role of faith in their lives. Further, by asking about the patient's spiritual history, the physician opens a unique line of communication that could cement bonds of trust and empathy between them. We need only remember the important role Dr. Ellen Beck played in easing the anguish of her elderly surgical patient by opening the dialogue about the woman's sources of strength.

Physicians should be made more sensitive to the role of their patients' religious beliefs that aid in coping with illness and recovery. Religious people, whose faith often underpins the meaning of their lives, almost always appreciate the physician's sensitivity to these issues. By making known this sensitivity, physicians can send an important message that they are concerned with the whole person, a message that could perhaps even increase the therapeutic impact of medical treatment.

The vocation of the physician is to cure sometimes, relieve often, *comfort always.* If a distressed and frightened patient asks for a prayer and the physician sees that such a prayer can bring comfort, then it is difficult to justify a refusal. The comfort conveyed when a physician supports the core that gives the patient hope is what many patients now miss in their encounters with caregivers.

Today, however, more than two-thirds of the medical schools in the United States teach courses on the importance of religion in the lives of patients. Without question, the recognition of the relationship between faith and medicine will continue to grow, particularly as our population ages and our healthcare system faces the inevitable strain of this demographic burden.

It is interesting that recognition of the connection linking a person's body, mind, and spirit, which is a growing trend in medical education and healthcare, is not a recent innovation. The fact is that religion and care of the ill and afflicted—both in body and mind—were intertwined for millennia before the advent of contemporary medicine. And now, in the twenty-first century, we are once more discovering the importance of this relationship.

Religion and the Long Tradition
of Caring for the Sick

6

"I swear by Apollo the healer ..."

TWENTY-FOUR CENTURIES AGO on the Greek island of Kos, a group of young men who had just completed their apprenticeship under Hippocrates, the most notable physician of his era, stood on the marble terrace of the Aesclepion temple at the edge of the Aegean Sea. They swore by their gods to discharge the duties of their profession honorably.

Two thousand four hundred years later, young men and women graduating from the University of Southern California School of Medicine stood together to take a modern version of the Hippocratic oath, swearing not only by "Apollo the Physician" but also by "whatsoever I hold most sacred" that they would lead their lives and practice their healing art "in uprightness and honor ... for the good of the sick." Like these California graduates, virtually all those completing medical schools in the United States and Canada now take some version of the oath.

The implications of this are obvious: For millennia, the sacred and the moral have been intertwined with the practice of medicine for the good of the patient.

But one of the best-kept secrets in medicine is that the entire notion of "caring for the sick" has religious roots.

In ancient Greece and pagan Rome, the wealthy consulted private physicians when ill. The poor were left to shift for themselves. But that situation changed with the Christian era. The connection between religious faith and the healing arts first became inseparably connected for the benefit of the average person—as opposed to only the wealthy—during the fourth century A.D. in the Roman Empire. It was then that Christians began to build hospitals and healing centers open to all and followed Christ's teachings to minister to the poor and afflicted. The well-organized, three hundred-bed hospital founded in 379 A.D. by St. Basil in Caesarea, a rich and cosmopolitan city in Asia Minor, and similar healing centers endowed by the patrician Lady Fabiola in Rome in the nearby Port of Ostia, were typical of this surge of religiously motivated charitable work. As the large Christian religious centers, such as the church of St. Sofia in Constantinople, were built, they acquired adjacent hospitals, many dedicated to the care of ill pilgrims—particularly the sick elderly—who had journeyed great distances to worship there. These hospitals later became "destinations" in their own right.

In the growing cities of the Eastern and Western Christian empires, religiously affiliated hospitals, foundling homes, and hospices (for the disabled and chronically ill) spread with the establishment of cathedrals and monasteries. And monasteries even welcomed society's ultimate outcastes, the lepers. Pilgrims' shelters providing treatment for the sick traveler had become a fixture of Christian Europe by the eighth century A.D. After the collapse of the Roman Empire, priests and monks worked diligently and made many of the slow but steady advances that laid the foundation for later medical breakthroughs and the system of caring for the sick as we know it today. For example, the ninth-century abbot of Monte Cassino in central Italy, the monk Bertharius, was not only the energetic spiritual leader; he was also a skilled and highly regarded physician.

Such religious communities and their dedicated healers carefully copied and preserved medical and pharmacological texts from the classical period, thus forging a vital link between the Roman and medieval worlds. The availability of these texts at monasteries and church hospitals across Europe assisted in the formation of guilds of Latin-speaking secular physicians who shared a common professional language with their foreign colleagues, an intellectual flowering that eventually led to dramatic advances in medical knowledge during the Renaissance and the Enlightenment.

But it was the direct therapeutic contact between members of religious communities—especially monks (and later nuns and deaconesses)—that alleviated the suffering of uncounted numbers of sick, especially the destitute elderly and the devout Christians who had become afflicted during pilgrimages to holy sites. The Knights Hospitallers of St. John of Jerusalem—now also known as the Knights of Malta—exemplify the Christian fervor to care for the ill and destitute. The order, founded in Jerusalem in 1113 during the First Crusade to recapture the Holy Land from the Muslims, established a large hospital near the Church of the Holy Sepulcher to treat sick and wounded crusaders as well as pilgrims. Members of the order serving under religious vows fulfilled the nursing duties, while there were five full-time physicians and three surgeons on the staff. Under the direction of the order's leader, Raymond of Provence, the knights also provided military escorts to guard pilgrims traveling between Christian enclaves. As long as the Christians held the Kingdom of Jerusalem, the system worked well, and grateful pilgrims and fellow crusaders of means contributed generously to the knights.

But by 1291 the victorious Muslims expelled the crusaders from Palestine. The Knights of St. John were given a corner of the island of Cyprus, where they once more built and staffed a large hospital. Later they moved on to the Aegean island of Rhodes. Even though they fought bitter land and sea battles against the advancing Muslim Ottoman Turks, the Knights of St. John established an elaborate hospital on Rhodes. When the Turks captured Rhodes after a long siege, the knights retreated to the Mediterranean island of Malta. There, despite harsh, desert-like conditions, they built extensive fortifications, which included their most sophisticated infirmaries and a well-staffed hospital. During the modern period, the Knights of St. John have served as medical volunteers and ambulance drivers in wartime and still conduct humanitarian work among those in need.

Although the knights were tested during centuries of ruthless conflict, they never forgot their underlying healing mission.

But dedicated Christians certainly did not hold a monopoly on religiously inspired medicine. There has long been a tradition of curing within Judaism. One of the legends surrounding King Solomon was that God had blessed him with the knowledge of healing and that he had written a book on medicine. The Jewish holy text, the Talmud, which many Orthodox Jews consider divinely inspired, provides counsel on diverse aspects of medicine and health. The Talmud recommended that scholars settle in communities served by physicians. Because Jews usually found themselves isolated within a Christian or Muslim majority, they often had to train their own physicians. Indeed, the study and practice of medicine became a complement to the Talmudic scholarship and other pastoral duties of accomplished rabbis.

One of the most notable of these physician-rabbis was Moshe ben Maimon, better known as Maimonides. He was born into a distinguished family in the early twelfth century in Cordoba, a prosperous city in Moorish Spain. Maimonides was one of the leading intellects of medieval Judaism and published a number of influential books on law and philosophy in both Hebrew and Arabic. Despite his energetic pursuit of law, theology, and philosophy, he found the time for thorough medical training and qualified as a physician while still a young man.

When Muslim fanatics gained control of Spain, they suppressed the Jews, and Maimonides' family fled to North Africa, where he practiced medicine. Eventually, as the persecution continued, the family was forced to move on to Egypt. His great accomplishments in practical medicine won the attention of the renowned Muslim military leader Saladin, whom Maimonides served as personal physician.

Although his fame was widespread among fellow physicians, Maimonides approached his profession in humility and never forgot that God was the source of all his talent and success. Nor did he ever lose sight of his purpose. The widely quoted Prayer of Maimonides summarizes his philosophy. It acknowledges that God "has appointed me to watch over the life and health of Thy creatures." He vowed never to forget "my lofty aim of doing good to Thy children. … May I never see in the patient anything but a fellow creature in pain." He also prayed that he might discover his errors of yesterday so that tomorrow he could obtain a new light on what he thought certain of today. The prayer ended with the confident statement: "Here I am, ready for my vocation and now I turn unto my calling."

Maimonides was just one of a growing number of equally well-motivated Jewish physicians who emerged in the medieval world and eventually served in the Vatican and in the royal courts of Europe. By the Enlightenment in the seventeenth century, Jews were permitted to study and teach in European medical schools. Their continuing contributions to medicine were notable, as evidenced by the high number of Jewish Nobel Prize winners during our own time.

The traditional role of Christian women in medicine was long limited to the contribution of nuns and deaconesses ministering to the needs of sick pilgrims and patients in church hospitals. But Florence Nightingale, a wealthy young Englishwoman of devout religious faith, broke that mold during the mid-1800s. An academically talented child who loved learning, she was not attracted to the Victorian ideal of making a "good marriage" within her social class. Instead, she was drawn to what she saw as a more meaningful contribution.

At age 18, while reading beneath a shady elm in the gardens of her family's summer home, Florence experienced an epiphany, which she would later describe as her "calling." She heard the voice of God directing her to fulfill His work on Earth. Deeply moved, she knew she had to comply, even though she had no idea what that work would entail.

She became interested in emerging social issues, particularly the plight of the sick in village cottages and squalid urban hospitals. This interest alarmed her parents, who found her visits to the bedsides of the afflicted poor unsuitable for a young woman of her social standing. They were especially concerned when Florence revealed her ambition to become a nurse, which at the time was a vocation considered fit only for the lower classes.

To prevent an open breach with her parents, Florence embarked with family friends on a grand tour of the classical sites in Europe and Egypt, a pursuit deemed much more suitable to a young woman of her position. But on the return trip in July 1850, the party visited Pastor Theodore Fliedner at Kaiserwerth near Düsseldorf, where he directed a hospital and school for nurse deaconesses. Florence was struck by the religious dedication and practical energy of the deaconesses, young women who were putting their Christian faith into direct action. Overcoming her parents' objections, she returned to Kaiserwerth the next year and took a nurses' training course. This led to her accepting a position as superintendent of the Establishment for Gentlewomen during Illness on London's Harley Street, the recognized center of British medical excellence. Although Florence Nightingale was now working in a secular establishment, her original Christian motivation remained strong.

When Britain, France, and Turkey declared war on Russia and invaded the Crimean Peninsula on the Black Sea in 1854, initial victories deteriorated into a stalemate. The carnage mounted. Soon the British press was filled with shocking accounts of the inadequate medical treatment afforded the ill and wounded. Because of her growing professional reputation in London, the British War Ministry appointed Florence Nightingale to direct the introduction of women nurses into the military hospitals in Turkey.

She took thirty-eight well-trained nurses with her to the largest British military hospital near Constantinople, arriving in 1854. They received a cold welcome from the military doctors. But when the facility was overwhelmed by large numbers of casualties, Florence Nightingale and her women nurses were put to work. For the next two years, they labored tirelessly, not only introducing new standards of hygiene and sanitation to the overcrowded wards, but also administering to the emotional needs of the sick and dying soldiers. Despite her superior social background and hectic schedule, Florence Nightingale herself always found time in each day to write letters home for illiterate soldiers, and to make sure that a wounded man's back pay was sent directly to his family. She also directed her nursing "sisters" to pray with the frightened, lonely men, and made sure there were Bibles available so that the literate could read comforting verses to their illiterate comrades.

Florence Nightingale became a legendary figure at age 25. Fundraising in Britain allowed her to introduce the same type of nursing and hospital reforms at home as she had done in Turkey. Throughout a long and productive lifetime,

Florence Nightingale continued her devotion to helping the afflicted and to building the foundation of the modern nursing profession that we know today.

Again, it was her unwavering faith that she was answering God's call that energized this remarkable woman.

⊙━━━━⊙

Religiously affiliated colleges and universities trained large numbers of physicians in the Victorian age. During the twentieth century, however, there was a trend toward purely secular medical education. This reached its apex in the 1970s and 1980s, when it became virtual dogma in nursing and medical schools that patients' physical or psychiatric afflictions — but not their spiritual needs — were the proper responsibility of medicine. Indeed, the concept that patients had spiritual requirements interconnected to their physical and psychological condition was generally viewed as unscientific.

This position began to change in the last decade of the twentieth century, as evidence from scientific research studies on the important connection between spirituality and health accumulated. Large, long-term studies linked religious faith and practice to improved longevity and lower rates and severity of depression. This research began to convince many in the medical education community to reconsider addressing the subject of spirituality in the curriculum to meet the "whole person" needs of patients.

Today, nearly two-thirds of America's 126 medical schools teach required or elective courses on the relationship between religion and spirituality and medicine, compared to only three such courses in 1992. In 1995, the John Templeton Foundation issued its first John Templeton Curricular Awards in Spirituality and Medicine, meant to stimulate this process. This medical school course award is given to outstanding schools that introduce and instruct their students on issues related to spirituality and medicine. The $25,000 award is divided between faculty and the institution. To date, thirty-eight Templeton Spirituality and Medicine awards have been presented to thirty-seven medical schools. (One school received two awards.) These are among our leading institutions and include Johns Hopkins, Harvard, Stanford, University of Pennsylvania, University of Minnesota, University of California at Los Angeles, Brown University, Oregon Health Sciences University, Case Western Reserve University, and Washington University at St. Louis, to name just a few. The Curricular Awards have been the key to stimulating the inclusion of education related to religion and spirituality in whole person, compassionate care.

Since 1997, the John Templeton Foundation has also presented the Spirituality and Medicine Award for Psychiatric Residencies. Twenty of these $15,000 annual awards have been made to psychiatric residency training programs that address religion, spirituality, and mental health in a high-quality manner. The psychiatric residency programs receiving this award include Baylor College of Medicine, Albert Einstein College of Medicine, the University of California at San Francisco, the Cleveland Clinic, and Emory University.

The John Templeton Foundation makes a similar award to primary care residencies in order to stimulate programs to begin educating residents about the role of religion and spirituality in patient care. Begun in 2000, sixteen primary care residency awards were presented in the first two years of the program to the nearly forty institutions that applied. These awards were divided among family practice residencies, internal medicine residencies, and mixed family medicine–internal medicine programs. The institutions receiving awards included Boston Medical Center, Brown University, Case Western Reserve, University of Colorado, Orlando Healthcare Center, and University of Pennsylvania.

Without question, awareness of the important connection between religion and spirituality and health has begun spreading among our leading medical educators and their students.

In October 1999, the Association of American Medical Colleges added a spirituality component to its "Medical School Objectives Report III," which provides a standard set of curriculum guidelines for all American medical schools.

One of the goals of the report was to present recommended learning objectives that medical students should try to fulfill to the satisfaction of the faculty before graduation. These included the ability to elicit a spiritual history; an understanding that the spiritual dimension of people's lives is an avenue for compassionate caregiving; knowledge of research data on the impact of spirituality on health and on healthcare outcomes; and an understanding and respect for the role of clergy, other spiritual leaders, and culturally based healers and care providers.

It is significant that the report addresses palliative care within the context of end-of-life issues and includes the spiritual dimension as well as the physical and emotional.

<hr />

Johns Hopkins Community Physicians has recently launched another major effort to foster awareness of the importance of spirituality in healthcare among clinicians. The program is centered on a thirty-minute video presentation entitled "Give Me Strength: Spirituality in the Medical Encounter."

Moderated by world-renowned Hopkins pediatric neurosurgeon Dr. Ben Carson, himself a physician of incredible skill and deep personal faith, the program offers a practical guide to physicians, nurse practitioners, and clinical psychologists on how to incorporate the important issue of spirituality in a fast, cost-effective, and nonintrusive manner into their everyday interchanges with patients. Dr. Carson stresses the relevance of the subject by stating that fully 95 percent of Americans believe in God and that 70 percent of these people consider religion and spirituality very important in their lives.

The role of religion and spirituality is shown to be part of the traditional healing process. The program's organizers, working with Jeanne McCauley, M.D., present research evidence on the benefits of combining a spiritual approach with contemporary medicine. Perhaps the most convincing sections of the video are the personal testimonials from patients whose health outcomes were positively affected by spirituality.

For example, Joe Conroy, a psychologically traumatized Vietnam veteran, tells of struggling with heroin addiction for twenty-five years—until he joined a spiritually oriented twelve-step recovery group and was able to kick the habit. Today he is a successful counselor in this program.

As a teenager, Joni Eareckson Tada became a quadriplegic in a diving accident. She was overwhelmed by depression for years following her injury. But one day, ten years after her crippling accident, she was being treated as an outpatient at Johns Hopkins Hospital in Baltimore. An orderly wheeled her gurney into the echoing rotunda and left it parked against a cold marble wall until a treatment room was ready. Joni felt as bleak as the chill stone beside her. *I'm useless*, she thought in despair. *No wonder they left me here alone.* Then something made her roll over painfully and face the center of the rotunda. She lay beneath the large sculpted figure of Jesus Christ, who stood above her with outstretched arms.

The physical and emotional chill vanished in a warm rush of recognition. She had *not* been forgotten, and she would never again be abandoned to grapple with depression. It had been no accident that the orderly had parked her gurney where he had. She had literally turned her back on Jesus Christ, but then rolled over to discover His healing embrace.

Joni's spinal injury was not cured in the scientific-medical sense of the term. But her emotions were healed.

The video also presents several role-playing scenarios that provide practical guidance to clinicians on how to explore a patient's spirituality and how to discuss the role that religious faith and spiritual practices might play in positively affecting the person's health outcome.

The Hopkins team tested the effectiveness of the video on sixty clinicians, only 15 percent of whom had previous training on the role of spirituality in healthcare. After viewing the program, the subjects were tested about their attitudes. The researchers reported a "significant decrease in clinician barriers to addressing spirituality with patients."

◦———◦

Religiously affiliated healthcare institutions such as the nationwide Catholic Ascension Health network and its affiliate St. Vincent Hospital system have continued into the present day the early Christian tradition of treating the afflicted poor. Indeed, St. Vincent hospitals follow the principles and mission of their movement's founder, the seventeenth-century French priest Vincent de Paul. He organized wealthy Parisian laywomen to feed and treat the sick poor and collaborated with St. Louise de Marillac to establish the Daughters of Charity, a religious order that became the Sisters of Charity of St. Vincent de Paul after his canonization. The Sisters of Charity are recognized as the first order of professional nurses, predating the Protestant deaconess movement mentioned earlier.

But, unlike during the fourth-century Roman Empire or Enlightenment France, most of today's sick and needy are also generally entitled to some form of government assistance, usually either Medicaid or Medicare, depending on their age and medical condition. Unfortunately, however, very low-income elderly Medicare recipients are often unable to afford the out-of-pocket expenses and co-payments required by the program's Part B insurance. This often results in beneficiaries avoiding needed treatment and skimping on essential but expensive prescription drugs. Because of financial hardship, their health can deteriorate drastically, ultimately resulting in long-term hospitalization in an acute-care facility.

To meet the needs of such poor, ill seniors, as well as the disabled whose meager Social Security disability pensions do not satisfy the costs of their supplementary Medicaid and minimum living expenses, the federal government has joined with states to provide relief. The Qualified Medicare Beneficiary/ Specified Low Income Medicare Beneficiary (QMB/SLMB) program can reimburse many poor seniors and disabled persons for the money they must spend in co-payments and other related healthcare expenses. This money is "paid back" directly into the recipient's Social Security or disability account. Although the payment might seem small, it can make a tremendous difference to an ill elderly person struggling to pay rent, eat a healthy diet, and buy prescription medications.

QMB/SLMB is a well-designed and well-intentioned plan. In theory, it should alleviate the needs of poor, at-risk seniors and the disabled subsisting on small pensions and Medicaid. However, the program often does not function as intended because of its bureaucratic complexity and the fact that government social workers are too overburdened to assist the sick elderly and disabled who need it most.

This was the prevailing situation when administrators of the St. Vincent's Hospitals in Indiana recently intervened to make sure that all the institution's "customers"—St. Vincent does not use the traditional welfare term "client" —derived optimal benefits due them. Prior to this effort, the large private hospital network was using about $51 million a year from its not-for-profit earnings to absorb the healthcare needs of its poor patients.

But proper administration of the QMB/SLMB program saved much of that outlay, which the hospital could use for other expenses in its generous Charity Care operation.

"When we identify a potential customer among the poor elderly or disabled people who come to us," program coordinator Sherry Gray explains, "our enrollment counselors make every effort to help. If they don't come back after an initial interview because they're confused by the paperwork, we'll drive to their homes to track them down. Their religion does not matter. We are following our basic mission to aid the poor, and we are determined to 'catch' those at risk."

Well-trained volunteers or full-time staff counselors work diligently with each customer to set up their QMB/SLMB enrollments at the local Medicare or Medicaid offices and to make sure reimbursements are processed correctly.

"We always keep an extra copy of all the paperwork," Sherry Gray notes. "It's amazing how often those forms are simply 'lost' during processing. That can be terribly discouraging for an elderly person already burdened by illness and poverty."

Another extra step St. Vincent enrollment counselors take for their customers is to guarantee they receive all the other healthcare benefits beyond QMB/SLMB to which they are entitled. One of the most important is Hoosier RX, Indiana's subsidized prescription drug program for seniors. Those eligible receive a 50 percent discount on drugs directly at the pharmacy, which is valid until a yearly limit is reached. For people who exceed that drug discount limit but still need assistance, St. Vincent enrollment counselors put them in touch with private charitable prescription drug agencies. During home visits, the counselors often discover that the elderly and disabled are malnourished. The St. Vincent workers put their customers in contact with local food pantries and even deliver the first emergency food shipments in their own cars.

"People come to understand that they have not been forgotten," Sherry Gray says. "Once they are enrolled in QMB/SLMB, they are not afraid to seek medical care because they can't afford to pay their bills."

But St. Vincent also respects their low-income customers' dignity. If people want to make a small effort by sending the hospital even a token payment of $10 a month, St. Vincent gladly accepts the reimbursement.

⸺

"Mary," one of St. Vincent's typical recently enrolled customers, is an African American woman in her late forties admitted to the hospital as an acute-care, charity inpatient. She was employed but had no health insurance. While in the hospital, her condition worsened dramatically and she accrued bills of almost $10,000. Before she was discharged, enrollment counselors interviewed her. A careful review of her medical and income records indicated she now qualified for Social Security disability and Medicaid and thus was entitled to QMB/SLMB assistance. Further, her three children qualified for free federal-state Children's Health Insurance Program (CHIP) coverage.

"When she entered the hospital," Sherry Gray recalls, "Mary was depressed that she would never be able to pay her medical bills. But when she left, her attitude had turned completely around."

A Hispanic man in his early sixties named "Jorge" was treated for a painful and disabling condition in the St. Vincent Primary Care Clinic. Although he had been afflicted for years, Jorge managed to perform hard physical labor to support his family. He spoke little English and did not understand that he qualified for Medicaid disability status. Again, the St. Vincent counselors intervened, relying on volunteer Spanish-English interpreters for communication. Soon, Jorge was enrolled in Medicaid—which provided free prescription drugs—and was receiving a small Social Security disability pension. Like Mary's, Jorge's children are now protected by CHIP coverage.

Program coordinator Sherry Gray emphasizes that the St. Vincent team has great sympathy for their overworked counterparts in the government agencies. Their intentions are good, she says, but they must cope with burdensome and discouraging regulations and huge caseloads.

But, she adds, her colleagues at St. Vincent approach their work from a different perspective—faith.

"We're known as the 'Little Program That Could,'" she says. "And we are very mission driven."

⸺

St. Vincent Hospital in Indianapolis is just one of a growing number of secular and religiously affiliated medical institutions nationwide that have demonstrated it is possible to meet the increasing healthcare requirements of the elderly. In coming decades, faith communities themselves will increasingly have to fill this responsibility.

Part III

The Role of Caring Communities

Religious Congregations and Retirement Communities as Support Networks

7

O VER THE PAST twenty years, an extensive body of research has shown that persons with larger, more satisfying, and supportive social networks experience better physical and mental health, live longer, and use fewer healthcare services. There is also growing evidence that religious involvement is correlated with social support of a higher quality than that obtained from secular sources. Research further reveals that the support of religious congregations is more strongly associated with improved mental and physical health than is the emotional bonding provided by groups such as card clubs, women's or men's social organizations, or other secular organizations.

The emotional and spiritual support found in religious communities is also more durable, especially during times of illness and disability, which people frequently experience as they grow older. Congregational sustenance often increases when people become ill, and that support persists long after the sick person can no longer provide anything of tangible social value in return. This is because religious support is *belief*-based and, in the Christian tradition, is grounded on the biblical imperative to "love thy neighbor" as a service not only to others but also to God.

Such friendship grounded in faith is especially important to bereaved elders who would otherwise be isolated when they move to new communities after retirement. The experience of Dorothy Thomas, a widow of 86, illustrates the important role a supportive congregation can play in the life of an older single person. When she left the Midwest to live with her daughter and son-in-law in a small town on the East Coast, Dorothy tried unsuccessfully to find a Lutheran congregation as warm and nurturing as the one she had left behind. Discouraged, she felt periods of emotional isolation and questioned whether she had made the right decision in leaving the only home she had ever known and the large, welcoming Evangelical Lutheran Church in America congregation in which she had worshiped for decades.

Her distress was exacerbated by a growing list of health problems. She developed a heart arrhythmia, which required the surgical implantation of a pacemaker. Then, on seeking treatment for nagging, incessant lower-back pain, the orthopedic specialist told Dorothy that she had an untreatable deterioration of her vertebrae. Dorothy next developed a serious bone infection in her right foot following surgery and suffered an acute allergic reaction to the antibiotic used to treat it. She was sent to a rehabilitation hospital connected to a local nursing home. Finally, she was diagnosed with the type of chronic kidney disorder that often afflicts the elderly.

Dorothy struggled to regain her previous optimistic outlook but almost surrendered to the hopelessness of depression. It was not easy to feel positive about the future. While in the rehabilitation hospital, as she fought to overcome her own multiple ailments, she was surrounded by people her age or younger afflicted by stroke and end-stage kidney disease. But Dorothy was a person of faith who drew great strength from prayer and was confident a loving God would not forsake her if she did not turn her face from Him.

When her condition improved, she decided, she would "shop around" to find a church that filled her spiritual and social needs.

"I knew the church wouldn't come to me," she recalls with a warm smile, "so I would have to go to the church."

Even though she had been a Lutheran most of her life, Dorothy had been baptized a Methodist. So she and her daughter decided to attend Easter service at the town's United Methodist church. The welcome they received from the congregation was genuinely heartfelt. People with whom Dorothy had a nodding acquaintance from her pharmacy, library, and clinic stepped forward to greet her and introduce themselves. Dorothy returned the next Sunday and was delighted that they all remembered her name. *They're treating me like I'm someone special,* she thought.

Dorothy had always loved church music, and the Methodist hymns were familiar. But what she found most pleasant and intriguing were the church's three handbell choirs. The musical phrasing was intricate, and each performance was obviously the result of hours devoted to rehearsal. Even the children bell ringers played with the same concentration and pride as the junior and adult handbell choirs.

The church's music program was just one of several devotional and social activities available. This was an established congregation where generations of families worshiped. A group of older members had formed a Bible-study group led by a layperson and advised by the pastor. It had been years since Dorothy had read Scripture in an organized manner and, on joining the group, she was pleased to find that the sacred text that had once seemed somewhat remote was now fully accessible.

Dorothy Thomas still had the same health problems that had emerged after she left the Midwest. But the fellowship and genuine concern for her well-being she received from the members of her new church strengthened her spiritual and emotional core. Although the number of activities in which she can participate is fairly limited, Dorothy has become an enthusiastic member of the Bible-study group. Before every Sunday service and on Tuesdays twice a month, she joins her new friends to explore the meaning of the sacred Scriptures. This has sparked in her an unexpected interest in the people and geography of the ancient Middle East. She has begun to read historical accounts and fiction set during the biblical period. For the first time in her life, she can see Jesus and His disciples as real people, living in a recognizable land.

Where so many others her age, burdened by the same health problems, would have submitted to despair, Dorothy has been virtually rejuvenated by her spiritual renewal. Although age has taken a toll, her devotional energy remains robust. In turn, this renewed interest in religion has kept her physically and mentally active.

"I'm too busy to feel depressed," she says. "Besides, I know now that everything is in God's hands and if I simply follow His will, my life will be fulfilled."

Dorothy has found a spiritually satisfying "home" in her new church. Like the hospitalized elderly patients who participated in earlier research studies, she draws emotionally protective sustenance from membership in the large and active congregation. In turn, this shields her from the depression that blights the lives of so many older people with multiple health problems. Maintaining a positive attitude based on faith and on the social support she receives at church, Dorothy Thomas has not surrendered to the "frail elderly" status that afflicts so many single men and women her age with deteriorating physical health. Every Saturday, she has her hair done at the town's beauty parlor in order to look nice for church. She drives her own car to Sunday service and Bible study. And Dorothy eagerly anticipates the church's annual cycle of bazaars, picnics, and the monthly ritual of Communion.

"I'm too busy now with church and all my new friends to feel sick," Dorothy says.

⊙══════╕

Dorothy Thomas is fortunate to live in a comfortable home with her daughter and son-in-law. For millions of other older Americans, this is not an option.

Retirement often means leaving behind the familiar and emotionally bolstering neighborhoods and religious congregations they have known for years. Many gravitate toward rapidly expanding Sunbelt states such as Florida and Arizona that offer warm weather, lower taxes, and more affordable housing.

But, whether or not they migrate south, increasing numbers of older people sell their homes and move into the thousands of continuing care retirement communities (CCRCs) around the country. These facilities offer three levels of accommodation: independent living, assisted living, and nursing home care. Retired people can choose among a wide variety of housing options ranging from rental studio apartments subsidized by the U.S. Department of Housing and Urban Development to luxury condominiums and villas. CCRCs are found in every state, and many are associated with religious denominations.

Luther Manor in the Milwaukee suburb of Wauwatosa is typical. Affiliated with the city's Evangelical Lutheran Church in America congregations, the community comprises several buildings on a quiet, tree-lined, twenty-nine-acre campus. Whenever possible, the not-for-profit organization encourages independence among the nine hundred residents. Almost half occupy comfortable studio, one-bedroom, or two-bedroom independent living retirement apartments. There are 157 supportive/assisted living one-room and two-room apartments for those who need limited weekly nursing or rehabilitative care. And the Luther Manor Health Care Center provides 254 beds in a skilled nursing home facility. To meet residents' needs, the community employs six hundred full- and part-time employees and relies on four hundred adult and teenage volunteers, many from local churches.

Like hundreds of other religiously affiliated CCRCs in America, Luther Manor emphasizes services and activities that benefit the whole person, physically, mentally, and spiritually. The dining room provides nutritious, appetizing meals, served in a relaxed and pleasant atmosphere. This is an important contribution to the well-being of the elderly, who often do not take the time to cook and eat well when living alone. Companionship is fostered through social gatherings such as informal card games in the comfortably furnished public rooms and sunny atriums. Craft and hobby clubs are active, and exercise classes are popular. Many residents participate in winter bowling leagues and summer golfing on the course adjacent to the campus.

Because Luther Manor's vision, mission, and philosophy are guided by a common Christian heritage and the shared values of the residents and staff, spiritual needs are emphasized. The official mission of Luther Manor is to "show God's love for older adults by providing a comprehensive and compassionate program of excellent housing, care and services contributing to the wholeness of body, mind, and spirit." This is meant to affirm and nurture the spirituality of each person, according to his or her individual beliefs and identity.

Religious services of several denominations are offered in the chapel. During Advent and Holy Week, the pace of devotional activity increases, with additional services and visits from church choirs. Even frail, bedridden elderly residents can maintain their spiritual connection to emotionally comforting worship. Chaplains visit Luther Manor regularly, their presence reassuring those afflicted by the inevitable health problems of advancing age. But, again, Luther Manor's guiding philosophy is to foster independence and personal autonomy among residents, no matter what their age.

Lucille and Ervin Platt, a couple in their mid-eighties who have lived at Luther Manor for several years, are typical residents. Erv Platt worked for decades as a skilled industrial craftsman after service overseas in World War II. Lucille Platt is a retired bookkeeper who still volunteers her services at their church. Their early retirement years were active and fulfilling, as each took great satisfaction in maintaining their suburban home and garden. Erv was proud of his rose bushes and bountiful vegetable plots. But as they grew older, keeping up the house and yard became increasingly difficult. Eventually, they decided to sell their home and move to Luther Manor.

But the idea of downsizing to a one-bedroom apartment—even a unit as large and modern as the one they chose—was initially intimidating. The Platts, however, soon discovered the many advantages of living at Luther Manor. Their building was a hospitable neighborhood, devoid of any institutional atmosphere. Although there were a variety of organized activities, they were free to participate or not according to their own wishes. And the first harsh Wisconsin winter spent in their new home made Erv realize that he would never again have to worry about shoveling a sidewalk or clearing a driveway. Because the community performed all maintenance, Erv was no longer responsible for house painting, cleaning rain gutters, or plumbing repairs.

But their third-floor apartment's balcony was an excellent location for a small flower-and-vegetable garden. By the middle of their first summer at Luther Manor, they had luscious tomatoes and flowering plants growing in pots on their balcony. An affable man with a trove of jokes, Erv was soon golfing regularly with other men from the community. The couple also quickly developed a circle of friends among the people they had met in the community dining room. Erv Platt continued his volunteer work, driving other elderly people to medical appointments, while Lucille volunteered as a receptionist in their building and donated crocheted crafts to the gift shop.

Several years after they sold their home and moved to the community, the Platts enjoy a life that does, indeed, enrich them—body, mind, and spirit.

"We are very happy living here," Lucille says.

One the reasons that Luther Manor is able to provide such a high level of service and specialized care — including day care for Alzheimer's and other dementia patients — is the unusually high ratio of volunteers to paid employees (400 volunteers to 600 paid staff). These volunteers — who devote over sixty thousand hours of their time each year — range in age from teenagers to over 90. Many are from local congregations; others are residents of the community. Their activities include operating coffee carts that serve home-baked cookies (and cheerful conversation) with coffee and tea to the residents. The volunteers' popcorn cart makes a regular circuit through the buildings, serving residents, staff, and visitors. Volunteers take part in sewing and craft classes, assisting those with limited vision or reduced manual dexterity. Volunteers also staff the old-fashioned ice cream parlor and gift shop. Transporting frail residents of the nursing home by wheelchair is one of the volunteers' most important responsibilities. This provides the bedridden with priceless mobility and a sense of belonging to a larger, caring community. In the adult day-care facility, volunteers patiently feed Alzheimer's patients, relieving paid staff of this task.

It is safe to say that Luther Manor would not be able to provide the high level of personal care and genuine concern for the physical, mental, and spiritual needs of the residents if it were not for the hard work and devotion of the volunteers. In turn, religious faith motivates many of these volunteers to serve.

And it is financial support for Luther Manor from local churches, businesses, and individuals that has helped the community build and maintain its tasteful facilities and comfortable accommodations over the past forty years, while keeping costs to a minimum. The nonprofit Luther Manor Foundation assists residents in all the housing areas of the community who have exhausted their financial resources. With these subsidies, no resident has ever had to leave because of inability to pay. The Luther Manor Foundation's Promise for Generations Campaign also provides ongoing support for renovations and capital improvements, and assists congregations and community-based services that help the elderly remain in their homes for as long as their health permits and they so desire. Charitable gift annuities offer an attractive option for contributors wishing to give to Luther Manor but who need a lifetime income. When the annuity holder dies, the balance is transferred to the foundation. A number of people contribute dedicated gifts in support of special needs at the community, such as nursing care or the Alzheimer's facility. Many remember Luther Manor in their wills. And congregations regularly give through the Luther Manor Auxiliary, direct financial gifts, or special donations.

This financial support is typical of church-affiliated retirement communities across the country. The security these contributions provide is not dependent on increasingly scarce government subsidies. And the quality of life in religiously associated retirement homes is usually superior to that of purely private or government-run and managed facilities that lack the important component of spiritual care.

But when a religious denomination takes an active role in a government-subsidized retirement community, the experience of both residents and staff is enriched. Canterbury Court, a low-income independent living community of 150 apartments sponsored by the U.S. Department of Housing and Urban Development, is located in West Carrollton just south of Dayton, Ohio. It is a perfect example of such a facility. As part of Episcopal Retirement Homes, Inc., the community overlooks a quiet courtyard and six acres of nicely landscaped grounds. All of the residents live on low incomes, including small Social Security retirement pensions or disability benefits.

But even though residents' financial resources are restricted, Episcopal Retirement Homes provides a variety of extra services and facilities to make life at Canterbury Court pleasant and fulfilling. The community offers free transportation to local banks, supermarkets, malls, and restaurants. The well-stocked lending library is a center of social activity. And the twice-weekly subsidized meals also foster social contact, as do the regular free exercise classes. Gardeners among the residents can take advantage of the large plot and the greenhouse. There is a full program of entertainment and recreation each week.

But the schedule of spiritual activities is perhaps the most personally fulfilling aspect of life at Canterbury Court for many people who live there. The Reverend Deacon Dolores Witt is the chaplain. She leads a vigorous ecumenical ministry that includes regular worship, healing services and Bible study, and pastoral visits to the sick. Chaplain "D.," as she is known, is an energetic person in her sixties who lived all over the world when her husband was a career military officer. She approaches her ministry with a mixture of deep faith, compassion, and practicality.

Dolores Witt recognizes that many residents have suddenly found themselves in greatly reduced financial straits because of the turmoil in the stock market and the downturn of the economy. They had not planned to retire to a low-income community, and react to the unexpected condition in different ways. Some retreat into an emotional shell, seldom venturing out of their apartments; a few abuse alcohol. But many others rediscover their religious faith and the spiritual side of their lives.

For those seeking spiritual enrichment, Chaplain Witt offers a variety of devotional activity that includes a Sunday healing and Eucharist service, twice weekly Bible study, and extra worship and liturgical music programs during Advent and Easter. She even gives an annual blessing of the animals to which the residents can bring their treasured pet companions for benediction.

"I'm fully aware that loneliness can gnaw at a person's well-being, especially someone elderly whose family doesn't visit very frequently," Dolores Witt points out. "So I always leave the door to my office wide open."

People often drop by to ask her to pray with them. "Sometimes their anguish is obvious, and I learn that they've just been diagnosed with a serious illness such as cancer, a heart condition, or heard of a death in the family. At times like these, a compassionate hug is perhaps just as healing as a formal prayer."

Chaplain Witt understands the deep need of a distressed person to be heard, or simply to be touched. "I talk about the healing touch that Jesus delivered to his flock," she says. "People empathize when I tell them, 'A hug a day keeps the doctor away.'"

This approach to her ministry at Canterbury Court seems to work. She is proud of the three devout sisters, aged 90, 92, and 97, who live independently in their own apartments and regularly join the community congregation for worship. One 96-year-old lady *never* misses a service or a Bible-study class. On Easter 2002, the chaplain baptized a woman 80 years old. "You're never too old to find faith," Dolores Witt says.

Norma Jarrett, 80, is a resident of the community whose faith and emotional well-being have actually been strengthened by overcoming the adversity of serious health problems. She suffered her first heart attack when she was only 54 and has also survived cancer. After moving to Canterbury Court four years ago, she became an active member of Chaplain Witt's faith community and devoted herself to volunteer work. She did kitchen duty and drove more frail elderly residents to supermarkets and medical appointments.

On August 6, 2002, she had driven another resident to a doctor's appointment and was sitting in the waiting room, paging through a magazine. Then the world around her went black. Norma Jarrett had suffered sudden cardiac arrest.

"It wasn't another heart attack," she recalls. "I just died."

Physicians from the clinic rushed to the waiting room to administer CPR, and the staff called paramedics. She remained in cardiac arrest for a prolonged period until she was revived at a local hospital. Norma had an internal pacemaker-defibrillator surgically implanted and remained, unconscious, in the intensive care unit for several days.

"Then I woke up," she says, "and they sent me home."

For the next two weeks as Norma recovered in her apartment, Chaplain Witt visited two or three times a day, and another resident, Helen Brooks, volunteered to spend nights with her.

As she regained her strength, a firm conclusion formed in Norma's mind: It had not been an accident that cardiac arrest had struck while she was sitting in the waiting room of the doctors' office and they could intervene immediately. Had she not been serving as a volunteer driver that afternoon, she would have been home alone, and no one would have found her for at least a day. "By then," she says, "it would have been too late."

Norma has no doubt about what occurred on August 6, 2002: "It was all the Lord's will, a miracle. Don't ever tell anyone that God doesn't revive the dead."

Obviously, it is impossible to test in a scientific manner the nature of the circumstances that took Norma Jarrett out of her apartment that day and placed her in the hands of skilled physicians moments after her heart stopped beating. But it is clear that she has experienced a complete recovery, with absolutely no lingering fears of recurrent heart problems haunting her. While people with less profound faith might be tormented by anxiety and sink into depression following such a crisis, Norma feels spiritually reborn.

Today, she has resumed her active role in the Canterbury Court community, volunteering and enriching the lives of those around her.

⚓

Beyond conventional spirituality, the residents also generously contribute their time and limited money to help those in need. Each Christmas, they buy toys for 150 poor local children. One person even dipped deeply into her small savings account to donate a brand-new bicycle. The residents of Canterbury Court also purchase kits of school supplies and toiletries for distribution to victims of disaster such as the hurricanes that devastated Central America.

"As a community, we may not be affluent in the conventional sense," Chaplain Witt comments, "but we enjoy priceless blessings."

⚓

If Canterbury Court represents a church-affiliated facility with a spiritual life much richer than the financial resources of the residents, the Shell Point Retirement Community near Fort Myers, Florida, is a center of affluence. A CCRC that has attracted thousands of residents to its tasteful independent and assisted-living units and its nursing home over the past thirty years, Shell Point has been called "the crème de la crème" of Florida retirement communities. It is located on the Gulf Coast and offers its residents an amazing variety of recreational activities, ranging from swimming pools, golf, tennis, and windsurfing to concert and lecture series. For those who can afford to live there, the community provides the "golden years" opportunities to which so many aspire, but that relatively few older Americans can actually afford.

Shell Point has not neglected the spiritual needs of its residents. The Village Church is located at the heart of the island on which Shell Point stands. It is a member church of the Christian and Missionary Alliance and is administratively separate from the overall community. The church owns its strikingly handsome modern building that includes a fifteen-hundred-seat auditorium in which musical presentations, lectures, and large assemblies take place.

A large number of the eighteen hundred current residents of Shell Point — who represent over twenty denominations — participate in regular services and small-group Bible study and worship. Although they live comfortably, Pastor Kenneth Nesselroade notes, many residents are searching for a deeper meaning in their lives.

"They've been 'successful' in the conventional sense for so many years," Rev. Nesselroade says, "that people often confront an emotional and spiritual void as they face their later years."

That turmoil is exacerbated among residents who have come to the community without family nearby and must confront loneliness on a daily basis. "Frankly," Rev. Nesselroade comments, "there are some people here who have come to die comfortably. But there are many others who want to live well and completely. We try to steer them toward volunteer work."

Seven hundred members of the community are in fact regular volunteers. Some help the frail elderly in the King's Crown Pavilion nursing facility (which includes an Alzheimer's unit and a hospice), where they distribute mail, dress hair, and offer their friendship to the residents. Again, religiously oriented compassion motivates this volunteerism. Both the recipients and the contributors of this generosity benefit.

Rev. Dr. Susan Stranahan, who has her graduate degree in public health and earlier spent seventeen years in nursing, is the chaplain at the pavilion nursing facility. Like Pastor Nesselroade, she is a compassionate person with deep insights into the needs of the elderly. Her work taxes all of her ability on a daily basis. The pavilion has four floors with one each devoted to dementia and hospice care. Almost all the residents of the pavilion have previously lived in other accommodations at Shell Point or are from nearby Fort Myers. Most are Protestant and possess a wide variety of individual faiths and spiritual values. Even though the pavilion's well-organized volunteer auxiliary is active in feeding, mail distribution, and individual personal visits with the bedridden residents, loneliness is still a concern.

So Chaplain Stranahan oversees a vigorous devotional program that begins with a Sunday afternoon service led by volunteer members of the church congregation. She also relies on volunteers to conduct hymn singing and Bible study during the week.

The recommended chaplain-to-patient ratio is a maximum of one to seventy, she remarks. However, she is the only trained professional chaplain for the 218 pavilion residents.

"I could certainly use two or three full-time assistants," Chaplain Stranahan says. "But the volunteers work so hard, we're not neglecting anyone's spiritual needs."

Her honest appraisal of the situation underscores an issue that will become more pressing as our elderly population grows inexorably. At first glance, there is a world of difference between the relatively small HUD-sponsored community of Canterbury Court and the sprawling, prosperous Shell Point campus with its palm trees, landscaped gardens, and marina. But, even in a community as comfortable and financially well endowed as Shell Point, the physical health consequences and emotional impact of aging are inevitable. And, whether older people are affluent or live on small fixed incomes, their spiritual requirements will have to be addressed along with their physical health. In this regard, aging is the great equalizer.

Rev. Dr. Chester Tolson, a Presbyterian minister from southern California, spent thirteen years as Rev. Robert Schuller's director of development at the huge Crystal Cathedral, known to millions of American and worldwide television viewers. Dr. Tolson is an active member of Churches Uniting in Global Missions, an alliance of approximately a hundred of the largest mainstream Protestant, Roman Catholic, and Pentecostal congregations in North America. One of the organization's main concerns has become how to address the "tri-level" nature—mind, body, and spirit—of elderly people.

"The leaders of our churches are aware that all healing is divine," Dr. Tolson comments. "What takes place in hospitals today is nothing short of miraculous. Medical intervention and prayer complement each other, not compete." Therefore, the spiritual life of the elderly is an essential part of their overall health and well-being.

Today, Dr. Tolson focuses on the retirement options of our rapidly aging population. The vast majority of the elderly, he points out, are religious, and hope that their spiritual needs can be met as they age.

"For most people," he says, "easy and guaranteed access to church is just as important a consideration as security, housing choices, and physical location." As the multi-million cohort of the Baby Boom generation reaches retirement,

Tolson predicts, most will seek a community near a church, or one such as Canterbury Court or Shell Point that offers a variety of devotional options.

Dr. Tolson says a growing movement will see large, "megachurch" campuses expand to include integral retirement communities of older people who share a bond of faith. Because membership in a congregation played a vital role during all their previous adult life, they do not want to enter retirement separated from active participation in their church.

"So offering senior housing will become a priority for large churches—not just in the traditional retirement zones of the Sunbelt—but nationwide," Tolson suggests. "I am very passionate on this subject. Tens of millions of today's Baby Boomers will soon need secure communal residential communities that meet their spiritual and health needs and provide the mental stimulus necessary for meaningful later life."

Older people want both to volunteer and to find fulfillment in mentoring and being in regular contact with school children. So, many church retirement communities will have their own K–12 schools at which residents can volunteer.

A practical model for this type of private, church-affiliated community is for retired people to use the proceeds from the sale of their homes to buy a condominium on the congregation's campus. The monthly fees are within reach of income from savings, pensions, and Social Security. These large church communities will provide "one-stop" social support, spiritual activities, and medical services. Alternatively, churches can offer accommodation on a rental basis, which is the case at the large First Assembly of God Life Center in Tacoma, Washington.

Rev. Tolson is involved in the planning of megachurch communities using innovative means to raise capital: After design is final and purchasers' down payments on their housing units reach 90 percent of development capital (or an agreed percentage), 70 percent of their down payment is returned so that residents can use it for monthly fees, food services, and medical expenses.

"This is the wave of the future," Dr. Tolson predicts confidently. "In coming years, we're going to see such communities rising on church campuses across America."

If he is right, the mental, physical, and spiritual needs of millions of elderly people will be met within the nurturing sanctuary of their familiar congregation.

But, whatever the retirement option the elderly choose—from remaining at home to more structured independent or assisted living—their growing numbers in coming years will place an increasing strain on America's financial and human infrastructure. It is obvious that there will also be a growing need for volunteers to meet the needs of our older people.

Successful Aging and Purpose-Filled Retirement: The Mutual Benefits of Voluteering

IN NOVEMBER 2002, Dan Tabler, 78, a "semi-retired" journalist from the small Eastern Shore town of Centreville, was nominated as his county's candidate for the annual Maryland You Are Beautiful award. Tabler, a World War II veteran, had worked for local newspapers for over fifty years, beginning as a teenage columnist earning a dollar or two a week in 1940.

As much as Tabler loved writing for small community papers, he was also drawn to volunteer work. He joined Centreville's Goodwill Volunteer Fire Department soon after coming home from his wartime service. His father, Ray, a banker, had always told Tabler, "Dan, you've got to give something back to the community." For Tabler, being a volunteer firefighter was an ideal way to meet this obligation. Not only was he helping protect his neighbors' lives and property, the work had practical advantages: "As a reporter, I was right in the middle of the action at every fire with my camera and notebook."

But as the decades passed, Dan Tabler derived much deeper satisfaction from his volunteer service. For every child rescued from a smoke-filled house or barn fire extinguished before a farm family's livestock were killed, Dan's sense of filling a vital role strengthened. Then, in the 1990s when he left full-time newspaper work, Tabler found he had more time to devote to being a volunteer. Even though he was in his seventies, Dan remained an active member of the fire department, serving as the unit's policeman. "I was getting a little old to lug ladders and those heavy rolls of hose," he observes. "But there was no reason I couldn't direct traffic at a fire or accident scene."

Tabler continued writing a weekly newspaper column, but had enough time to seek other volunteer opportunities. A life-long member of the Centreville United Methodist Church, Dan became the "more or less permanent" secretary of the United Methodist Men. He and his wife, Ruth, are both church ushers, and have missed very few services over the years that they have been members of the congregation. Ruth, retired as a registered nurse, became a volunteer at the Queen Anne's County Hospice. Dan joined her, taking on the responsibility for the group's public relations, which included the vital task of fundraising, as well as working as a volunteer driver.

"I drove patients to their medical appointments—often for pain treatment—all over the Shore," he says. "Sometimes it took most of my day, but these were terminally ill people who really needed help. I knew they were counting on me. It was the least I could do."

Dan also volunteered at the Queen Anne's County Free Library, work that quickly grew into a paid part-time staff position. He had always been active at his American Legion post, and retirement gave him extra hours to volunteer at the Legion's community suppers and breakfasts.

A member of the Lions Club for years, Tabler volunteered for extra duties once retired. In early 2002, he joined other Lions Club volunteers on trips to New York to work in warehouses supplying donated clothing and equipment for firefighters at Ground Zero, site of the World Trade Center terrorist attack. Despite his age, Tabler patiently lifted cartons of donated coveralls, boots, and gloves. He stacked heavy cases of bottled water and soft drinks. "I wanted to be down there helping the men and women digging through the ruins," he says. "But I was needed at the warehouse, so that was where I worked."

Dan Tabler recently celebrated his fifty-fifth year with the Goodwill Volunteer Fire Department. "I have no plans to quit," he says, noting that his friend, Wes Thompson, recently observed his seventieth year as a volunteer with the department. "I guess I'll try to match Wes's record."

What drives a person like Dan Tabler to go beyond a comfortable retirement devoid of responsibility? Certainly, the sense of connection to his community that he developed as a boy is part of the answer. But more important is the personal reward Tabler gains from his work as a volunteer.

"I really get a deep sense of satisfaction and fulfillment from volunteer work. It keeps you busy. Your mind stays active, and you can't just sit around at home thinking about growing old. I don't *feel* old. Every time you go out on a fire call, you know you're helping your neighbors. That's all the pay I need."

⟡━━━⟡

Dan Tabler's sense of satisfaction and fulfillment is indeed a rich personal reward. And he's certainly not alone. Several carefully designed, peer-reviewed research studies have shown that men and women who volunteer—especially elderly people—gain significant physical health benefits and increased emotional well-being compared to their peers who do not volunteer.

In his book, *Give to Live: How Giving Can Change Your Life,* co-author Doug Lawson discusses the health-promotion aspects of personal involvement in volunteer activity. He has emphasized that people who volunteer live happier, healthier, and longer lives than non-volunteers. The motivations behind such volunteer behavior also seem to make a difference. When volunteer activity is based on the fundamental tenets of a Judeo-Christian faith, for example, both the emotional and physical benefits are enhanced. Community involvement through volunteerism gives people the opportunity to find happiness through the self-fulfillment and self-esteem gained through acts of kindness and love for others.

Volunteering significantly reduces the levels of toxic stress in our lives, thus offering protection from depression and perhaps even from some physical illnesses. When depression afflicts elderly people, it often becomes a chronic condition that is generally overlooked as a normal symptom of aging. The difficulty in treating the depressed elderly was underscored by Dutch researchers who conducted a six-year study of 277 depressed people aged 55 to 85. About two-thirds were repeatedly assailed by the affliction. At the end of the six-year follow-up period, less than 25 percent had remitted from their depression.

Aarjan Beekman, the Vrije University psychiatrist who led the study, concluded, "In later life, depression is a common disorder, with well-documented consequences for well-being and mortality."

Because working as a volunteer appears to combat depression and improve mood in the elderly, the medical community should give serious consideration to this type of "therapy."

Volunteering also provides a sense of self-acceptance, which allows us to feel compassion and empathy for others in our emotionally detached and personally isolated society. Being a volunteer may actually affect brain chemistry, causing the release of endorphins, which produce a feeling of joy and mental clarity that has been called "the helper's high."

Consider these findings:

- Today approximately half of all adult Americans undertake some kind of volunteer work, donating an average of about four hours a week. The level of volunteerism waxes and wanes—it declined in the late 1990s—but is now rising again, probably due to greater community solidarity following the 9/11 attacks and the hardships of the economic slump.

- Most of the estimated 99 million adult volunteers perform scheduled work within a formal group (religious congregations, local groups, or one or more of 800,000 national organizations).

- These volunteers produce a staggering annual total of more than 20 billion work hours, equivalent to the efforts of 9 million full-time employees. Volunteer work has an annual value of over $150 billion.

- There is a strong connection between religious faith and volunteerism: More than 60 percent of members of religious congregations are volunteers. The Barna Research Group, which conducted a national survey of 1000 randomly chosen adults in January–February 2003, found that volunteering by older adults in church is down 7 percent in the last five years, a trend that causes concern.

- People offer many reasons for volunteering. Some follow long family traditions—think of the advice that Dan Tabler received from his father, Ray. Others participate because they had been urged to do so by relatives, friends, or community leaders. Some volunteer simply to help friends.

- Among the millions of American volunteers, only 21 percent create their own assignments; the vast majority accept jobs available in an organized group, such as a congregation or a community service organization.

- But people who volunteer on an informal basis—helping friends and neighbors—also derive rewards. Researchers Barbara McIntosh and Nicholas Danigelis randomly sampled 1,644 people aged 60 or older about their levels of satisfaction in retirement. The study concluded: "It is clear that the most important productive activity for predicting well-being among seniors is informal volunteering, and the least important is paid work."

- A Gallup poll found that most people said they volunteered to be of use in their community and to find more meaning in their lives.

Years of scientific research confirm that volunteers receive at least as much as they provide. This is not just an anecdotal notion. Studies have found that volunteers enjoy better physical and mental health and greater longevity than non-volunteers.

Research published by a number of institutions and in popular reviews, including the Institute for the Advancement of Health, *Psychology Today*, and *American Health*, has explored the physiological mechanism of the helper's high. As noted, volunteering may trigger the release of endorphins—naturally occurring brain proteins — that make us feel more expansive, even euphoric. Endorphins are closely related to a sense of pleasure and satisfaction; they have a soothing effect that ameliorates daily stress. Dr. Herbert Benson, an acclaimed Harvard cardiologist and researcher who has studied the mind-body connection for decades, says that altruistic acts can produce a relaxation response equivalent to a deep state of rest.

And recent pioneering research on the effect of altruism at the biological level has discovered further intriguing connections between selflessness and emotional well-being. Investigators led by Dr. Gregory S. Berns of Emory University in Atlanta employed magnetic resonance imaging (MRI) to chart the differences in brain activity between experimental subjects exhibiting either greedy or cooperative behavior. Participants in the experiment played the standard psychological game called the Prisoner's Dilemma, in which they received different cash rewards for either cooperative (selfless) or greedy (self-serving) responses. The subjects played either with other people or with pre-programmed computers, and had the chance to either work in partnership or "defect" by withdrawing with the money they had already earned. While they played, the subject's brain activity was monitored using MRI scanning.

As Dr. Berns told the *New York Times*, the scans revealed that when players formed "cooperative alliances" rather than ruthlessly competed, the areas of their brains known to respond to pleasure glowed brightly on the screens, indicating they had been activated. Close analysis of the scans showed that the precise portions of players' brains active during cooperative behavior were rich in neurons responsive to dopamine, the chemical associated with pleasure, including the response to addictive substances. In other words, the researchers' MRI scans were actually revealing the helper's high in real time.

This result was surprising because traditional evolutionary theory had predicted that humans were biochemically predisposed for competition: the survival of the fittest. But no one had anticipated that there were even stronger inherent survival mechanisms thrusting us toward altruism. Apparently, humans are more willing to forego personal gain for the common good than researchers had anticipated.

Describing this unexpected response, Berns says, "In some ways, it shows that we're wired to cooperate with others."

Other research studies have found that altruism helps people avoid premature physical and emotional deterioration by staying active in the service of others. This effect is particularly strong for the elderly. University of California at Berkeley scientists Doug Oman and Dwayne Reed examined the effects of volunteering on survival in 1973 residents age 55 or over living in Marin County, California. Among participants, 31 percent (n = 630) participated in some kind of volunteer activity, and about half of these subjects volunteered for more than one organization. Those who volunteered for two or more organizations experienced a 63 percent lower likelihood of dying during the five-year study than did non-volunteers. Even after taking into account the subjects' age, gender, number of chronic conditions, physical mobility, exercise, self-rated general health, health habits, social support, and psychological status, the beneficial effect was reduced by only 19 percent to a still highly significant 44 percent reduction in mortality. They also found that among weekly church attenders, any level of volunteering reduced mortality by 60 percent. They concluded that the positive effects of volunteerism on mortality were particularly strong for the actively religious.

Another intriguing study recently described in the *New York Times* was led by University of Michigan Institute for Social Research psychologist Stephanie L. Brown, Ph.D. She focused on 423 men aged 65 and older and their wives. Those who provided emotional support to a spouse or other types of help to friends and neighbors were about half as likely to die during the five-year study period than those who made no such contribution to the well-being of others.

"What is beneficial about being in a close relationship," Dr. Brown commented, "is rooted in the contribution we make, not in the support we receive."

Personal involvement has an impact on one's sense of worth, significance, and purpose. But lack of purpose and its associated chronic boredom are among the most serious consequences of later life for millions of Americans. And research has shown that boredom and inadequate control over life's events can have devastating health consequences. Professor Benjamin C. Amick III of the University of Texas School of Public Health studied workers trapped in boring jobs with little control over their tasks. During a ten-year period, these workers were one-third more likely to die than people in challenging jobs with ample opportunity for decision making. Older Americans living on small fixed incomes who also have few meaningful social contacts often complain of boredom and a lack of control over their lives. Like the workers in Professor Amick's study, these emotionally isolated elderly people might risk being literally bored to death.

But volunteering provides a sense of purpose and responsibility, which helps counter the negative health effects of aging. Consider the benefits derived by senior citizen volunteers at the Capital Area Food Bank in northeast Washington, D.C. Retired beautician Velma Hammond, 75, is one of a dozen elderly people who call themselves the "Reclaimers." These people are far from bored with their lives; they know they are needed. Every weekday morning, the volunteers work through huge bins of donated groceries, salvaging dented cans of vegetables, torn cereal boxes, and crumpled cartons of macaroni, searching for food that is still safe to eat. "I keep coming because I'm doing something to help people," Ms. Hammond recently told the *Washington Post*. Working to serve their neighbors takes these elderly people out of their houses and helps prevent them from dwelling on their own arthritis, diabetes, or heart disease. They gain a sense of satisfaction in the knowledge they are performing a desperately needed community service.

Such dedication to the service of others — in effect, "loving thy neighbor as thyself," an article of faith common to most of the world's major religions — frees people like Velma Hammond from negative emotions such as anger, hatred, suspicion, guilt, and anxiety. These emotions have been proven to be literally "toxic" because they increase the stress hormones cortisol, epinephrine, and norepinephrine, which can elevate blood pressure and heart rate to dangerous levels, exacerbating underlying cardiovascular disease. The impact of chronic stress on an elderly person can be devastating. But the sense of purpose and joy enjoyed by older volunteers combats stress on a daily basis and helps prevent stress-related negative physical and emotional health effects.

This is also important because research has shown that the overproduction of the stress hormone cortisol can impair the immune system. Too much cortisol circulating in an elderly person's system can cause him or her to become vulnerable to infection, to poor wound healing, to a build-up of artery-clogging plaque that often triggers heart attacks and strokes, and possibly to some types of cancer.

But research conducted at the UCLA School of Medicine and elsewhere has found that a positive attitude — including optimism and altruism — can open beneficial pathways between the mind and the body that help strengthen the immune system. In one fascinating study, Drs. David McClelland and Carol Hirshnet of Harvard University discovered that people who watched a filmed documentary of Mother Teresa's work with the dying of India showed a significant increase in immunoglobin-A, one of the body's first lines of defense against infection. But movies that focused on the opposite of compassion had little or no impact on immunity. Intriguingly, McClelland and Hirshnet also found that people strongly motivated by a drive for power and success had lower levels of immunoglobin-A than those who were more altruistic. They concluded: "This suggests that one way to avoid stress and illness associated with a strong power drive is to … turn the power drive into helping others."

Cardiologists such as Dr. Dean Ornish and Dr. Herbert Benson, as well as cancer specialists such as Dr. Bernard Siegel, have argued that we can speed recovery from illness and reduce our risk of life-threatening disease by improving our personal relationships and emotional attitudes. Certainly, volunteering promotes an optimistic, emotionally healthy attitude and leads to strong, ful-

filling personal relationships. *Psychology Today* quoted Dr. Benson on the healing power of selfless service to others: "For millennia, people have been describing techniques on how to forget oneself, how to experience decreased metabolic
rates, lower blood pressure, lower heart rates and other health benefits. Altruism works this way, just as do yoga, spirituality and meditation." It is therefore
reasonable to assume that the health benefits of altruism might be enhanced
when motivated by religious faith or spirituality.

The late Dr. Hans Selye, often called "the father of stress reduction," led many
of the pioneering studies on the connection between emotions and illness. He
coined the phrase "altruistic ego" to describe a person involved in charitable
activities or volunteering. The benefit they derive is the "love and gratitude" of
those they help. Significantly, Dr. Selye observed, "Like stress, love has a cumulative effect." By this he meant that good deeds performed over a period of time
have a sustained positive effect on our well-being. Dan Tabler and Velma Hammond are well into what used to be considered old age; the cumulative impact
of their advanced years takes its toll on mind and body. Yet they—like millions
of other senior citizen volunteers—have more energy and better health than
their chronological age would suggest. There is clearly a connection between
their tireless community service and the robust health they enjoy. Further, both
—again, like millions of other older volunteers—draw on inner reserves of
spiritual faith to sustain their strength.

The optimism and general sense of satisfaction experienced by volunteers is
a well-established fact. For example, a study of 188 companies by David Lewin
of the Columbia Business School showed that employee morale was three times
greater in firms with a high degree of community involvement than in companies that were uninvolved. Toxic levels of stress, leading to depression and
physical ailments, are a serious problem in the workplace. But it is reasonable
to suggest that a corporation's community altruism might provide a solution
to the problem. Granting employees two or three afternoons off a month to
serve as volunteers in company-sponsored projects might well make bottom-
line sense. It is more profitable in the long run to have a happy, self-fulfilled
workforce than it is to have large numbers of employees using every bit of
available sick leave due to stress-related illness.

This is not just wishful thinking. Sociologist Allen Luks studied fifteen hundred women volunteers, many of who mentioned the pleasurable physical sen-
sations they experienced while helping others, which continued for days or
weeks after the volunteer activity. This was the helper's high, and Luks concluded that it likely combated toxic stress, which too often led to chronic illness.
Such stress increases blood cholesterol levels that play a role in heart disease
and elevates blood sugar, a precursor to diabetes. As previously noted, stress

disrupts the immune system. In contrast, the women volunteers Luks studied showed low levels of stress. They described increased energy, a pleasurable, satisfying state of calm, and a feeling of warmth and well-being derived from their volunteer work.

Co-author Dr. Douglas Lawson once visited a man in his early nineties living in a Dallas retirement home. His mind was sharp as a teenager's, his movements nimble as someone half his age. Like Dan Tabler, this gentleman had "retired" years earlier, but ever since had volunteered as a student counselor at a nearby junior high school. This role gave him a well-defined sense of purpose. At eight every weekday morning, he reported to his "job" at the school. His attendance was perfect. Sometimes he counseled the children of parents he had helped twenty-five years before when he began serving as a volunteer. Sharing his insight and compassion with these youngsters gave him a sense of sustained energy. People needed him; there was a tangible purpose to his life. By contrast, men who retire with no special plans often experience health problems within a year of leaving work. Again, there may be a direct connection between improved health and volunteerism.

Time after time, research has linked altruism and mental health. Dr. George Vaillant monitored a group of Harvard graduates over a forty-year period, resulting in the pioneering study *Adaptation to Life*. He found that altruism was one of the personal qualities that helped even the most poorly adjusted in the study group to improve their lives emotionally and physically. In a similar study, researchers at Cornell University followed a group of people for thirty years and found that those who volunteered were happier than those who did not. It was clear that the volunteers had a greater sense of self-satisfaction, had a purpose in life, and were happier overall than non-volunteers.

Such findings might be because personal isolation from the larger community is almost invariably associated with maladjustment and unhappiness, which in turn lead to emotional and physical illness. Such isolation often provokes a sense of emptiness, of having no purpose in life. When a person is younger, involved in work or raising a family, life's purpose is as close as the morning alarm clock. But when children have grown and moved away from home—the empty-nest syndrome—or the long-awaited golden years of retirement suddenly become reality, many people confront an emotional void, not the fulfillment they had anticipated. As the Reverend Deacon Dolores Witt, chaplain of the Canterbury Court retirement community in Ohio, has found, some retired people try to fill this void with alcohol. But that only widens their separation from the larger community.

However, those among the elderly who reach out to their neighbors, providing whatever service they can, whether it be cooking a meal, baking a cake, or pushing someone's wheelchair, are rarely plagued by loneliness. They feel empowered; their lives have meaning and purpose. Equally important, volunteering allows the giver to be active, to exert control over life's events. And the more active a volunteer is, the greater the sense of connection and personal involvement. Volunteer work requires focusing on other people, not on one's own problems. And when a volunteer helps others—as soup kitchen volunteers can attest—the day passes quickly, leaving a glow of satisfaction that cannot be duplicated in any other way.

Spirituality is among the most important motivating factors of senior citizen volunteers.

Let's reexamine the story of Karen Williams, 62, of Eudora, Kansas, who sought some way to secure adequate housing for herself and her three grandchildren (see Chapter One). Karen's deeply rooted Baptist faith led her to pray for guidance and strength. And when the local Habitat for Humanity chapter approved her application to become the organization's first homeowner in her small town, Karen was certain that this "miracle" had been in answer to the long hours she had knelt with the children, hands clasped, heads bowed, praying for a home to replace their overcrowded trailer. Even though Karen suffered from chronic health conditions, she had unshakable confidence that God would give her the strength to perform the "sweat equity" Habitat requires of every partner homeowner.

By traditional social standards, Karen Williams had little reason to be so optimistic. But research has shown that older people with health problems living on small fixed incomes in below-average housing are often happier in retirement than their much more affluent peers. It should be recalled that a number of wealthy residents of the luxurious Shell Point Retirement Community in Florida have not found happiness or satisfaction in their comfortable circumstances. People such as Karen Williams, however, often have a positive outlook that is linked to their strong religious faith. This leads to a rich network of social relationships, which often are strengthened through volunteer work. Karen eagerly anticipated such a rewarding experience as the project began.

What she didn't know when her application was accepted was that many of the Habitat volunteers who would help build her house were also guided and motivated by faith. Marilyn Laws Porter, who became the coordinator for Karen's home, was a retired stockbroker whose traditional Roman Catholicism had evolved into a broader spirituality that encompassed a deep sense of commitment to her community. But, at the outset, Marilyn was far from sure that the small town of Eudora had the financial or volunteer resources to support the project. She confronted her doubts, however, and then went to work to help transform Karen Williams's prayers for a new home into planks-and-shingle reality. In doing so, Marilyn drew on her confidence that God would see the project through to completion.

It was good that Marilyn had this faith-rooted confidence, because building the new home for Karen and her grandchildren proved to be a tougher challenge than anyone could have imagined. As in all Habitat projects, raising money was the highest hurdle to surmount. The estimated budget for the lot and material for Karen's home was $54,000. But Habitat would have to raise that money from a town of only four thousand people. Marilyn's first success came when the City of Eudora sold the lot for just $10,000, less than half its actual market value. Then, to her surprise, local contractors then stepped forward to generously donate expensive building materials and to serve as expert volunteers. The cash contributions came in steadily. By early autumn 2002, it was clear there would be enough money to complete the house.

The small core of day-to-day volunteer builders included retired men and women from the Eudora Methodist Church's Neighbors Helping Neighbors program.

"Those people almost built the house," Karen Williams recalls.

Through summer heat and the cold of fall and winter, these committed Methodist volunteers worked steadily on the house. Each weekend, they were joined by other volunteers, some from the University of Kansas in Lawrence, others from churches in the larger community.

"I had a sense that they were doing God's work," Karen says. "They were careful, patient, and generous in teaching me how I could make my own contribution. To me, these people are real saints."

Evenings when Karen returned to her mobile home to cook the children's dinner, her mind was filled with images of rafters being hoisted into a solid grid work, of living-room walls taking shape, of windows fitted into casements. Her prayers were being answered.

For Marilyn Laws Porter, who modestly describes her role as a "worker bee," not a supervisor, helping build Karen Williams's Habitat home provided immense emotional and spiritual satisfaction. "Every time another contractor donated timber or drywall, or when an electrician came out on Saturday to work on wiring for free, I knew God was also at work."

Marilyn saw religious faith made manifest through the contributions of the volunteers. "Helping build this house was one of the most important things I've ever done. To know that you have been called to participate in a project like this is close to the Beatitudes, the blessings that you read in Scripture. The day that Karen and the children moved into their home, all of us who had contributed felt this blessing."

Perhaps this is why so many local Habitat for Humanity programs work in partnership with "Covenant Churches" in their communities. The pastors and congregations of Covenant Churches support Habitat's goal of building decent houses for those in need both in the United States and around the world. Habitat strives to establish ongoing relationships with Covenant Churches in every community in which the program is active.

Each Habitat for Humanity church signs a covenant to provide spiritual, financial, and material support for the organization. Covenant Churches are asked to encourage their congregations to work as hands-on volunteers on building projects. One purpose of this partnership is to bring the affluent and poor together to achieve a common goal, and, in the process of working side by side, for them all to become aware of their common heritage as God's children. Throughout the decades, Covenant Churches have provided tens of thousands of volunteers as well as vital financial support to Habitat for Humanity.

Such spiritually rooted volunteer efforts are not limited to large national organizations such as Habitat for Humanity. Maida Apodaca of El Paso, Texas, is a dedicated volunteer who has worked for years with the nondenominational Christian organization Casas por Cristo (Houses for Christ) that builds modest homes for needy Mexican families. The group has worked in Ciudad Juarez, across the Rio Grande from El Paso, replacing cardboard-and-tarpaper hovels in the *colonia* shantytowns with solidly built two-room houses.

A devout Roman Catholic, Maida Apodaca describes her efforts as "the Lord's work." Once you begin volunteering, she says, you can't stop. And she is thankful for the chance to serve: "You always get more than you give."

<hr />

Although Habitat for Humanity and Casas por Cristo have a strong component of spiritual commitment, less formal secular efforts akin to old-fashioned barn raisings have also achieved spectacular results when volunteers band together to help their neighbors. The *New York Times* reported on just such an effort in the 1990s. Kansas City nurse Cheryl Woods lost her paycheck, which she had already endorsed, just before Christmas. She needed the $400 to pay for her family's holiday, and thought it was gone forever.

But Rosemary Pritchett, a homeless mother of three young children, found the check. She had just deposited the last of her money to secure a bid on an abandoned inner-city house that was up for auction. Rosemary used the final quarter in her coin purse to call Cheryl Woods to say she had found the missing paycheck. When Cheryl came to the homeless shelter, she offered Rosemary a $25 reward. Despite her circumstances, Rosemary Pritchett refused the money. "Just write me a note of thanks that I can show the children," she said. "I want them to know that when you find something, somebody has lost it."

Cheryl had to threaten to leave the reward money on the floor before Rosemary would accept it. The next day, Rosemary and her young family moved into the ramshackle abandoned house. Vandals had stripped the building of wiring and plumbing, and there was no electricity or running water. When Cheryl paid a visit, she found Rosemary and the children trying futilely to make repairs using only a bent screwdriver and a rusty hammer.

I've got to help, Cheryl realized. She began working through the Yellow Pages, searching for contractors willing to work on Rosemary's house as volunteers. She finally found one experienced contractor willing to become supervisor for no charge. Another offered to install a free water heater, while a building supplier built new windows and provided fixtures. Cheryl's retired uncle volunteered to work on the restoration.

Soon Kansas City newspapers and television stations focused on the story and more contractors came forward to donate material and skilled labor. Strangers arrived each day at Rosemary's house to help. By the time the project was completed, over $30,000 worth of labor and supplies had been donated. This was as much a miracle as the building of Karen Williams's Habitat house in the small town of Eudora.

The transformation of Rosemary Pritchett's abandoned house into a modest but comfortable home for her family would not have been possible without the confidence, faith, and determination of one woman who refused to break the human bond of trust that linked her to this young mother who had found her paycheck.

Without question, all those who helped rebuild Rosemary's house likely received the same satisfaction and sense of fulfillment as Habitat for Humanity volunteers and Maida Apodaca. A similar quest for personal connection to the needy in the community motivates those who participate in Volunteers in Medicine (VIM), an innovative service program for retired and practicing health professional volunteers created in Hilton Head, South Carolina, in 1992. Retired physician Jack B. McConnell, M.D., found that, although Hilton Head was a retirement community for the affluent, one-third of the people living there had no access to healthcare. Even though most of these ten thousand

people were employed and paid taxes, they had no health insurance, nor sufficient income to pay for care. Yet, a large number of retired physicians, dentists, and nurses lived in Hilton Head. These retired health professionals
expressed an interest in finding a way to continue practicing their professions
on a voluntary, part-time basis to help those in the community who had no
access to care.

Among the reasons the retired health professionals sought volunteer work
was their deep connection to the healing professions, as well as their desire to
deliver care to those in need in a more relaxed, less stressful setting than the
high-pressure, earnings-driven clinics, hospitals, and HMOs from which they
had retired. By 1993, the first Volunteers in Medicine clinic was created as a free
healthcare facility staffed by retired professionals. Soon, fifty-five physicians,
sixty-four nurses, and fifteen dentists, all of whom had retired in Hilton Head,
came forward to staff the clinic. They all wanted to continue practicing the
healing arts in this "hassle-free" environment.

These retired healthcare professionals sought to reestablish as volunteers the
traditional ethical standard in medicine in which the manner that people are
treated during a clinic visit is as important as the medical care they receive.
Patients who came to the Volunteers in Medicine clinic were not seen as charity cases, but rather as good people in need of help. They deserved respectful
and dignified treatment because they survived on limited incomes, coura-
geously struggling to do the best for their families under difficult economic
circumstances.

A "culture of caring" emerged at the Hilton Head clinic that recognized
patients not for their weaknesses but for their strengths. They deserved all the
respect and dignity the retired professional caregivers could provide. And the
clinic staff sought to heal not only the physical illnesses of their patients, but
also the injury caused by years of bias, prejudice, and indifference. When a
groundskeeper at one of Hilton Head's famous golf courses, painfully limping
through his workday with a torn knee ligament, came to the Volunteers in
Medicine clinic, he received the same skilled and compassionate care as a
retired CEO millionaire was given at one of the community's modern private
hospitals. Children of migrant workers who had never visited a doctor's office
were examined by skilled retired pediatricians and were given the inoculations
necessary to attend local schools. Older patients among the working poor who
did not qualify for Medicaid and were too young for Medicare came to the
clinic, where they received free treatment for specific ailments, as well as advice
on preventive care and nutrition.

But retired healthcare professionals are not the only essential staff members. Over 150 lay volunteers support the work of the retired professionals.

Active members of the healing professions have also come forward to volunteer. The clinic now offers the services of twenty-two volunteer mental health and social work professionals, as well as three part-time nutritionists. Some of the lay volunteers work as "Partners in Care," who greet patients and escort them through the healthcare process, explaining clinic procedures and services and letting the patients know that someone hears their problems and cares about them as individuals. Community volunteers also provide essential operational and administrative support to the healthcare staff. The Joint Underwriter's Association has provided full malpractice insurance coverage for all volunteers in the VIM Clinic.

Ten years after it opened its doors, the clinic offers free care in pediatrics, general medicine, family practice, dentistry, immunization, ophthalmology, otolaryngology, cardiology, internal medicine, gynecology, dermatology, neurology, orthopedics, urology, radiology, minor surgery, laboratory support, nutrition counseling, social services, and mental health counseling. These services represent a truly astounding achievement that demonstrates the vast potential of healthcare professional volunteers to meet the growing needs of our low-income and aging population.

The success of the first Volunteers in Medicine clinic in Hilton Head was that it matched the untapped resource of the highly motivated retired medical professional with the obvious need of the low-income members of the community. Today, there are twenty-one VIM clinics in eleven states from New Jersey to Louisiana. Many VIM programs have attracted more practicing than retired healthcare professionals. The fact that these busy professionals are willing to serve as volunteers is a tribute to the VIM concept and to those who staff the independent centers.

Sister Lois McDonough, a member of the Sisters of Mercy order, has served as an administrator and fundraiser at Gwynedd-Mercy College near Philadelphia for thirty-five years. In 1999, she sought some way to work directly for the poor. Eugene Jackson, a successful local publisher and philanthropist, contacted Sr. Lois with the idea of creating a health center to meet the needs of their community's working poor.

"I can't do this job alone," Jackson told Sr. Lois. "You're going to have to come join me."

Working together, and mustering the energetic efforts of other dedicated organizers, they began fundraising and "networking" in the healthcare community. Their goal was to create a modern medical center that would provide a variety of professional services and specialties to the working poor who "fell between the cracks," not qualifying for Medicaid, too young for Medicare, but not having sufficient income to afford health insurance.

Eugene Jackson made a major contribution by purchasing a large old stone-façade home in Bucks County. The Turner Construction Company and its subcontractors went to work to completely rebuild the structure into a modern medical center with four examination rooms, a small pharmacy, three dental suites, a reception area, and staff offices. All told, this reconstruction was worth $325,000, but did not cost the new VIM center a penny. The program opened its doors in March 2001, and by the end of that year was treating over thirteen hundred medical and dental patients. Today, twenty-six physicians and twenty-one dentists, most still practicing their professions, join retired colleagues as volunteers.

The program is called the HealthLink Medical Center. "We didn't want to use the word 'clinic' because that has a slight connotation of charity care," Sr. Lois says. "These patients are our neighbors. We treat them with dignity and the care they receive at HealthLink is first class in every way."

Sr. Lois has been "overwhelmed" by the generosity of the volunteers. Primary care physicians donate hours of their time each week, and specialists in a variety of disciplines volunteer on a regular basis. To qualify for treatment, patients must be employed with an income under 200 percent of the federal poverty guidelines. Once enrolled, they receive treatment at no cost. Volunteer pharmacy students from local institutions work at the center, where they fill prescriptions with free medications donated by local physicians and pharmaceutical sales representatives. Because the volunteer staff professionals have wide-ranging contacts in the medical community, they are able to refer patients for advanced treatment, which is delivered free of charge.

"The volunteers just keep coming in," Sr. Lois points out.

After the HealthLink Center was featured in a nursing magazine, scores of experienced nurses signed up as volunteers. The knotty problem of malpractice insurance coverage was overcome in June 2002, when the Pennsylvania state legislature passed a bill that allowed practicing physicians to extend their insurance coverage into volunteer work. The retired physicians at the center obtain volunteer medical licenses and are covered by the program at much lower than commercial rates.

Sadly, Eugene Jackson died shortly before the center opened its doors to patients. But his energetic vision of marshalling the volunteer spirit of the medical community lives on. The HealthLink Center is a model volunteer medical organization. Hundreds or thousands of similar institutions will be needed in coming decades as our low-income elderly population grows inexorably and Medicare coverage inevitably shrinks.

Healthcare professionals either currently practicing or retired who are interested in serving their communities on their own terms in a relaxed, respectful atmosphere can find out more about Volunteers in Medicine by visiting the Web site www.vimi.org/volunteer.htm. Each volunteer—either a medical professional or a layperson—can commit as much time as he or she desires. VIM recommends retired professionals volunteer a minimum of a half a day per week. Many actually choose to provide a few hours' care every day. Practicing professionals can provide as much care as their schedules permit. The goal is to arrange their volunteer time to maximize continuity of patient care; thus, some volunteer physicians work in clinics every Wednesday and Thursday afternoon, and see the same patients each week. To maintain high standards, all professional volunteers are required to attend the same ongoing education as their peers still working in regular practice. But serving as a VIM volunteer is far from a burdensome obligation. Almost universally, the healthcare providers develop an esprit de corps that has all but disappeared in the more stressful professional working place. They find their service relaxing and even fun, and undoubtedly experience the expansive joy of the helper's high.

Although these retired health professionals are uniquely qualified to give to their communities as volunteers, their non-medical peers without such experience can make their own important contribution to their neighbors' health and well-being.

We have discussed the activities of Shepherd's Centers in an earlier chapter. Because they illustrate how older volunteers can help themselves by helping others, we return now to this exciting program. The Shepherd's Centers of America are probably the most successful volunteer programs meeting the needs of the elderly principally through the work of senior citizen volunteers. When Rev. Elbert C. Cole created the concept of the Shepherd's Centers in 1972, he was confident that older religious people represented a huge untapped community resource, not just in Kansas City, but also across the country. Cole was spurred forward in this effort by local retirees who sought new and meaningful volunteer work in a society that had traditionally viewed the elderly as powerless.

"They wanted to continue to serve," Cole recalls, "to give, to have a responsible role."

Cole and his volunteers rejected the myth that most senior citizens were frail and needy, dependent on the benevolence of others. Certainly, Cole recognized, there were many elderly people facing challenges in old age, particularly those with chronic health problems. But he believed that the majority of older people were capable of contributing to their communities, not drawing on scarce resources. He was certain that the religious elderly could harness their faith and volunteer to work with community partners for the common good.

Thirty-one years after the first Shepherd's Center was organized at Rev. Cole's United Methodist church in Kansas City, there are seventy-nine centers active in nineteen states.

Thousands of people of all faiths cooperate to help older adults sustain and enhance their lives. The primary purpose of a Shepherd's Center is to enrich the lives of retired people with opportunities to serve others, to experience self-expression, to engage in meaningful volunteer work, and to enjoy the close friendships that flourish at the centers.

An equally important goal is to help the elderly live independently in their own homes for as long as they choose to do so. This aim lies at the heart of Shepherd's Centers' programs. Shepherd's Centers volunteers do not view older people living alone—many of them disabled—as burdens on society, but rather as members of the family of God who deserve love and respect. And volunteers are prepared to offer whatever is necessary to help their less-fortunate brothers and sisters live as comfortably as possible with dignity and autonomy. To help preserve this independent living, volunteers deliver meals to homebound elderly people, help repair their houses, and provide full-time caregivers—often family members—much-needed relief. And it is important to note that the volunteers are themselves always older adults.

Reflecting on the importance of this work for today's underfunded and over-burdened healthcare system, Elbert Cole observes, "We keep people out of nursing homes left and right."

Like Dan Tabler and Velma Hammond, the "retired" senior citizen volunteers of the Shepherd's Centers are probably as busy as they ever were in their traditional working lives. They have a sense of involvement and responsibility. Every Shepherd's Center is freestanding, self-funded, planned, developed, and administered by the people who use it.

Beyond the volunteer outreach to the homebound, a typical center might offer classes in foreign languages, local history, healthful exercise such as T'ai Chi Chih or yoga, and the use of computers. Traditional crafts such as quilting and pottery are also popular. Some centers have bands, choruses, or glee clubs that visit local retirement communities and nursing homes. The range of activities is as diverse as the centers themselves.

What Shepherd's Centers have in common—their real genius—is that their programs are a ministry by and with older adults rather than a ministry to them. Shepherd's Centers' volunteers have authority to make decisions and to take responsibility for implementing them. Volunteers feel a sense of empowerment and ownership. They know they are needed. And they recognize that their motivating religious faith has been harnessed to accomplish specific tasks for the greater good of the community. This provides Shepherd's Centers' volunteers with ongoing purpose and meaning in later life, just like their volunteer peers in other organizations around the country. As with the congregational volunteers and covenant church workers on Habitat for Humanity projects, Shepherd's Centers' volunteers experience the same type of joyful "blessing" as the people who came forward to build Karen Williams's home in Eudora, Kansas.

Russ King, 80, is a retired Little Rock, Arkansas, life insurance actuary who completed a successful forty-year career in the 1980s. A Navy veteran of World War II, King saw combat in the Pacific as a radar man aboard the battleship USS *Tennessee.* Like millions of other former servicemen, King came home from the war, married, and attended college on the GI Bill. For forty years, his life revolved around his job, his family, and the Roman Catholic Church.

Once retired, however, he looked for activities that would provide personal fulfillment. He was attracted to the Little Rock Shepherd's Center's Adventures in Learning program, which offers the same level of education as an open university, but with no tests or homework. Always interested in history, King studied the Civil War, then moved on to Great Books and art appreciation. The "Swinging down the Lane" music course featuring the compositions of Glen Miller, Tommy Dorsey, and the other giants of the Swing Era was a favorite of King's World War II generation.

He became a regular in the Shepherd's Center's classes and discussion groups. But King quickly recognized that the Center's volunteer programs offered an outlet that he wanted to explore.

"I recognized there were a lot of older people who needed a little help," he says. "And I had time on my hands to help."

The Center's Faith in Action services relied on volunteers to help older adults remain independent and living in their own homes. Among the services provided were Caring Wheels (volunteers driving the people to medical appointments); Handy Hands (volunteers repairing older people's homes); Friendly Callers (volunteers calling to chat with shut-ins); and Meals on Wheels (volunteers delivering nutritious meals to homebound older people).

Russ King became a Meals-on-Wheels volunteer, first filling in as a replacement driver before receiving his own weekly route. Today, he delivers hot meals to about a dozen people every Friday. They always appreciate the food, which includes fresh fruit and a half-pint of milk. But not just the meal brightens their day.

"Most of these folks are all alone," King says. "I'm probably the only person they see that day, and some of them feel kind of low. I always stay a few minutes to chat with them."

One of the people King visits is a man near his own age who suffers from macular degeneration that has almost stolen his vision. But the man always perks up when King arrives. Recently, the man proudly demonstrated his computerized text enlarger that allows him the freedom to read on his own.

"He was so proud of that machine," King says, "and now every time I visit, he reads some of the newspaper to me. That's a little thing, but I know it makes him feel good."

From Meals on Wheels, King volunteered as a Caring Wheels driver. Several days a month, he drives people to their medical appointments, waits, then takes them shopping before delivering them back home. "It's important for them to see the doctor, of course," King says, "but it's also important for them to just get out of the house and go to the supermarket."

The advantages of being a volunteer are reciprocal. "I'm not 80 years old," King jokes. "I'm 80 years *young*."

There is no doubt that his being a volunteer fills a practical need and raises the spirits of those he serves. But there is also no doubt that King's own life is enriched by this volunteer service.

Fred Williams, 67, is another Shepherd's Center volunteer in Little Rock. He retired as a section chief in the state highway department at age 58 and found plenty of time on his hands. Williams worked as a volunteer bus driver at his United Methodist church and also began attending Adventures in Learning classes at the Shepherd's Center. Like Russ King, attendance at the center's classes naturally led to his serving as a volunteer. Williams was drawn to Caring Wheels because he knew the roads and streets of the local community intimately from his years with the highway department.

"I knew I wouldn't get people lost," he says.

But Williams also recognized the people with whom he interacted were often lonely shut-ins in need of simple human contact. Williams and his siblings drove their elderly parents to medical appointments and on errands, but he knows many of the elderly in his community live a long way from their children. They are isolated, vulnerable to depression. When he drives people to a medical appointment, Williams always chats with them, trying to be a good listener. "Sometimes folks just need to talk to someone face-to-face, to hear another voice," he says.

And like Russ King, Fred Williams receives deep satisfaction from his work. "I get as much or more from driving these people as they do," he says.

There are millions of retired people who want to become volunteers, but who wish to earn a minimum additional income to supplement their pensions. For them, the Experience Corps offers an ideal solution. This program, overseen by and funded through the national nonprofit private agency Civic Ventures, recruits retired people to serve as teachers' aides in overcrowded public schools.

Annette Mitchell, 70, is a typical Experience Corps volunteer. She receives a small monthly stipend for working sixteen hours a week with kindergarten teacher Aurora Milas's large class at Montgomery Elementary School in Washington, D.C. A former government worker with an artistic flair, Annette Mitchell brings a mature patience and understanding to her work. Because she feels a deep sense of responsibility to these children, she devotes extra attention to their classroom assignments. As described in a recent issue of the *Washington Post*, she read the five-year-olds the children's book, *A Chair for My Mother*, then had them pick up their crayons and draw the chair they would like to give their own mothers. "You want it to be a very nice chair," she told them, bending over the low tables to praise each child's work. "This is an important chair."

Certainly, Aurora Milas would like to have the time to devote such personal attention to every child in her class. But the fact is there are just too many students. Having Annette Mitchell available as an assistant is invaluable. For Ms. Mitchell, the rewards go far beyond her modest salary. She has the satisfaction of knowing that she is needed and that she fills a responsible position in her community.

Shirley Juarez, 63, an Experience Corps volunteer in Port Arthur, Texas, also derives great personal satisfaction from her work. A former payroll supervisor in a private company, she retired early because of the stress of her job. But she found retirement an empty reward after decades of work. Shirley did not have the attitude that she had labored hard all her life and that society now owed her a living. "No," she reflects. "What you give, you're going to receive. So, if you're going to sit back and not do anything, you're not going to get anything. You have to go out and become involved."

One day she read about Experience Corps in the church bulletin at St. Joseph's Parish.

That's what I really want, to work with children in school, especially bilingual students, she thought.

She went to work as an aide in a kindergarten class in the same school that she and her siblings had attended decades earlier. Many of the students in her kindergarten were recent Mexican immigrants who spoke little English. Although she never married or had children, her heart went out to these little boys and girls, and she saw in them both the frustration and the potential of her own Spanish-speaking brothers and sisters. When her oldest brother had entered this school, there were no Spanish-speaking teachers and he struggled. He didn't even know how to ask permission to use the bathroom.

Combining her Christian compassion with an ingrained sense of professional responsibility, Shirley took extra time working with each child. She learned to value these eager, resourceful five-year-olds. "Some of them don't speak or understand English well, but those who do translate for the others. They help one another. They're good kids."

Like Annette Mitchell, Shirley Juarez brings patient maturity to her role as a volunteer. She takes extra time to guide the children through basic English vocabulary and to pronounce the letters of the alphabet. Some are quick to learn; others are slow. Shirley Juarez treats them all equally, with dignity.

Her reward comes each day when a shy child finally speaks up to say "dog" or "cat" instead of *perro* or *gato*.

"The children need all the help they can get because it all boils down to kids," she says. "It makes you feel so good when you've had even a small part in helping them."

Ed Blystone retired as a Teamster truck driver in Chicago in his sixties and moved to Portland, Oregon. But retirement became a directionless emotional void. He ended up homeless, sleeping on the docks, caught pneumonia and nearly died. After four years on the streets, he turned his life around. But he recognized he needed a deeper purpose, a way to find meaning in his later years.

The burly, streetwise former trucker became an Experience Corps volunteer. Like Annette Mitchell and Shirley Juarez, Ed Blystone works as an aide in a kindergarten class. The children captured his heart, transporting him beyond his own troubles, giving him the human connection and direction that had been missing from his life.

Speaking of his first year as a volunteer, Blystone comments, "You get hooked. There are times you want to take the kids home with you. I'm salty and hard, but times I just want to cry. It's a wonderful thing. I had one of 'em come up to me and throw her little arms around my neck and say, 'Grandpa Ed, I love you.'"

Without question, Blystone's experience as a volunteer has transformed him. "I am a different person than I was thirty or forty years ago."

He has learned to "really listen" to the children. "I think a child can tell, and a child can also tell whether you really care or not."

Reflecting on the value of his volunteer work, Blystone says, "I think we are leaving a legacy. I don't think the children will ever forget us. I really believe they would miss us. I know I would miss them."

Like most other volunteers, Ed Blystone has gained immeasurably more than he has given.

Retired persons interested in this type of volunteer work should contact www.experiencecorps.org or e-mail info@civicventures.org.

Even though about half of retired Americans serve as volunteers in some capacity, half do not and fewer are volunteering now than they were five years ago. This means that millions of older people are missing the emotional and physical health rewards that come through volunteer work.

To correct this situation, we have developed practical, concrete steps to help those who wish to explore volunteering opportunities.

It's important that a person not just plunge into the first volunteer job he or she hears about. Take some time to investigate. And while you're doing it, consider the following points:

- Think about the kind of work you like and that you do well. Some people love to organize an office; others hate paperwork, but take great pleasure in personal contact. In every Shepherd's Center, for example, there are volunteers working as office managers and others like Russ King and Fred Williams who find real satisfaction in regular face-to-face encounters with their Meals-on-Wheels or Caring Wheels friends.

- There are 800,000 nonprofit volunteer organizations in America, many serving the elderly and staffed *by* elderly people. Your local United Way can put you in contact with dozens of such groups.

- But before you actually sign up as a volunteer, honestly assess your skills, which may include: teaching (anything from local history to first aid) fundraising; administration or clerical work; helping with support groups or grief counseling; construction or repair; physical assistance or care taking. And every hospice in the country needs volunteers devoted to meeting the needs of the terminally ill.

- You may already be involved in volunteering in your religious congregation and simply wish to expand that effort. Habitat for Humanity or Building Together with Christmas in April may offer you the added volunteer opportunities you seek.

- But, if you are a first-time volunteer, take the time to be sure the job you have in mind matches your skills and interests. Ask yourself these questions: Do you work well with people? Can you handle stressful situations—perhaps working with troubled youth or serving at a hospice? Do you prefer well-structured or loosely organized work? Are you comfortable working in fundraising or in asking for other types of support? Do you seek immediate feedback on your work, or do you prefer to work with little or no recognition? Do you like to work independently? Do you want to learn news skills? Do you truly enjoy a tough challenge—work in an inner-city clinic, for example? Try to remember jobs or activities in which you "lost yourself," became completely immersed. Finally, just jot down ten activities that you know or think you would enjoy. Try to match one of them to a volunteer job.

■ Don't knowingly take volunteer work in an organization or among people with whom you are not comfortable.

■ If you're bogged down by inertia and reluctant to take the first step toward the rewarding work of a volunteer, take a realistic look at what you *can* do. Remember, most people only spend a few hours each week in volunteer work. Ask yourself when you have a little spare time. Are mornings best? How about afternoons or evenings? Do you spend too much time on weekends vegetating in front of the television set? If so, it would be easy to find a Saturday morning or afternoon volunteer assignment.

■ Don't hang back because you really believe you have no special talent. Spending friendly time with lonely old people in nursing homes does not require great skill, just patience and compassion. Every retirement community in the country with an acute-care facility needs volunteers to help feed and groom the bedridden. Faith-filled volunteers find immense satisfaction in sharing this loving concern for those in need.

■ If you live on a low income, find a volunteer job that doesn't require driving a long distance or travel by using public transportation. Remember, some organizations contribute to their volunteers' travel expenses.

■ Pace yourself. Don't take on overly heavy responsibilities. One of the biggest mistakes new volunteers make is to accept a burdensome schedule or too many tasks. These volunteers can quickly burn out and become discouraged. They might become over-stressed—just the opposite effect of satisfying volunteer work—and drop out. As Doug Lawson puts it, "Take small bites. Don't overextend yourself. Don't over-promise. Don't try to do the whole job alone. Don't overreact when conditions are not perfect. *Do* find time to enjoy yourself."

■ Remember that effective volunteering almost always involves successful teamwork. Learn to moderate your efforts and share the burden.

■ Try to enlist the entire family. Many volunteer organizations provide a role for people of all ages. Kids can stuff envelopes or stock shelves; teenagers can push a wheelchair; the elderly can call shut-ins. Volunteering at religious congregations almost always provides opportunities for family groups. The burden is small; the rewards are immense. Children who grow up volunteering reach maturity with a healthy sense of self-worth and purpose.

Co-author Douglas Lawson has virtually "written the book" on becoming a volunteer and on the rewards to be gained from volunteering. Those interested in reading his practical advice should consult: *Give to Live: How Giving Can Change Your Life* (La Jolla, Calif.: ALTI Publishing, 1991); *Volunteering: 101 Ways You Can Improve the World and Your Life* (San Diego, Calif.: ALTI Publishing, 1998); *More Give to Live: How Giving Can Change Your Life* (San Diego, Calif.: ALTI Publishing, 1999).

For more practical information on volunteering, please see Chapter Eleven.

What "Caring" for the Elderly Truly Entails

9

B Y TRADITIONAL CRITERIA, retired librarian Sue Kann, 89, fits the definition of the "frail" elderly. Due to a recent broken hip and a fall resulting in a shoulder injury, she now moves with the aid of a walker. Some might consider her disabled. But they would be wrong. Sue may not be as physically robust as she once was, but she definitely is not an invalid. Living independently in her own apartment at the Marjorie P. Lee Retirement Community, a subsidized facility in Cincinnati, Ohio, Sue has days rich with companionship, stimulating conversation, and spiritual fulfillment.

Twice widowed in the past forty years, she has both older and younger friends in the community with whom she shares her interest in books, music, and religion. Sue is a devout Episcopalian with a curiosity about other philosophies and faiths. This past year she re-read works by pioneering psychoanalyst Carl Jung and Christian philosopher C. S. Lewis. Then Sue began studying a long history of Byzantium.

The retirement community's religious services form an important part of Sue Kann's week. She always attends Sunday chapel, at which the chaplain, Father David Cottrill, offers the spiritually elevating Communion liturgy and lay readers provide familiar and comforting scriptural passages. Sue finds special satisfaction in Advent and Holy Week leading up to the profound joy of Easter.

"I've always been a seeker," she says, reflecting on her combined spirituality and intellectual hunger. "I guess that's why I get along so well with Father Dave. He *responds* to us. We're not just old people for whom he's officially responsible. We are his friends."

Sue realizes and accepts that there is a limit to the healing she can expect from her physicians. In spite of modern medicine's incredible scientific advances, she is approaching the natural end of life. Reflecting on this, she says, "I am not afraid of dying. I have great faith in heaven, and I'm looking forward to seeing it. I sometimes tell Father Dave, 'Don't be embarrassed, but I hope that I can die while you are here as chaplain.'"

Meanwhile, she intends to live each day to its maximum potential. "I'm used to this old walker," she says cheerfully, "and I get around quite well with it."

While depression afflicts many institutionalized elderly people, Sue remains positive, alert, and eager to greet the morning. Her community provides a warm and nurturing environment in which she can spend her remaining years in contentment. And for Sue, the most important aspect of the Marjorie P. Lee Retirement Community's environment is the spiritual care she receives from Father Cottrill and the members of the congregation.

⌁━━━⌁

"Sue Kann is a perfect example of the importance of *care* versus *cure*," Father David Cottrill points out. "We're not doctors, so we cannot heal her fragile bones or lift the years from her shoulders. But we certainly can and do care for her spirit. That's the vocation of chaplains at communities such as this. We address the needs of the whole person, but our specialty is spiritual care."

There are about 220 residents at the Marjorie P. Lee Retirement Community, half in nursing beds or assisted-living units, half, like Sue Kann, living independently in apartments. The community accepts residents of all denominations, although many are members of the Episcopal Church. For those of other faiths, visiting chaplains frequently offer worship service, and a van is available to take people to congregations in the city.

The community has a permanent Catholic deacon who leads devotions every Wednesday evening in the chapel or in the Lee Library. Recognizing the importance of spiritual care, Father Cottrill also provides nondenominational services throughout the week. The Sunday morning ecumenical community worship includes Holy Communion. He does not evangelize for his own denomination, however, and always encourages people to attend their own church whenever possible. But if the weather is bad, he reminds them, "Think of me as an extra pastor. You're always welcome to worship with us."

One of the most popular of Father Cottrill's services is the one devoted to healing. Held each week, the worship includes sacred music and group prayer.

"By 'healing,' I mean a sense of spiritual renewal. We're not advertising miraculous cures. But the inner peace and tranquility afflicted elderly people can receive through focused group devotion can be quite dramatic."

Father Cottrill adapts this approach every Wednesday night when he and lay volunteers conduct worship service for Alzheimer's patients. He has tailored these devotions for their special needs. Calming sacred music issuing softly from a CD player draws their attention as Father Cottrill or one of his lay volunteers reads simple, familiar passages from the Book of Common Prayer. The high point of this worship is the Baptism of Jesus, during which Father Cottrill soothes each patient's cheeks and hands from a bowl of warm water.

"The devotion is very tactile," he says. "It's amazing how people who are agitated or almost totally withdrawn from the world will respond to familiar hymns, the touch of warm water, and the sound of prayer."

Father Cottrill understands full well that he and his volunteers are in no way curing the incurable affliction of Alzheimer's disease. "It's a terminal condition," he says. "We accept this. But we also believe that some of these people have been healed on a different level."

And what is true for the Alzheimer's patients also applies to people suffering from cancer, end-stage kidney disease, or the crippling effects of stroke. Society often considers them victims of "terminal" disease who have lost some of their human value because they cannot be cured by modern medicine and are thus closer to death than to life. But to the members of the Marjorie P. Lee faith community, all their friends and neighbors, no matter their medical diagnosis, are children of God. Their bodies cannot be cured, but their spirits can be healed.

Father Cottrill depends on motivated and trained volunteers from among the residents to help conduct the specialized healing and other services. Volunteers serve as lay ministers, serve on the altar guilds, assist people in getting to the devotions, and perform the many other duties that keep the Episcopal and other denomination "parishes" within the community running smoothly.

Mel Dickerson, an elderly man who, like Sue Kann, many might believe needs help himself, is one of Father Cottrill's most devoted and productive workers. He takes full responsibility to be at the assisted-living or nursing units in time to push the patients' wheelchairs to the chapel and makes sure each worshiper is safely returned. This is his way of showing loving care for his friends and neighbors. Mel Dickerson derives as large a psychological reward as he delivers through his selfless action.

Speaking of the volunteers on whom he depends, Father Cottrill says, "I couldn't do my work as chaplain without them."

Concerning Marjorie P. Lee residents in general, Father Cottrill continues, "There is no cure for old age and death. But there's anecdotal evidence that coming to a caring community such as this, which provides intense and varied spiritual support, can extend life by up to four years. And there is no question that the spiritual care available here improves the quality of life of our people. In many ways, we're like a small, tranquil village."

The views of medical ethicist Daniel Callahan, Ph.D., director of International Programs at the Hastings Center and a senior fellow at the Harvard Medical School, coincide with those of Father David Cottrill. At the heart of their theoretical and practical work lie important questions: How does a family member, a neighbor, a resident of a retirement community, or a volunteer demonstrate valid, compassionate "care" toward the elderly and the afflicted?

Often, the chronically ill and disabled experience great emotional upset and grieve over the loss of their independence. Irritability and social withdrawal frequently accompany their ensuing depression. Such people can also become resentful toward those who want to help them, seeing them as "do-gooders" who threaten to take away even more of their precious remaining independence. Providing care for others is a skill, an art that must be learned. Otherwise, the volunteer may only add to the burden of the sick elder, be quickly rejected by that person, soon become frustrated, and burn out. Thus, volunteers can benefit from well-structured training on how to provide effective care to others—how to develop the art of caring that meets the true needs of those they wish to serve. This will maximize the benefit both to the volunteer and to the care receiver.

As Daniel Callahan has pointed out, in the current clinical paradigm, money and prestige accrue to those who cure patients. But as Father David Cottrill reminds us, there is as yet no cure for Alzheimer's disease—or for severe stroke and many metastatic cancers—and there never will be for old age itself. And as the growing numbers of elderly are burdened with chronic medical conditions and disabilities that cannot be cured, they will be ill-served by a healthcare system that puts curing first and often discounts the concept of emotionally supportive care, which includes a focus on a person's spiritual requirements.

Callahan has developed a hierarchy of curative and caring priorities:

- The maximizing of mental and physical function: Think of the inclusiveness and the spiritual/intellectual stimulation available at our best retirement communities.

- The prevention of dependency and the pursuit of autonomy: Shepherd's Centers volunteers help tens of thousands of elderly living independently through programs such as Friendly Callers, Caring Wheels, and Meals on Wheels.

- The relief of pain and suffering: The hospice movement has led the way in this regard.

■ Enhancing the sense of physical and psychological security: Most modern retirement communities offer a mix of independent, assisted-living, and nursing facilities.

■ And the realization of psychological and spiritual needs: Increasingly, institutions serving the elderly recognize their vulnerability to depression and their need for spiritual support.

Often the trained physician cannot affect a cure while chaplains such as Reverend Cottrill or sincere, well-trained volunteers such as Mel Dickerson can devote adequate time to the afflicted individual and thus alleviate that person's suffering to a significant degree.

"Caring may be the focus," Callahan says, "when the highest curative aims cannot be achieved."

A number of exemplary congregations provide support and care for their members, especially those with chronic health problems. Such facilities exist within both the Christian and the Jewish religious traditions; within Protestant and Catholic communities; within megachurches and small congregations; within Caucasian and black churches. There are organizations such as Shepherd's Centers of America that have mobilized thousands of healthy elderly volunteers to provide support and care for sick or disabled peers, thereby helping to reduce healthcare costs and delay nursing home placement. And there are smaller groups such as the Marjorie P. Lee Retirement Community or the Luther Manor in Milwaukee, where volunteers fill such a vital role in the spiritual and emotional care of their friends and neighbors.

———

But it is when Alzheimer's disease, perhaps our most demoralizing affliction, strikes that the devotion of the caregiver is truly tested. Alzheimer's causes the deterioration of the brain itself and, before inevitably ending in death, robs the victim of memory and other mental capacity.

Stephen G. Post, Ph.D., a professor of biomedical ethics at Case Western Reserve University in Cleveland, is a world-renowned expert on the compassionate care of Alzheimer's patients. He is the author of the highly regarded book *The Moral Challenge of Alzheimer's Disease: Ethical Issues from Diagnosis to Dying*, 2nd ed. (Baltimore, Md.: Johns Hopkins University Press, 2000), as well as other notable books and journal articles on caring for dementia victims.

One of Dr. Post's special interests is the role of *agape*, which Webster defines as "spontaneous self-giving love expressed freely without calculation of cost or gain to the giver or merit on the part of the receiver." In Christianity, agape reflects God's love for man, and has parallels in all the other major religions. Post suggests that this unselfish love is particularly important in the care of those he calls "the deeply forgetful." He also cites persuasive research evidence that indicates agape or its equivalent helps sustain caregivers of Alzheimer's patients. As the disease progresses, these victims invariably lose the attributes such as responsiveness to others, recognition of relatives and friends, and even their own unique individuality that we traditionally associate with "person-hood."

For the caregiver—often a close relative—to continue to value Alzheimer's patients for their God-given spiritual identity, which even the disease in its most ravishing terminal stages cannot strip away, is the ultimate trial of this altruistic love.

And Post is convinced that spiritual strength, the long-neglected element in modern medical science, is exactly the element that will help sustain the millions of Alzheimer's patients who will be diagnosed as our society ages over coming decades. Spiritual strength, he adds, also bolsters the devotion, courage, and perseverance of those who care for them.

He describes the touching story of "Jan," who was an optimistic, well-adjusted, and forward-thinking woman who had just turned 40 when she noticed that she was beginning to forget names, addresses, and even relationships within her family. As the condition quickly progressed, Jan consulted a neurologist. After tests and brain scans, the diagnosis was unequivocal and devastating: Jan had a very aggressive form of Alzheimer's disease. Because of its early onset, her prognosis was bleak. The disease would quickly consume her mind and then kill her body.

Jan was crushed, overcome by the unanswerable "why me?" anguish that assails so many newly diagnosed victims of incurable diseases. Like all those who must face the reality of an Alzheimer's diagnosis, she mourned the imminent loss her life's hopes and dreams, of the very essence of herself. Jan's torment deepened as the illness followed its relentless path, and she lost more precious fragments of memory and personality each day. In the coming months, Jan tried to reassure herself that much of her mind remained intact even as she struggled to understand why she had been struck such a savagely cruel blow during what should have been a productive and fulfilling period of her life. But she found no answer.

Then one winter morning, she wandered to the kitchen and gazed out the window. It had snowed hard in the night, the sun was now emerging, but a few large white flakes were still spiraling soundlessly down to disappear into the white blanket of the yard. Her son was clearing the sidewalk, bending and rising to deposit each shovelful of sparkling crystals. Jan was fascinated by the different textures of the snow: the soft flakes still falling and the clouds of gleaming gems drifting from the shovel blade. Time passed. She studied the snow in perfect contentment. From some deep trove of memory rose the image of a kindergarten paper cutout of a snowflake's unique multiple facets. Her eyes filled with tears of gratitude.

If Jan had been a *normal* person in her early forties, leading a typically hectic life in the suburbs, she probably would have seen this snow as a nuisance, not as one of nature's miraculous gifts. But it was her affliction that had widened Jan's perspective. Her torment began to subside.

God, she realized, *has granted me the ability to see the world with the innocence of a child's eyes.*

Faith overcame Jan's anguish. Despite the cruel disease, Jan realized that she was a divinely created being graced with the limitless love of her creator. *I'm still here,* she thought, *and there will still be wonder in my life.*

Like Sue Kann, Jan's religious renewal allowed her to cope and indeed thrive under conditions that drive so many into depression. In fact, Post notes, research has shown that more than 85 percent of people with Alzheimer's disease cope through prayer and other spiritual ritual.

In Post's opinion, this religious and spiritual coping offers clear clinical advantages to the Alzheimer's patient. Post cites research led by David Bennett, M.D., of the Rush-Presbyterian-St. Luke's Alzheimer's Disease Center in Chicago, that indicates the personality trait of serenity might be a protective factor in the progression of the disease. Virtually all major religions embrace a sense of Providence, which tends to enhance serenity among the faithful. Thus, Post says, Alzheimer's patients who cope through prayer—and who share prayer and religious ritual with their caregivers—might strengthen their basic serenity and thus help combat the affliction.

Agitation exacerbated by disorientation can be a serious problem among people with Alzheimer's. Post describes the case of an elderly Roman Catholic man so confused by the disease that he could no longer speak and was reduced to inarticulate moaning. But when a rosary was placed in his hands and a caregiver spoke the first words of the Lord's Prayer, "Our Father, Who art in heaven …" the man took over in a strong, clear voice and completed the prayers, word perfect, and in their proper order. And on completing the rosary, his agitation and moaning always ceased and he was calm.

The serenity found through religion also helped Peter, another Roman Catholic Alzheimer's patient Post describes, face the disease. Like Jan, Peter was diagnosed at the most productive time of his life. His corporate career was flourishing and his professional future was bright. Then the disease struck. He quickly lost his ability to function in the fast-paced corporate world and had to retire. Peter was crushed. The prestige and salary of a high executive position had been snatched away just when it seemed within his grasp. All the years of hard work, he thought bitterly, had been wasted.

Then, in an effort to understand the disaster that had swallowed his life, Peter started attending mass more frequently than he had before his diagnosis. Whereas he had previously been a Christmas-and-Easter churchgoer, he now attended each Sunday and also acquired the habit of regular private devotion, including reading from a missal that offered a prayer for each day. One of his favorites was, "My Lord God, I do not see the road ahead. But I trust in You, who will never leave me."

Just as Jan had found a purpose in her affliction, Peter came to understand that God had removed him from the career rat race in order to slow down and learn to appreciate what was truly valuable in life: his loved ones and friends, and being of service to others.

Once, when his anguish threatened to return, Peter had a vivid dream in which a warm, infinitely benign light appeared and spoke to him: "Remember, I will always stand beside you." He was convinced that light was God. Peter's torment disappeared.

He became a volunteer at an adult day-care center for Alzheimer's patients. Many were people whose conditions had deteriorated much further than his own. Each morning, Peter was first on the van, and then he greeted each new passenger and made sure his or her seat belt was securely buckled. This responsibility was far removed from his duties as a corporate vice president who chaired meetings every day and flew off regularly to confer with colleagues or clients.

But Peter came to realize that his work as a loving volunteer carried a responsibility far greater than anything he had known in the business world. He was a patient himself. He was now following the same life path of those who rode with him in the van. No one could be more compassionate toward them. God, he realized, has a plan for us all. By the time Peter would no longer be able to work as a volunteer, God would provide someone to replace him.

This is a splendid example of what we call "religious coping." Those who are able to benefit from it are often shielded from depression.

Stephen Post emphasizes that spiritually based compassion—agape—is perhaps the single most important tool available to nonprofessional caregivers. Prayer and religious ritual link volunteers such as Mel Dickerson at the Marjorie P. Lee Retirement Community and millions of others nationwide with the Alzheimer's patients for whom they care. Faith helps alleviate the stress of the caregiver's endless duties, which have been aptly described as "the thirty-six hour day." Post highlights research that suggests spirituality and faith are the strongest factors determining successful coping among African American women caring for a relative with Alzheimer's disease. He notes that, as a social group, these women are often the victims of depression triggered by the stress inherent in their environments, and that it might be expected that the added burden of this stressful caregiving would overwhelm them emotionally. But many of those who cope through faith and see their responsibility toward their loved ones within the context of God-ordained love (agape) are shielded from depression.

"It's clear that spirituality really counts," Post concludes, "both for the patient and the caregiver."

Post calls on faith communities — churches, synagogues, and mosques — to remember their sacred covenant to protect the weak and care for the sick. As the grim statistics of Alzheimer's progression through our expanding elderly population continue, he says, people of faith must rise to the challenge.

"Loss of memory is like the loss of a limb," Post says. "It can be replaced by a prosthesis. Congregations must serve as an alternative source of memory for the deeply forgetful."

He cautions, however, that contemporary worship — like much of today's society — has become "hypercognitive," overly reliant on linear logic, not on emotionally satisfying ritual that involves music and basic prayer. Hypercognitive devotion is meaningless to people suffering from dementia.

"Liturgy must be tailored for them," Post says. There should be recognizable sacred music, hymns with a strong, familiar melody, hugs, and clasping of hands. "If patients are in wheelchairs, the caregivers should sit close beside them during devotion, make eye contact, smile and share the joy of worship."

One obvious practical advantage to such worship with the deeply forgetful, Post adds, is that caregivers themselves also benefit from communal warmth of agape; they experience a renewal of energy and are reassured that their work has value.

This sense of worth and the confidence to continue are essential for caregivers facing one of the most stressful challenges imaginable: Even as the patient's condition worsens and they require ever-increasing care, they become increasingly withdrawn or agitated and are unable to express appreciation for the care they receive. It is then that the caregiver's selfless love is sorely tested.

Carol J. Farran, DNSc, is a professor of nursing and a member of the faculty of the Rush-Presbyterian-St. Luke's Alzheimer's Disease Center. She is an internationally recognized expert on caregiving who has specialized in mental health with an emphasis on caregivers of Alzheimer's patients. Since most of these caregivers are family members, Dr. Farran has focused on the factors that allow some to cope well with their difficult circumstances, while others do not.

Her research has revealed that the ability to preserve hope, maintain optimism, and find meaning is essential to effective caregiving. Conversely, a sense of hopelessness is the single most significant factor in *in*effective caregiving.

Caregivers of people with Alzheimer's are most often successful when they are able to rely on a positive emotional foundation on which to build their problem-solving strategies. They recognize that—by its very nature—their loved one's Alzheimer's disease will test them in new, often frustrating ways every day. If caregivers lose hope that they will be able to cope, frustration prevails, and they relinquish the ability to think clearly.

Dr. Farran has found that successful caregivers must remain emotionally and mentally nimble. And this requires an optimistic attitude. But how can they remain optimistic in the face of an undeniably terminal condition that is inexorably eroding their loved one's very identity? For many, hope and faith are inseparable: The caregiver relies on faith in accepting his or her burden; faith lightens the weight of that burden. Again, it is the personal connection with God-given love, agape, that allows the preservation of hope and lightens the caregiver's load to a manageable weight. It is faith that gives purpose and meaning to this difficult task, helping the caregiver realize that caring for a loved one with this disease is the same as caring for God himself, who exists in that person.

This does not mean that faith will completely alleviate the complex, emotionally draining struggle. But without faith or a sense of spiritual support, the caregiver can quickly burn out, surrender to hopelessness, suffer impaired thinking, poor decision making, and stress-induced guilt, and often slip into depression.

Indeed, Dr. Farran has found hopelessness to be perhaps the single greatest enemy of the caregiver of the afflicted elderly. Hopelessness is in every way the opposite of a positive, inventive, problem-solving attitude. The caregiver who has given up hope and surrendered to despair feels powerless, trapped in the situation. His or her thoughts are often muddled. He or she is unable to learn caregiving techniques or to adapt to the afflicted loved one's changing needs.

"Hopelessness includes a behavioral process in which a person attempts little or takes inappropriate action," Dr. Farran concludes.

Indeed, hopelessness per se can be a symptom of encroaching depression. And, as we have seen, people sliding into depression generally cannot see the wider purpose of events around them. Unlike Alzheimer's victims Jan and Peter, caregivers who have lost hope feel alienated from God. Dr. Farran describes this condition as "spiritual muteness … the inability to cry out to a Higher Power." The spiritually mute feel alienated and isolated, as much victimized as the person for whom they must care.

To help families of people with Alzheimer's, Dr. Farran and her colleague Eleanora Keane-Hagerty have devised a guide: "Twelve Steps for Caregivers." Based on other successful twelve-step programs, this framework urges caregivers to acknowledge that their normal human resources of education, intelligence, and endurance are insufficient to meet this new challenge, that they must accept the help of a Higher Power, and depend on it whenever the burden seems too heavy.

In Step 1, the caregiver recognizes that modern medicine can do relatively little to treat Alzheimer's. The caregiver must learn to help reduce disruptive behavior and adapt his or her own attitude toward that behavior.

Step 2 reminds the caregiver of the need to "take care of myself." If people become burned out and depressed, they cannot care for their loved ones. Here they are encouraged to consult health professionals and volunteer organizations that provide respite care so that family members can take time away.

Step 3: "I need to simplify my lifestyle." Caregivers must recognize that the life led before their loved one's diagnosis is over and that former activities must be adapted or dropped.

Step 4 urges caregivers to accept the help of others; this is not a sign of weakness. No one can bear this load alone.

In Steps 5 and 6, caregivers are reminded to take responsibilities one day at a time and to structure their days. As the memory impairment of Alzheimer's increases, regular daily structure, routine, and ritual for the affected family member become important.

Step 7: "I need to have a sense of humor." The ability to see comedy and irony in potentially embarrassing or otherwise painful situations allows the caregiver to preserve a human connection with the loved one.

In Step 8, caregivers are urged to remember that their relatives' behavior and emotions are distorted by the illness. Don't take disruptive behavior personally.

Step 9: "I need to focus on and enjoy what my relative can still do."

In Steps 10 and 11, caregivers are reminded that they have additional resources for love and support: other family members and friends and the wider community. Interacting with them will remind caregivers that they will not have to handle every situation perfectly and allow them to develop a sense of self-acceptance in a wider context.

Step 12: "A Higher Power is available to me." Many caregivers find that their connection to a Higher Power has assisted them through difficult situations and that this same Power has helped them to find meaning through their caregiving experiences. There are books of prayers specifically related to Alzheimer's disease that some caregivers have found quite useful.

Throughout this book, we have referred to "faith communities" and "congregations," meaning not just Christian churches, but synagogues and mosques as well. Indeed, if the wider American faith community is to address the social and healthcare needs of our aging population, it will have to draw on all of these resources.

Rabbi Richard F. Address, D.Min., is director of the Department of Jewish Family Concerns at the Union of American Hebrew Congregations (UAHC). He oversees the department's mission of creating "caring congregations" and is particularly interested in the role of Reform Judaism in facing the challenge of what he has called the "longevity generation," the growing cohort of the elderly who will live decades longer than their predecessors. Turning to Torah, the theological bedrock of Judaism, for guidance, Rabbi Address is developing training material for the clergy and lay members of the Jewish community to help them face the tasks ahead. As the Baby Boom generation melds with that of their parents and traditional designations such as "middle-aged" and "elderly" become less relevant, Rabbi Address believes we must all reassess our responsibilities toward each other.

In his book, *That You May Live Long: Caring for Our Aging Parents, Caring for Ourselves* (New York: UAHC Press, 2003), Address develops the concept of "sacred aging," which emphasizes the role of spirituality for caregivers and the entire faith community. It is essential, he says, that congregations begin to train volunteer caregivers to prepare for the undeniable burdens they will face in the years ahead. As with the rest of our population, Alzheimer's disease will pose a special problem. But Rabbi Address frankly admits that there is "a huge denial factor" among most congregations with which he has raised this subject: "Alzheimer's is something that happens to *other* people, not themselves."

He finds that congregations also wish to avoid the unpleasant issue of broader looming healthcare problems for the elderly.

"People recognize the threat intellectually," he says, "but they cannot emotionally come to terms with it."

But Rabbi Address intends to work beyond this denial. In his approach to the Sacred Aging initiative, he reminds congregations that 20 percent of American Jews are already over 65 and that the ratio of elderly to younger people will only increase steeply in coming decades. Once more, however, Rabbi Address is able to draw on Torah for the theological basis of this contemporary project:

the Sixth Commandment, "Honor your father and your mother that your days may be long in the land which the LORD your God gives you."

In motivating congregations, Rabbi Address and his colleagues urge synagogue members to think beyond "pediatric Judaism," faith communities focused on young families, and traditional programs such as fundraising for new buildings. The true need as our population ages, Address emphasizes, will be for training volunteer caregivers and other volunteers to interact with the growing numbers of the elderly.

"Developing such relationships will be more important than bricks and mortar," Rabbi Address says.

On a practical level, his department is preparing a syllabus for a Caring Academy that can be taught in synagogues nationwide. This is a one-week program for lay leaders and clergy that provides guidance for developing specific caregiving techniques and volunteer activities, somewhat similar to those underway in the Christian community, including the Friendly Caller and Caring Wheels programs of the Shepherd's Centers.

"Judaism has faced many crises in its long history," Rabbi Address comments. "I am confident that it will meet the challenge of the longevity revolution."

———

Eileen Rogers, a para-rabbinic fellow, a liturgically trained Jewish lay leader roughly equivalent to a Christian deacon, is a virtual model for the type of energetic volunteer Rabbi Address envisions. Rogers, a professional woman in early middle age from Rockville, Maryland, came to her vocation unexpectedly.

"I was raised to be *culturally* Jewish," she says. Her family observed High Holidays, but she did not develop a deep emotional connection to her faith.

Then, in the early 1990s, she was diagnosed with breast cancer and underwent surgery and chemotherapy. The disease was both physically harsh and emotionally wrenching. Trained as a classical pianist, Eileen had always relied on music as an emotional balm. Indeed, she listened to soothing music as she received her chemotherapy. During her recovery and remission, she began to attend Temple Emmanuel in Kensington, Maryland, where the cantor was renowned for his beautiful voice.

"It was the sacred music that opened the door to faith for me," she recalls.

Once through that door, Eileen was eager to explore the rich and spiritually nurturing aspects of Judaism. During her cancer treatment, she had learned a lot about the importance of a loving family and the strength a spiritually supportive caregiver can extend. As much as anyone, Eileen's daughter Johanna, a rabbinical student, taught her mother about the role of faith in healing. Eileen began to visit elderly Jewish people in institutions and retirement communities around Washington, D.C. She found that, although their physical needs were usually well met, they often were not equally cared for spiritually.

As a volunteer at the Hebrew Home of Greater Washington, she worked with a small group of Alzheimer's patients. Her experience was similar to that of Father Cottrill's. The people with whom Eileen Rogers worked responded to music, touch, and other noncognitive forms of devotion. She recalled earlier visiting a great-aunt at the Hebrew Home. The woman's mind was so shrouded with dementia that the only way Eileen could draw her out was by softly chanting Hebrew prayers or singing old Yiddish songs. When Eileen did so, the old lady would smile wanly and join her.

Eileen Rogers "learned through experience" and soon became a regular volunteer at local retirement communities. Then she underwent her formal liturgical training. At Riderwood retirement home in Silver Spring, Maryland, she is the visiting clergy person who performs the Friday evening Sabbath service once a month and leads the congregation of approximately 125 elderly people in High Holy Day worship. With the assistance of Rabbi Dennis Jones, this small faith community was able to secure a long-term loan of a Torah scroll from Temple Emmanuel.

"This is very important to these people," Eileen points out. "They no longer feel cut off from their faith. Most of them don't drive and many had felt severed from their old congregations."

Such isolation can be a real problem for the elderly, she says. "Among seniors, there can be a sense of disenfranchisement because they are living on small fixed incomes, can no longer contribute financially to the congregation, nor worship there regularly." But it is exactly these people—many suffering from chronic illness—who need spiritual support the most.

With them in mind, Eileen has tailored her work as a volunteer lay leader. A few years ago at her synagogue, she helped lead a healing service that involved music and poetry. A friend recorded the worship for her homebound mother who is almost totally blind. Then Miriam, this older handicapped person, asked Eileen to repeat the ceremony in her home. Since then, the worship has evolved into a well-attended, twice-monthly healing service.

As the sacred liturgy is chanted and the menorah candles are lit at local nursing homes where she volunteers to conduct Sabbath services, Eileen can see the appreciation glow in the eyes of even the oldest, most afflicted people.

"They know that they are not forgotten, that they are loved," she says.

British physician Cicely Saunders founded the modern hospice movement in London in the 1960s. Hospice is derived from the Latin *hospitium*, a traditional guesthouse that provided shelter for tired and sick pilgrims. As envisioned by Dr. Saunders, a hospice was a place "between a hospital and a home, with the skills of the one and the hospitality, warmth, and the time of the other." In other words, a hospice would become a place of comfort and shelter for people with terminal illness, for those embarked on the final stage of their life's journey.

As Daniel Callahan reminds us, modern medicine has long been devoted to finding cures to illness. However, there are not yet cures for many afflictions to which the elderly are especially prone. It was with this in mind that Dr. Saunders established St. Christopher's Hospice near London, the first facility to combine advanced pain management with compassionate care for the terminally ill. The goal of St. Christopher's was not to cure a person's terminal cancer or kidney disease, but to allow them to die with dignity, free of pain, and surrounded by loved ones or spiritual supporters.

By the mid-1980s, Congress made the Medicare Hospice Benefit permanent, and later extended Medicare hospice coverage for as long as patients needed the service. Hospices are nonprofit institutions that rely on approximately one volunteer for every two paid employees. And hospices have done much to overcome the old, illogical medical prejudice against effective pain management for the terminally ill. Under that paradigm, dying people often suffered needlessly out of fear that they might become "addicted" to their narcotic pain medication. In hospices today — and indeed in most hospitals — patients are adequately medicated to control pain.

With physical needs met in the comfortable environment of the hospice, the dying person is free to spend time with loved ones and friends outside the more institutionalized atmosphere of an acute-care hospital. It is in this environment that hospice chaplains and spiritual caregivers play an important role. One of these chaplains, Sr. Caryn Brennan, a member of the Community of the Sisters of St. Joseph, is a board-certified Catholic chaplain who performs many of her duties with hospice patients. She reminds them and their families that she believes God is the true provider of spiritual care and therefore her first responsibility as a chaplain is to pray for her patients and their families. And she always advises and helps her patients to bolster their spiritual strength.

Sr. Caryn tells the story of Ken, a dying patient in his eighties in a hospice. Visiting him, she learned that he had received the anointing of the sick (or last rites) while at an acute-care hospital and suggested that he invite his pastor to come to the hospice to administer Communion, which she knew was very important to Ken. But during a slow, emotionally painful conversation, Ken revealed that he felt hurt that no one from his congregation had visited him in the hospital, despite his decades-long involvement with that church. He felt isolated from the faith community, which he believed had rejected him when he needed them the most.

This admission strengthened the growing bond of trust between Ken and Sr. Caryn. He eventually was able to unburden himself of other rejections he had suffered throughout his life and finally voice his deepest fear.

"Sister," he said, his voice breaking, "I'm just afraid that God might also reject me when I die."

She assured him that this was not the case, that God's love was limitless. Slowly, Ken's fears were replaced with a sense of acceptance and peace. He felt free to invite his pastor to the hospice. When the priest administered Communion, Ken's face was warm with peaceful joy.

He told Sr. Caryn, "Everything is okay. I know I'm going home to a welcome."

Sr. Caryn Brennan attributes this transformation from resentful torment to joyful tranquility to the simple human gift of listening with openness as Ken unburdened himself. She recognizes that people have unique responses to the Holy and respects whatever means they find for spiritual comfort, whether it be prayer, music, nature, friendship, or religious ritual.

Like Father David Cottrill, Rabbi Richard Address, and Eileen Rogers, Sr. Caryn understands that she cannot cure the incurable. But, also like these others, she recognizes the vital role of the spiritual caregiver who has the ability to help heal the spirit.

As our population ages and healthcare requirements expand beyond the capacity of traditional privately and publicly funded programs, the country will have to turn to clergy such as these and to volunteers from faith-based communities and institutions to form innovative partnerships to meet these needs.

Part IV

Implementing the Vision

The Partnership of Government, Philanthropy, and Faith-Based Communities

10

CARLTON ZIEBELL, a tall, robust man of 81, is a retired Wilmington, Delaware, teacher and a former Lutheran minister. He and his wife, Doris, have led an active retirement life, dividing their time among their grandchildren, their garden, cooking, classes at the nearby university, and singing in the choir of the Church of the Good Shepherd.

Carlton has also been an energetic community volunteer who derived great satisfaction working at a kitchen that served the homeless. But perhaps his greatest fulfillment came as a volunteer advocate for the mentally ill in a program that fellow church members Dorothy and Dick Patterson introduced to the congregation.

The Pattersons helped create the Delaware chapter of the National Alliance for the Mentally Ill (NAMI) more than fifteen years ago. Started as a small Wilmington support group for family members, the Delaware NAMI branch eventually spread statewide to include hundreds of volunteers such as Carlton Ziebell, many recruited from local faith communities. The secular organization's goal was to serve as advocates for the hospitalized mentally ill and to help facilitate their successful reentry into society after discharge from the Delaware Psychiatric Center in Newcastle, the state's sole public treatment facility.

"We started out at the grassroots level, discussing the issues around the kitchen table," Dick Patterson, a retired Dupont chemist recalls. "Then we talked to former patients about their experiences and needs, and moved on from there to consult professionals, both inside and outside the medical community and government."

Soon, the growing NAMI branch was meeting regularly in local churches and eventually established a permanent office. The group developed a program to educate family members of newly diagnosed patients. In turn, these families were able to help orient others who were experiencing the same confused anguish that often accompanies a diagnosis of mental illness in a loved one. One of the chapter's most useful accomplishments was developing the "warm line," a phone bank that volunteers staffed to provide comfort and support to nonhospitalized mentally ill people in emotional pain.

The NAMI program that Carlton Ziebell joined was the volunteer monitor team that paid frequent unscheduled visits to the Delaware Psychiatric Center. Modeled on the effort in Massachusetts, the team's goal was to remove the traditional barrier between the publicly funded treatment institution—most of the long-term patients were Medicaid recipients—and the citizens it served.

"We speak for those who cannot speak for themselves," Dick Patterson says of this NAMI advocacy.

The volunteers monitored both the facility's physical environment and treatment. Were the walls painted, the kitchens clean, the food wholesome and tasty? Did the dayroom television sets work, were there adequate books and magazines to read? Did patients receive therapy? Were they medicated at appropriate levels that brought emotional comfort without rendering them too lethargic? The teams arrived at the hospital unannounced, day and night, and discussed what they found with both staff and patients.

"Just knowing our program existed improved conditions," Carlton Ziebell observes.

Early in the monitor program, there were no curtains in the shower rooms.

"I guess the staff thought hospitalized men and women no longer had a sense of privacy," Patterson recalls.

Another problem the monitors found was that there were no housekeeping workers assigned on weekends, so dirty clothing or linen was not changed between Friday and Monday. And patients complained to the monitors that there were no personal visiting rooms to spend time with their families.

But when the volunteers brought these oversights to the attention of the hospital director, they were corrected.

However, the monitors encountered a far more serious problem when they visited the institution's geriatric building. Here they found scores of elderly residents who were not suffering from mental illnesses such as schizophrenia or clinical depression, but rather from Alzheimer's disease and other forms of dementia.

"There was no reason for them to be in a psychiatric institution," Carlton Ziebell says.

But treating Alzheimer's disease and dementia patients requires an expensive caregiver-to-patient ratio. And the Medicaid funding of their care at nursing homes did not cover its cost.

"So, in my opinion, when nursing homes found treating them was too costly," Carlton says, "they just dumped these helpless elderly at the hospital."

The Delaware Psychiatric Center did not have enough trained staff to meet the special needs of elderly Alzheimer's and dementia patients. "They were just being warehoused there," Carlton points out.

At the urging of the Delaware NAMI chapter, the Alzheimer's and dementia patients were eventually moved to a facility away from the psychiatric center, where they now receive more appropriate care.

This is an excellent example of the improvements in government healthcare programs that well-organized volunteers — many motivated by a religious sense of duty toward their neighbors — can help bring about. Medicaid was funding the Alzheimer's and dementia patients at the Delaware Psychiatric Center, but they needed better care. And the Delaware NAMI volunteers made sure they got it.

Today, there is a mutually respectful and efficient working relationship between the NAMI volunteers and the Delaware Psychiatric Center.

———

This might seem a relatively minor footnote in the looming nationwide healthcare crisis. But, in considering the success of the Delaware volunteers, we should recall the scenarios that UCLA gerontologist Dr. Edward L. Schneider projected concerning the adequacy of government-funded healthcare in coming decades. By 2030, many of the huge Baby Boom generation will be over 85. A number of these seniors will be what Schneider calls the "frail elderly," in failing health and suffering from multiple disabilities.

They will require greatly increased care in their homes and frequent treatment in acute-care hospitals. Schneider also predicts that the need for nursing homes will grow far beyond today's requirements and implicitly beyond the ability of Medicaid to fund them. If the overall health of the elderly does not improve from today's condition, he suggests, nursing homes will become "semi-acute hospitals with long waiting lists."

The elderly will still be entitled to some form of publicly funded healthcare, but those scarce dollars will have to be spent in the most efficient manner possible. The partnership between government and community will have to become closer. Groups such as the National Alliance for the Mentally Ill, made up almost entirely of volunteers, many acting from the inspiration of their religious faith, will become increasingly important.

———

What can local, state, and federal governments do today to encourage health-care systems to form such working partnerships with religious communities? The ongoing debate over public funding for religiously based social programs obscures the fact that government has traditionally provided some form of financial or material support to the charitable efforts of religious communities. These include the food Salvation Army volunteers distribute at disaster sites, Meals on Wheels delivered by church volunteers, and congregate meals prepared each weekday in tens of thousands of church and synagogue senior centers nationwide.

But more support and a closer government-faith community partnership will be needed as our population ages in coming decades. Before such initiatives reach their final form and exert a widespread effect at the level of the community and congregation, however, a number of key questions need to be answered. Will this effort pass muster before the Supreme Court or be rejected for violating the constitutional mandate on the separation of church and state? At the state level, what laws must be changed that presently act as impediments to such partnerships? For example, many congregations are reluctant to send volunteers into homes for fear of being sued in the event of an accident; these liability issues can pose a huge barrier to more effective community outreach.

Another issue is whether state or federal government should subsidize the salaries of parish nurses. This question will become urgent as Medicare costs inevitably rise and the co-payments for routine preventive care now covered in the program become too expensive for beneficiaries on low fixed incomes.

Should government support expanding pastoral care departments in hospitals? What kinds of partnerships could be developed between religious congregations and government in the publicly funded Medicaid sector?

These important questions preferably should be addressed sooner rather than later.

To understand these complex questions, we must briefly examine the recent history of the government-faith community relationship.

As part of welfare reform in 1996, the second Clinton administration launched a legislative initiative called Charitable Choice, designed to remove unnecessary barriers to faith-based organizations that provide social services from receiving specific federal funding available to secular groups offering similar services. The legislation prohibits states from discriminating against religious organizations when choosing community service providers eligible to receive these federal grants.

Then, in 1997, Housing and Urban Development Secretary Andrew Cuomo established the Center for Community and Interfaith Partnerships; a Jesuit priest led it. Former President Bill Clinton proposed allocating $20 million in the fiscal 1999 budget to encourage greater federal government-religious community cooperation. During the 2000 presidential campaign, Democratic candidate Vice President Al Gore backed a social-service partnership between government and the faith community.

George W. Bush campaigned on the even more ambitious promise of "compassionate conservatism." He proposed a multi-billion-dollar Faith-Based and Community Initiative, which included funding for selected social-service programs of religious charitable organizations.

The appeal of a government-faith community partnership is obvious. Recently, *Worth* magazine rated five religious charities among the country's most effective. The selection criteria involved philanthropies that spent more than $75 out of every $100 in donation income on services, as opposed to fundraising and other "administrative costs," such as salaries. The most efficient was America's Second Harvest, which spends $95 of every $100 providing food directly to needy families or to feeding programs, two-thirds of which are at religious institutions. The country's largest charity, Lutheran Services in America, averages 88 percent of its $7.6 billion annual income on services, a record matched by Catholic Charities, the fourth largest in terms of contributions. The Christian organization Volunteers of America spends $85 of every $100 in contributions serving those in need. The venerable Salvation Army spends 72 percent of its $1.9 billion annual income on services, but keeps a large reserve to meet disaster-relief needs. By any measure, these charities are more cost-effective than similar government operations.

But when the original initiative legislation stalled in Congress, the White House authorized the departments of Health and Human Services, Labor, Justice, Education, and Housing and Human Development to use their discretionary spending authority to advance the initiative.

These cabinet departments established new initiative "centers" that consider grant requests from religious institutions based on the same criteria used to weigh those of secular organizations, a process that Health and Human Service Secretary Tommy Thompson calls "leveling the playing field." Through these centers, the executive branch created programs that channel millions of dollars to faith-based communities working with the poor, the unemployed, and the elderly.

To assure the strict separation of church and state, funding passes through state or local "intermediary groups" that in turn make grants to churches and other faith communities. But even moving through this indirect channel, the grants are a highly efficient use of tax dollars. Labor Department funds, for instance, are spent on educational and job-skill counseling at faith-based centers that draw heavily on congregation volunteers, have a low operating overhead, and are not overly burdened by complex workplace regulations.

The one requirement community nonprofit groups must meet is to avoid proselytizing or mixing worship with the social service they deliver.

<hr />

This has not been difficult. As Jane Brown from Virginia's Department of Social Services recently told the *Washington Post*, her state will use its $1.28 million Labor Department grant to "strengthen the network" that already exists between faith-based organizations and government employment centers. Southern Virginia has been especially hard hit by layoffs as plants closed. The state's One-Stop Centers have facilitated unemployment compensation and other services for several years. Now, with the Faith-Based Initiative federal grant money, these centers have forged links with religious communities that provide volunteer mentors and advisers—including many older people—who help the unemployed seeking new skills or wishing to further their education.

On October 1, 2002, the U.S. Department of Health and Human Services released scores of grants totaling $25 million to intermediary organizations for distribution at the grassroots level. These included faith-based groups focused on the needs of our growing elderly population.

However the partnership between government and faith communities providing social services develops in coming years, such cooperation will be inevitable as our population ages and public funding must be stretched.

The cost effectiveness of such cooperation is undoubtedly its strongest selling point. Research, however, is needed to document that cost effectiveness.

<hr />

Florida is about ten years ahead of the rest of the country in terms of its proportion of elderly population, and has already actively begun to encourage state-faith community healthcare partnerships. Under the leadership of former Florida Secretary of Health Robert G. Brooks, M.D., the state expanded cooperation between government and volunteer health initiatives, many based in religious congregations. Brooks considers such cooperation essential to the most efficient and cost-effective use of both increasingly scarce state revenues and private sector healthcare funds.

"The success of this partnership has been its emphasis on disease prevention and health promotion," Dr. Brooks comments.

These efforts include programs to prevent adult-onset diabetes, cardiovascular disease, obesity, lead poisoning (a special risk to inner-city minority children), and HIV/AIDS, among many other health promotion activities.

He notes that federal, state, and local government resources combined will never be adequate to fund the country's more than one trillion-dollar annual healthcare expenses, which will only increase as the Baby Boom generation ages.

"We're going to have to draw on other resources," Brooks says.

And the vast potential of America's more than 350,000 religious congregations offers just such a resource. Dr. Brooks sees the faith community broadly, not only as individual congregations but also as whole denominations and religiously affiliated charitable and volunteer organizations such as the Salvation Army, Lutheran Services in America, Catholic Charities, and similar Jewish groups.

"One major benefit for governments," Brooks says, "is that they can leverage their budgets by working with these groups on social and healthcare programs of mutual interest."

He cites the case of the Florida Department of Health, whose budget is only 3 percent of the state's annual $17 billion healthcare expenditures.

"Using just a fraction of our budget to form partnerships with community nonprofit groups and faith-based organizations," he points out, "allowed us to reach more people at much less cost."

To government, the advantages of such cooperation are manifold:

- Community and faith-based volunteers are energetic, joyful, and dedicated.

- They work at the neighborhood level and are available around the clock, seven days a week.

- Since volunteers are members of the community, they have no problem gaining people's trust. This is particularly true among members of a faith community.

But Dr. Brooks cautions that there can also be disadvantages in these partnerships, which must be recognized and addressed:

- Because volunteers are not salaried employees, absenteeism is a potential problem. (Organization should always have stand-by volunteers available.)

- Volunteers usually lack specific skills (respite care for dementia clients, exact record-keeping procedures in health surveys, etc.) and must be trained.

■ Volunteer programs often do not have enough experienced managers; they, too, must be recruited or trained.

There are distinct advantages in these partnerships from the perspective of faith-based organizations, Brooks observes:

■ They fulfill their traditional mandate of service to others.

■ Community service and outreach to those in need builds respect for the religious institution.

■ As this need increases, faith communities will inevitably be called on to fill the gap, so those that begin early will be the most effective.

However, Brooks frankly admits that there can be disadvantages to the partnerships from the viewpoint of the faith community. These include:

■ Distrust of close cooperation with government agencies because of fear of "cultural contamination," in which an agency might attempt to secularize a religious institution. This problem can be avoided if groups within a congregation split off to form nonprofit organizations separate from the church, synagogue, or mosque.

■ "Mission creep" toward nonreligious social-service outreach, which dilutes a congregation's resources away from its core spiritual purpose.

But, from his experience, Dr. Brooks is confident that all of these disadvantages can be surmounted to the mutual benefit of government and faith-based community.

To help cement effective partnerships, government agencies should be prepared to assist faith-based institutions by training members in the skills of grant-request writing. Training volunteer managers is also an important contribution that government can provide.

And once a community or faith-based volunteer organization is prepared, Brooks says, the results of its efforts can be very impressive. He points to Shepherd's Hope, an Orlando volunteer group that provides free healthcare to the uninsured of all ages living on incomes of less than 150 percent of the federal poverty level. These people are mainly the working poor, who, like so many others, cannot afford food, rent, and health insurance. So they are forced to do without essential care, including testing for such chronic conditions as diabetes and cardiovascular disease. Again, if left untreated, these afflictions can prove very expensive for the Medicare system once the middle-aged working person reaches 65, and it is much better to prevent the illnesses from progressing.

Shepherd's Hope is a partnership of healthcare professionals, hospitals, schools, and the Orlando faith community. More than seven hundred physicians and hundreds more other healthcare professionals as well as lay volunteers donate their time to provide treatment to the working poor in the clinics of local schools. Many of the professionals and most of the volunteers come from faith-based communities.

In other volunteer programs established under a $500,000-state government start-up grant, more than eighteen thousand Florida healthcare professionals now offer healthcare to the uninsured poor.

One of the most important factors in the success of such programs was the passage in 1992 of the Florida Health Care Access Act, pioneering legislation that eliminated the threat of malpractice lawsuits to programs treating the working poor and indigent. Under the act, professionals cannot be sued while volunteering their services, except in cases of willful or wanton negligence. To date, no one has been sued.

Dr. Robert Brooks foresees the need for such efforts and legislation in every state. Government cannot carry the entire burden, he stresses: "I believe that the demographics of our aging society will require us to all work together to meet looming healthcare needs."

As noted earlier, about 33 percent of people over age 85 around the world currently suffer from Alzheimer's disease. In the United States, annual per-patient care in residential facilities is extremely expensive. And, as noted earlier, researchers estimate that there could be between 11 and 16 million Americans living with Alzheimer's in 2050. If all of them have to be cared for in nursing homes or other long-term assisted-living facilities, Alzheimer's costs could soar to $25 billion a year for direct professional care.

But if caregivers in the family receive adequate training and support by members of their religious congregations, homecare offers a less expensive and more compassionate alternative.

Because of its demographic makeup, Florida is among the states that Alzheimer's disease has hit the hardest. As in Delaware, Florida's private nursing homes have found that the cost of providing residential care to Alzheimer's patients usually exceeds Medicaid reimbursement. This has led to an intense effort to expand the system of effective, humane homecare.

In 1991, Elaine Maxwell's father, Charles "Chuck" Emerson, the former executive vice president of the Fort Lauderdale Chamber of Commerce, was diagnosed with an aggressive form of Alzheimer's at the age of 60. He was a tall, husky man who had spent thirty years as an officer in the National Guard and was looking forward to his retirement, when he and his wife planned to tour in a Winnebago recreational vehicle. But the disease destroyed those dreams. Elaine lives in Orlando and drove to Fort Lauderdale every weekend, and more often when she could get away, to relieve her mother's burden as caregiver. But after a few years, it became impossible to keep her father at home, and the family eventually made the wrenching decision to place him in a nursing home.

"I tried to visit him there as much as I could," Elaine says. "It was important for people from the family to come often, even if he did not recognize us, to show the staff how much we loved him."

During this difficult period, Elaine's religious faith supported her. She is not a regular churchgoer, but she has a deep personal spirituality, which sustained her. "Near the end," she says, "as painful as it was, I knew I would see Dad again."

Her father died in October 1999.

Elaine missed him terribly. She even missed the challenge of caring for him. After her father's death, she fell into depression. But four months later, in February 2000, she decided to put her eight years' experience as an Alzheimer's caregiver to use to help others. Elaine contacted the state Alzheimer's Disease Resource Center to inquire about becoming a volunteer caregiver. They put her in touch with Share the Care, a private Orlando nonprofit organization that assists central Florida families caring for aging loved ones with disabilities, including dementia.

For twenty years, Share the Care had been part of the Christian Service Center, a faith-based social-support organization. Today, Share the Care has incorporated as a separate nonprofit, but still maintains its volunteer base in the greater Orlando faith community. The organization has three adult day centers, open five days a week, where families can take their loved ones who suffer from dementia. At these centers, the clients receive personal care from both professionals and trained volunteers. Other neighborhood care centers, many located in churches, are open one day a week to provide respite for family members caring for their loved ones at home.

Share the Care also offers in-home respite, during which a trained volunteer companion spends time with the Alzheimer's or dementia client while the family caregiver is free to leave the home for shopping or other errands.

Crisis care is also available if a family caregiver has a medical or personal emergency but cannot leave the afflicted loved one alone. Similar respite is available through overnight care in assisted-living facilities, at which family members can place their loved ones several times a year in order to "take a break" from the grinding challenge they face.

In-home counseling is another service Share the Care provides. Because approximately 70 percent of family caregivers suffer some form of depression yet cannot leave their loved ones to seek psychological help, the organization provides trained counselors who come to the home.

Elaine Maxwell now works two mornings a week as a volunteer at a Share the Care adult day center in Lake Mary north of Orlando. She has been able to put her experience helping to care for her father to good use with her clients.

"Dad was always a good eater and enjoyed food far into his illness, even when he had lost interest in other things," she recalls.

So Elaine makes a point to bring the clients Danish pastry and fruit. She takes them on walks when the weather is nice and encourages them to absorb the beauty of flowerbeds and watch birds in flight. "It's important to keep people's minds as active as possible."

The volunteers play music and sing with their clients. One volunteer brought 78 rpm records of old *Hit Parade* songs that kindled a spark of memory in some of the clients. This spring, the volunteers at Elaine's center planted tomato seedlings with the clients. They will water the plants every day and watch them grow. This is a simple project, but it brings both clients and volunteers great satisfaction.

Today, Elaine regularly offers training sessions for new volunteers. Above all, Elaine tells them, it is direct personal interaction that holds the interest of people with dementia. The most successful home caregivers provide this type of interaction. But they burn out unless they have some respite. Providing that is the role of the volunteer.

Elaine also draws on her experience when speaking with family members. There may come a time at the end of the illness, she explains, when their loved ones will have to enter an institution. And, if they do, Elaine has practical advice. Decorate your loved one's room with displays of photographs, picnics, reunions, weddings, and vacations. These pictures will remind the nursing home staff that the patient has a loving family and is not just another burdensome case to be managed. Talk to the staff in a friendly manner, but make it clear that you expect them to treat your loved one with the same care they would extend their own mother or father.

In speaking to volunteers and to clients' families, Elaine also talks of the positive side of her experience at the Share the Care center. "It's very satisfying when you come into the room and these old people are so happy to see you that they smile and put out their arms," she says.

Elaine's experience is typical of Share the Care volunteers. Currently there are more than two hundred, most members of Orlando-area churches and synagogues. The award-winning program was one of the state's Alzheimer's Disease Initiative original grant recipients in 1986. Its first adult day center was a modular building on the grounds of a Methodist church. Currently the three adult day centers serve about a hundred clients daily. The neighborhood care centers provide respite care for scores of families. And in-home respite visits relieve the burden of many additional caregivers.

Today Share the Care has an annual budget of $1.3 million, which is funded from private fees, state and federal revenues, and foundation grants. Under Medicaid's home- and community-based waiver program, guardians of eligible clients can use these funds to pay for Share the Care services without placing their loved ones in nursing homes.

"Such flexible funding will become very important in the future," Mary Ellen Ort-Marvin, Share the Care's director, observes. "The current paradigm will have to shift away from institutions and back to the community because nursing homes are extremely expensive and cannot provide the same level of care as clients receive at home."

Indeed, Florida's annual per-person nursing home costs — borne by federal and state Medicaid revenues — now average $39,000, and can be much higher for dementia patients. But Share the Care can help guarantee quality homecare for a fraction of that cost by providing family caregivers with needed respite.

Partnerships of government and faith communities meeting the challenge of Alzheimer's disease are also expanding elsewhere in Florida. The Florida Department of Elder Affairs administers Support Through Alzheimer's Relief System (STARS), a faith-based initiative centered on churches in four northern, predominantly rural counties. This is a demonstration outreach project involving eighty-one volunteers from seven rural and small-town congregations, most made up of ethnic minorities and low-income families. The goal of the project, funded through a Faith-Based Initiative grant made by the Administration on Aging of the U.S. Department of Health and Human Services, is to identify and educate rural families about Alzheimer's disease. The volunteers have gone door-to-door gauging the extent of the illness in their communities, and to date have contacted 2,250 families providing care at home.

"So many of those families have kept very quiet about a loved one with Alzheimer's disease," remarks Dorothy Myles, who heads the STARS program.

"But because they trust a fellow church member, they'll open up to talk about the problems they are facing."

The basic message the volunteers carry is that the families are not alone. Once this contact is made, informal support groups spring up within the congregations. On two Sundays each month, the congregations include Alzheimer's-specific information in their church bulletins. STARS will use these church support groups as the sites at which Alzheimer's professionals can provide formal training, including instruction to volunteers offering respite care.

"The STARS volunteers often reach those families by walking down country roads," Dorothy Myles says. "They showed true love and dedication. That's the kind of compassion you can find in a faith community."

———

Josefina G. Carbonell, assistant secretary of the Department of Health and Human Services in charge of the Administration on Aging, lauds the work of STARS and says similar projects will become increasingly necessary in the future.

Noting the "huge demographic shifts" that will sweep through our population in coming decades, she says, "the demand for home-based care and respite services to assist and support caregivers will increase dramatically."

Assistant Secretary Carbonell states that the Administration on Aging is "committed to shifting the balance of care from institutional to home- and community-based services."

Without question, such services can be made more cost effective by tapping the resource of volunteers from religious congregations who have demonstrated their ability to work so efficiently.

———

One of the most successful private-public-congregational healthcare partnerships in recent years was the multi-year Wilson Health Ministry (WHM) project in Franklin County, a largely rural area of central Pennsylvania. Between 1998 and 2002, over seventy churches took part in a health education project that Wilson College, a Presbyterian women's institution, initiated and led. Under grants from Summit Endowment (an affiliate of Summit Health) and with the participation of the Pennsylvania Department of Health, WHM educators worked with parish nurses to host a wide variety of monthly seminars in churches. The seminars covered prostate and breast cancer, diabetes, diet and obesity, emotional health, and the mental and spiritual aspects of health. Selected church lay representatives learned how to take blood pressure readings, to be patient advocates at physical examinations of congregation members, and to promote physical fitness among parishioners. Some of this training took place at the Chambersburg Hospital, which was one of the healthcare institutions participating in the project.

A symposium attended by congregation members featured Dr. W. Dan Hale, professor of psychology and director of the Center for the Study of Aging and Health at Stetson University in Florida. He taught a brief workshop using his instructional manual, *Health Ministries for the 21st Century: Building Healthy Communities through Medical-Religious Partnerships.*

In the second year of the program, WHM helped establish congregational care teams—groups of members in each participating church dedicated to linking spiritual energy to improved health. Weight control and diabetes awareness and management emerged as key objectives of these care teams. Using Summit Endowment funds and support from the Pennsylvania Department of Health, a professional diabetes educator worked with the care teams. A total of thirty-six meetings with twelve focus groups for diabetes care teams took place in the 2000–2001 grant year. Care team members learned specific nutrition and exercise techniques. The diabetes educator and nutritionists taught cooking methods using low-fat, low-calorie ingredients. In February 2000, a number of congregations joined a cooking contest at which a wide variety of healthy recipes were presented. Out of this contest, a cookbook was prepared and distributed among the participating care teams.

Walking programs became the predominant method of exercise. Soon, walking competitions emerged with participants wearing pedometers that counted their daily steps. At King Street United Brethren Church, members joined two teams to compete for prizes that included a gift certificate to Foot Locker. Altogether the two teams walked a total of 4,473,195 steps or about 2,450 miles.

Among the participating churches, there was a notable increase in care team members regularly testing their blood sugar. An impressive 82 percent of the participants reported that they could better choose appropriate foods to control blood glucose levels. And, equally notable, 57 percent of the participants lost weight, with an average loss of sixteen pounds.

To quantify the results of this program, WHM and Summit Health helped track the Hemoglobin A1c (HbA1c)—the standard indicator of long-term diabetes control—of the care team participants. Among the ninety-eight participants tested, 64 percent had an HbA1c within a normal range at the end of the program.

Marilyn Ross, Ph.D., who helped implement the WHM program, stresses that its success is due in large part to the spiritually focused nature of the ministry. Participants trusted the healthcare professionals they met in their churches; a large proportion of these churches already had active parish nurses who endorsed and supported the care team effort. Prayer was a prominent feature of care team meetings.

"There's no doubt that the spiritual component played a large role in the impressive success of the Wilson Health Ministry," Dr. Ross comments.

———

Private foundations and individual philanthropists are increasingly essential in supporting the social work of religious communities. Foundation contributions include seed grants, sustaining funding, and grants for research that improves program efficacy.

This research helps determine the most effective way for healthcare systems to cooperate with religious communities. Pilot projects can be designed to study how to maximize client or patient satisfaction and minimize costs, while maintaining respect for a person's religious beliefs. Results from such research can be used by government and private groups to select programs likely to have the highest payoff for any given investment of increasingly scarce resources.

A number of large private philanthropic organizations support such research. They include: the Pew Charitable Trusts, which have funded both demonstration programs and research; the Anne E. Casey Foundation; the Lilly Foundation; and the Robert Wood Johnson Foundation.

The Retirement Research Foundation is America's largest private organization devoted expressly to meeting the needs of the elderly and enhancing their quality of life. Begun in 1978 by the late John D. MacArthur, one of the country's leading philanthropists, the foundation has invested more than $115 million to help develop networks of innovative and skilled individuals and institutions devoted to meeting the challenges of our burgeoning retired population. Currently, the foundation spends about $9 million annually to support programs that enable older adults to live at home or in residential settings that facilitate independent living, improve the quality of care in nursing homes, coordinate the insights and experience of older adults to promote community involvement, and increase understanding of the aging process and age-related illness.

Specific research that the foundation supports includes: performing studies to improve services and care for the elderly; educating local, state, and federal policymakers about the needs and capabilities of senior citizens; attracting trained and skilled professionals to the service of the elderly; expanding employment and volunteer opportunities for older people; and working directly with older Americans to identify and address their concerns.

The Retirement Research Foundation's goal is to assure that seniors remain vibrant, vital participants in society to the fullest extent possible.

The Brookdale Foundation is also an active and well-funded philanthropic organization devoted to community healthcare, especially to programs concerned with Alzheimer's disease. For the past fourteen years, the Brookdale Foundation's Group Respite Program has awarded start-up seed grants to organizations providing adult day services to thousands of persons with Alzheimer's disease and to their family caregivers. This effort has reached many inner-city and rural organizations that have often been isolated.

Nationwide in scope, many of the more than 250 Brookdale-initiated programs are associated in some manner with religious communities or charities. In fact, when the Orlando Share the Care program began under the Christian Service Center for Central Florida, it relied on a Brookdale grant for start-up funds. Every year, more Brookdale-funded respite organizations open, demonstrating that cost-effective adult day services can address the pressing needs of individuals and their family caregivers impacted by the devastation of Alzheimer's disease.

Brookdale respite programs are required to meet certain criteria. First, they must be dementia-specific, serving both the afflicted client and the family caregiver. They must provide structured group activities that include socialization and cognitive stimulation. The group size should range from about five to around fifteen. Professional staff must support trained aides and volunteers. The centers must be open at least one day a week, four hours per session, and keep regular hours. Each center must offer a secure, comfortable, and homelike environment. Counseling, education, and training programs must be made available for family caregivers. Brookdale-initiated respite centers have served as a focal point for community service providers to join together in meeting the needs of Alzheimer's families.

The Brookdale Foundation is committed to continuing its expansion of the Group Respite Program.

Among large faith-based community service organizations, the spiritually centered Volunteers of America provides technical assistance and workshops in many areas, including grant writing and program design and start-up.

———

The Robert Wood Johnson Foundation—the nation's largest philanthropy devoted exclusively to health and healthcare—endows the uniquely successful Faith in Action volunteer organization. Over one thousand local coalitions have received grants of up to $35,000 to organize Faith in Action volunteer programs that provide the chronically ill in their communities with many needed services. The coalitions can include as many as twenty congregations and several hundred volunteers who meet the needs of the elderly, children with chronic illnesses, the mentally ill, and AIDS patients. Most volunteers come from Christian, Jewish, Islamic, and other faith communities. But secular civic organizations such as Rotary clubs, schools, and youth groups also provide Faith in Action volunteers.

The effort began in 1983 as the Interfaith Volunteer Caregivers Program, which continued until 1993 when the Robert Wood Johnson Foundation introduced the much more ambitious Faith in Action project. Since then, the Foundation has funded more than eleven hundred local Faith in Action coalitions in every American state, the District of Columbia, Puerto Rico, and the Virgin Islands. At least 80 percent of these coalitions continue to operate. Because of this success, the foundation has dedicated $100 million to expand Faith in Action to three thousand sites by 2007. This ambitious undertaking easily makes Faith in Action the nation's largest faith-based volunteer effort.

Elderly people with chronic health conditions comprise the majority of clients that Faith in Action volunteers serve. Over 60 percent of Faith in Action clients are 65 years of age or older. More than 40 percent of these clients live independently. Faith in Action volunteers working with the elderly divide their time between friendly visiting, which relieves loneliness and provides a needed emotional lift; shopping, often with the elderly person, an "outing" that boosts the person's sense of autonomy and independence; and transportation to medical appointments and worship service. These contacts with volunteers ease the sense of isolation that can grip chronically ill elderly people living alone. Without question, the regular human interaction helps stave off depression, which all too often accompanies physical and emotional isolation.

Another essential service that Faith in Action volunteers provide is respite for the full-time family caregiver of a cognitively or physically disabled elderly loved one. Nationwide many of the volunteers in such programs as Share the Care and Shepherd's Centers are also members of Faith in Action coalitions.

But above all, the human contact between Faith in Action volunteers and the elderly is a warm, personal, and mutually beneficial exchange. Some of the programs transcend traditional generational barriers. In Greeley, Colorado, for example, young people from Weld Opportunity, an alternative high school for academically underachieving and disadvantaged students, have become Faith in Action volunteers and regularly visit local nursing homes. Rosanna Munoz and her fellow Weld students call on the elderly residents of Greeley Manor every few weeks. At first, the students were shy with the old people because many of the teenagers came from broken homes and had never known their grandparents. But soon the emotional gap was closed.

Mary Orleans, director of Catholic Charities Northern, a Faith in Action coalition agency, comments on the unexpected success. "It seems like we have found a fit," she says. "We brought these two groups together, and they both get something out of it."

Playing bingo is one of the simplest yet most satisfying activities the students and elderly residents share. For many older people in assisted living, a game of bingo is simply a meaningless time killer, akin to staring blankly at a television screen. But when two generations, their ages decades apart, form competitive teams, the game becomes exciting for everyone.

"It's really fun playing bingo with the seniors," Rosanna comments. She never played the game until she became a Faith in Action volunteer. "They get into bingo so much. When they win, they really get excited."

Rosanna's fellow student, Dave Gonzalez, enjoys leisurely conversations with the old people, which he finds both fascinating and informative. "They talk about all the things they've lived through," he says. From the perspective of a teenager, distant history such as the Great Depression and World War II comes alive in the voices and gestures of newfound older friends. The elderly people themselves take satisfaction in passing on the wisdom they have acquired under difficult circumstances. They are usually more patient than the teenagers' parents, more willing to listen and less judgmental.

"We look forward to seeing them," says Greeley Manor resident Caroline Schmidt. "We sure would miss them if they didn't come."

Are such volunteer intergenerational programs merely a superfluous tangent to the serious practice of geriatric medicine in an institutional setting? Definitely not. Clinical depression is a major threat among both nursing home residents and adolescents who lack meaningful purpose in their lives. Bringing these two groups together helps stave off the threat of depression for both.

One of the goals of the Faith in Action program is to keep chronically ill or disabled elderly people living independently as long as they can and as long as they choose to do so. Dr. Liliane Clement, a retired Arizona physician, 84, is typical of such older people living alone in their own homes. As a professional her entire adult life, she values her independence. But then Liliane began losing her eyesight and worried that both her independence and the quality of her life would be threatened. Reading several newspapers a day and several science fiction novels a week was her main interest. But, as her vision weakened, reading became impossible, and her future seemed bleak.

That was when Sally Elliott, 70, a Faith in Action volunteer from the Verde Valley Caregivers Coalition—consisting of eight congregations with over 220 volunteers who assist homebound adults—entered Liliane's life. Sally began to read to her new companion, first the newspaper, and then a chapter or two from books by Liliane's favorite science fiction authors. The reading sessions were soon accompanied by long conversations during which both women spoke of their lives. They became close friends.

Reflecting on her experience with Faith in Action and her friendship with Sally Elliott, Liliane Clement notes her initial reluctance to seek help. "I didn't want to ask in the beginning, and then I realized I couldn't be so proud."

When Sally took a trip to Asia, Liliane gave her a leather-bound journal in which to record her experiences each day. On her return, Sally read a day's journal entry to Liliane on each visit.

"It was so rejuvenating," Liliane recalls. "It was just like taking the trip myself."

Instead of being isolated within the dim confines of her failing vision, Dr. Liliane Clement has literally had her perspective widened through the eyes of her dear friend, Sally Elliott.

———

Personal outreach to the elderly in need is certainly not limited to Christian and Jewish volunteers. In metropolitan regions such as greater Washington, Atlanta, and New York, increasing numbers of young Muslims are joining volunteer programs. Islamic high school students in the New York boroughs of Bronx, Brooklyn, and Queens have been especially active at Muslim institutions for the elderly.

Leila, 17, whose family were immigrants from Syria, volunteers three afternoons a week at a Muslim day-care center for cognitively impaired seniors.

"I was a little scared at first," she says, "because the people seemed too *old*. But then I thought of my granny, who died last year, and I kind of realized that the ladies at the center are just like her. I really like going there now."

———

The cabinet-level Faith-Based and Community Initiative centers, Share the Care, STARS, the Brookdale Foundation, and Faith in Action all offer successful models for marshalling the energy of religiously motivated volunteers to help meet the growing healthcare needs of America's elderly population.

But, as we see in the next chapter, there are many additional practical programs and methods available to tap this wellspring of compassion.

Practical Steps for
Putting Faith into Action

11

As we have seen in this book, the programs of Shepherd's Centers of America are among the many religiously motivated services offering practical solutions to the mounting needs of our aging population. Other faith-based volunteer and community service organizations that have formed partnerships with local private and public healthcare systems are flourishing in every state. Churches, synagogues, and mosques are seeking ways to transform their congregations into more effective caring communities. And these congregations are increasingly aware of the upcoming healthcare crisis involving older adults within their communities. Through efforts such as Faith in Action and religious youth groups, faith communities are training their younger members to value older adults and motivate these young people to volunteer to help those in need. Healthcare professionals such as participants in Volunteers in Medicine are reaching out to those in need. Other professional healthcare volunteers in programs like Shepherd's Hope in Orlando and the Central Dallas Ministries have established practical interaction with religious communities to encourage care within the community itself, rather than in expensive institutional settings.

⊶――――⊷

These programs are examples of successful, practical partnerships between faith communities, philanthropic foundations, volunteer organizations, and local, state, and federal governments. But they are only a tiny fraction of the kinds of cooperative efforts that will be needed to meet the needs of our aging population in the years ahead.

How will the United States draw on the vast potential of these partnerships in coming years and multiple them by a hundredfold? Surveys indicate there are literally millions of would-be volunteers among America's diverse faith communities who haven't yet become involved in serving their communities. Further, many congregations have not reached their full potential in this area. Lack of concrete information—Who? What? Where? When?—about resources and opportunities is often the stumbling block between nebulous, unfulfilled desires to help others and thriving practical community organizations.

The news media represent the best means of spreading that information, either locally or at the national level.

Newspapers, television, and radio can also play a crucial role in educating people about the demographic and worsening healthcare economic trends we now face, which will soon escalate to a crisis level. This public education can emphasize the positive relationship between religious faith, spirituality, and health both among the young and the elderly, as well as the historical relationship between religion and healthcare. Without sounding alarmist, the news media can also stress the importance of government, religious organizations, and faith-based volunteer groups addressing problems now, rather than waiting until demographic and healthcare trends merge into disaster in coming decades.

G. William Nichols Jr., Ph.D., is a former Baptist minister and the founder of the nation's largest cable television channel on health, wellness, and disability, Kaleidoscope Television Network. He has extensive experience in all forms of media, including the Internet. As a Baptist theologian, he has published numerous books and articles on faith and spirituality.

"Bill" Nichols, as he prefers to be called, has acquired decades of knowledge transforming the spirituality and vision of faith communities into film and television productions that have been broadcast widely on commercial networks and on the U.S. Armed Forces Television Network. He understands the opportunities and challenges inherent in spreading a congregation's or faith-based program's message through the print or electronic media.

"The news media are the most powerful tool available to healthcare institutions and faith communities to bring about change and disseminate information about their work," Dr. Nichols says.

Conversely, he warns, any new social-outreach effort of a healthcare organization or faith community will fail unless it uses the news media carefully and effectively.

"Too many visions go no further than the eye of the visionary," Bill Nichols says.

New organizations seeking community support, or established institutions attempting to expand, "must become partners with the media if they truly wish to succeed."

Traditionally, however, both healthcare institutions (such as hospitals) and faith communities (such as individual congregations or denominations in a town or city) have kept a distance from the news media. This stems from institutional self-perceptions in which both healthcare and faith communities have seen themselves as separate from the purely secular (and commercial) news media.

But today, hospitals, clinics, and faith-based institutions with social-outreach programs, as well as local news media, all have a greater sense of connection to community. For example, every day in any average-sized "media market" in America, hospitals run skillfully produced commercial advertisements promoting their commitment to local people. Often hospitals highlight a particular aspect of healthcare, such as cardiac surgery, pediatrics, or obstetrics. Assisted-care facilities and nursing homes have also followed this example. In the competition for health consumers' dollars, this makes good business sense. Bill Nichols suggests that faith communities should also emulate this practice.

"The media are important because they have the power to produce 'mind share,'" he says.

By this he means news media can cause people to think about an issue or institution that they might normally ignore in the hectic pace of daily life. "In order to get noticed, you first must get your message out."

Another important aspect of media is that they deliver believability. People seek truth and understanding, but often distrust what they see or hear in the incessant blizzard of commercial hype that bombards us every day. Yet survey after survey has shown that a sixty-second news segment on television catches people's attention and causes them to *believe* what they see and hear. Research tells us that most Americans obtain their health information, in which by definition believability is a priority, from their local and network television news broadcasts. People trust this information even more than the advice they receive from their own doctors. This demonstrates the level of believability woven into the fabric of the news media.

Television and print news stories can also build a sense of community from disparate individuals. For example, the brief taped television news items on Rebuilding Together (Christmas in April) that appear on the evening news on the last Saturday of April every year in communities across the country have brought thousands of volunteers to the organization. What makes Rebuilding Together's efforts appealing to local television news producers is that the work is rich in both "visuals"—repair crews, ranging in age from 10 to 80, sawing boards, pounding nails, and installing donated windows, water heaters, and furnaces—and fresh interviews with volunteers and sincerely appreciative homeowners. The effectiveness of these short television segments is greatly enhanced when they carry a local telephone number or the Web address.

But in small communities that television crews don't normally cover, cultivating good relations with local news media pays dividends for Rebuilding Together. In 2003, on the front page of the April 30 edition of the weekly Queen Anne's County, Maryland, *Bay Times,* for example, staff writer Rose G. Spik's three-column story was headlined, "Despite Rain, Volunteers Repair Homes." Six color photographs showing volunteers wielding tools and beaming elderly homeowners accompanied the article. Dave Rausch from Safe Harbor Presbyterian Church was prominently featured installing new windows, doors, and rain gutters on the rural home of Mary McGee.

"Every year is just as amazing as the year before," Safe Harbor volunteer crew leader Rauch says in the article. "You have everyone from expert carpenters to people like me who just fix things around their own homes."

As Mrs. McGee, an elderly widow who lives alone, watched the energetic volunteers install handrails in the house to help her move about, she told the reporter, "I can't believe this. I can't imagine the energy of these people."

This is the kind of media attention that high powered public relations executives rightfully describe as priceless. It is safe to assume that the *Bay Times* article will be among the organization's most effective recruiting tools for next year's effort.

On a national scale, Habitat for Humanity receives equally effective public attention. Having celebrity volunteers such as former President Jimmy Carter and his wife Rosalyn is certain to attract the news media. But Habitat goes beyond using VIPs to capture media interest. The organization actively cooperates with television news producers and correspondents, newspaper editors, and reporters in every community in which it is active. When Habitat builds a home for the first time in a community, the organization rightfully treats the occasion as a newsworthy event, alerting local media contacts and keeping them informed on the progress of construction. Habitat prepares brief, quotable, "media-friendly" news releases and guides reporters to its well-organized interactive Web site.

Bill Nichols notes that such skillful coordination of multiple media resources —television, radio, newspaper, and Internet—represents one of the most essential future trends that healthcare and faith-based community social-service organizations must learn to employ if they are to succeed in fulfilling their vision.

Yet he also finds that too many well-intentioned social-service organizations —especially among faith-based groups—remain wary of the secular news media. These groups see the media as too expensive, too complex, and too threatening for practical access. But Nichols contends these are artificial obstacles. The media coverage that Rebuilding Together and Habitat for Humanity receive every year in the communities they serve costs nothing other than the efforts of volunteers to maintain their contacts in the media and to prepare releases and coordinate journalists' visits. Once relations are established with the news media, organizations find them cordial and straightforward, certainly not complex. And the news media are hardly threatening to volunteer organizations: In almost every television media market, there are three commercial network channels competing for the most relevant local stories. They are virtually hungry for the type of human-interest material volunteer organizations such as Shepherd's Centers of America, Faith in Action, and Habitat for Humanity can provide.

In order to meet the needs of the news media, nonprofit organizations must understand significant emerging trends.

First, there is a shift of focus from what Bill Nichols calls "control to convenience." By this, he means that traditionally healthcare and faith-based organizations have viewed the communities they serve from a position of control—in other words, "We have the truth (or the requisite skills). Come to us, we will help you." But Nichols says a new message is needed to cultivate the prevailing American mindset; it is a message of convenience: "We'll come to you. We're in your neighborhood." The best example of this shift to convenience can be found in the optometry industry, which has moved almost entirely from small independent practitioners to large franchise operations in shopping malls. The analog for nonprofit faith-based healthcare programs is the periodic health fair held at a house of worship or community center, a "one-stop" service at which people can receive a variety of free consultations and referrals to professional care.

Nichols also notes the shift from "isolation to connectivity." In this transformation, organizations no longer continue their traditional posture of authoritative separation (long the position of healthcare specialists and many religious congregations), but rather move toward community outreach. "We don't have all the answers, but we want to be your friend."

Nichols describes the shift from "maintenance to convergence" as moving from an organization mailing out the occasional news release to actively coordinating media campaigns that bring together print and electronic media and the Internet, which provides multiple Web site links to related organizations. This multimedia convergence is one of the most significant current trends.

In the shift from "brand loyalty to value loyalty," Nichols describes the trend of organizations moving away from their traditional static identity (a religious denomination or a charitable organization) to a more textured public image of the actual value they provide.

An organization shifting from "individuals to communities" entails providing the media with information on what they can offer the entire local community rather than simply standing as traditional separate entities with their distinct clientele or congregations. "People want to be connected to those around them," Nichols says. Once more, combining print and electronic media with the Internet promotes this connectivity.

When organizations work with the news media, Nichols recommends that they learn to communicate in a direct, straightforward manner. "They should move from complexity to simplicity." Healthcare and faith-based organizations' informational material has traditionally been wordy and laden with "in-house" jargon; they must move beyond this practice and write in concise, readily understood language if they wish to reach a wide audience through the media.

This approach works well with another current media trend: delivering broader information through true, "human-face" anecdotes. "It used to be you had nothing but celebrity spokespeople on television," Nichols says. "But now one brief, honest story from an average person carries more weight."

Bill Nichols recommends several practical methods for faith-based and non-profit social-outreach organizations to spread their messages more effectively:

- They should create strategic partnerships with businesses that are respected in the local community and have experience working with the news media. He cites the case of the San Antonio, Texas, Heart Association, which has partnered with Wal-Mart. The company, which has some of America's most effective media experts, has helped the Heart Association spread its health-education message in the community.

- Engage the audience: Do not try to reach the community as a faceless institution, but rather as a group of committed people who believe in their cause.

- Prioritize the message; think of it as a simple persuasive or selling tool, not as a complex piece of theology or healthcare research.

- Be honest and humble: Speak as a concerned neighbor, not as a technically or morally superior institution.

- Develop a simple media plan with clear goals. Then "work the plan."

- Put one person in charge of the media campaign, a person who can organize people and provide reporters with simple, honest stories and interview sources.

"These are practical steps that faith-based and healthcare organizations can follow with the news media for significant and far-reaching results," Nichols says.

Since the tragedy of 9/11, many of our leading news media have refocused their attention on religious faith and spirituality. Today, every large and medium-sized American newspaper has a full-time religion editor or reporter. Scores of religion editors and reporters belong to the Religion Newswriters Association (RNA), which is an excellent source of contact information for organizations that want to spread news of their work. The RNA's Web site is: www.religion-writers.com.

In the Frequently Asked Questions page of this Web site, veteran religion reporter Gayle White of the *Atlanta Journal-Constitution* responds thoughtfully on the subject, "Why should the secular media cover religion?"

"Often, religion provides the 'why' in the equation of a story," she says. "Faith motivates people, groups, and, at times, nations.... It also gives impetus to acts of heroism and massive humanitarian efforts.... Statistically, polls show that most Americans believe in a higher power, consider religion important and identify with a religious group. These same Americans make up the reading, viewing and listening audience."

On the RNA Web site, members also provide excellent practical information and guidance of interest to both aspiring religious journalists and faith-based organizations that wish to understand the news media better.

Here, for example, is some advice from Michael Paulson, religion editor of the *Boston Globe,* to would-be religious journalists:

"In my experience, editors are always hungry for good stories about any subject, and religion is no exception. To get more religion stories into the paper, apply the same rigorous reporting and writing standards you would apply to a story about politics or business; choose an interesting—and with luck, surprising or revealing—event or phenomenon, report it fully and fairly, and write it clearly, cleanly and brightly."

This suggestion from one of America's most respected religion editors presents a trove of information for faith-based social-service and healthcare organizations seeking better media coverage. Obviously, they need (as Bill Nichols emphasizes) to have an honest and interesting story to tell, one that will stand up to the rigorous scrutiny of a neutral reporter. In this regard, a clear and concise news release on an event of potential community interest represents merely a means of cutting through the welter of information that crosses a busy journalist's desk each day. There has to be more to satisfy a curious reporter—and his or her editor.

New York Times religious editor Laurie Goodstein recommends that her colleagues "Speak softly and carry a long letter opener." By this, she means that a responsible journalist specializing on spiritual matters should be familiar with as many religious publications as possible. It is from these specialized magazines, journals, and books—which cover information on charismatic Pentecostals, mainstream Protestants, Roman Catholics, Jews, Muslims, and Buddhists—that a reporter can reach out and find story leads.

This should suggest to a faith-based organization's resourceful media-campaign leader with an interesting story to tell that the best place for a story might initially be in a denominational publication that will be read by a national religion editor.

To promote excellence in religious reporting, the Religion Newswriters Association organizes an annual competition open to journalists working at small, medium, and large newspapers and electronic media outlets.

Many members of faith communities are surprised to learn the extent of interest on religious matters in the secular news media. But, as the *Boston Globe*'s Michael Paulson suggests, editors are always "hungry" for interesting material.

One of the best examples of this interest was the award-winning five-month series of articles the *Washington Post* ran in 1998, "Faith Stories: Moving from Uncertainty and Despair to Spiritual Fulfillment." These weekly articles profiled twenty-three people telling in their own moving words the stories of their spiritual journeys.

Among the profiles was the story of Kim Marie Lamberty, a well-educated Washington professional woman and a nominal Protestant who found herself slipping into depression after the failure of a personal relationship and disillusionment with her job. As she increasingly sought emotional and physical isolation from her friends, Kim Marie found sanctuary in the gardens of the Washington National Cathedral. Then, one day as she sat steeped in misery beside the fountain listening to the choir practice, she heard the silent voice of God: "I have always been here for you."

This epiphany led her to reach out to friends once again. Some were Roman Catholics who introduced her to that faith. Eventually, she attended a mass on Ash Wednesday. Then Kim Marie began receiving instruction on entering the faith. Today she is a devout Catholic.

When asked about the personal benefits her conversion has brought, she talks about Holy Communion. "When I take Communion with the countless other Catholics in the world, it gives me hope. The hope is that despite all our divisions, our violence, hatred, anger, injustice and poverty, that someday humanity will be one. This hope is what gets me through each week."

Reading Kim Marie Lamberty's story and those of the spiritual voyages of the others profiled in this series is testimony that the news media are among the most important resources available to faith communities in spreading their message.

It is for that reason that the John Templeton Foundation, named for philanthropist Sir John Templeton, offers an annual award for excellence in enterprising reporting and versatility in the field of religion in the secular press. Contestants submit one breaking news story, one feature story, one analysis piece or column, one profile, and one story of the writer's choice in any category. The past winners of these prestigious awards include America's leading religion journalists. Details on the Templeton Award are available by e-mail at: contests@religionwriters.com.

As we have seen, social-service systems can be linked with religious communities to provide less expensive, more satisfying healthcare to the elderly in their homes. The growing parish nurse program and volunteer ministries such as Faith in Action and Shepherd's Centers of America are excellent examples of this trend. Private and public secular healthcare systems are following this pattern in order to lower their costs and to reduce the need for people to enter acute-care or rehabilitation hospitals. (Hospitalization is the most expensive form of healthcare, accounting for about 70 percent of current costs.)

As we have discussed throughout this book, the innovative parish nurse program plays a key position in this linkage. Located within the church or synagogue, the faith-community nurse keeps in touch with the patient's hospital or doctor's office nurse or with the hospital chaplain to establish a link on the medical side, which insures compliance to clinical instructions (proper use of medications, etc.); on the religious side, the parish nurse communicates with the congregation leaders and the members, mobilizing lay volunteers to provide patient support, training these volunteers, conducting health screening, performing health education, and providing spiritual care to sick members and their families. In this way, the resources of the congregation (its healthy members, including the elderly) are put to work to help provide practical support for the sick, thereby greatly reducing the need for hospitalization.

With the parish nurse program growing rapidly nationwide, educational institutions have expanded their curricula to provide the specialized practical and academic training needed to meet this demand. Today, a number of healthcare organizations, universities, and healthcare schools offer degrees in parish nursing or health ministry. They include: Georgetown University in Washington, D.C.; Lutheran General Healthcare System in Chicago; the College of Mount St. Joseph in Cincinnati; Gardner-Webb University in Boiling Springs,

North Carolina; and numerous independent programs such as the Partnership in Parish Nursing in Baltimore.

Duke University in Durham, North Carolina, is one of several institutions offering a master's degree program in parish nursing. Duke's Divinity School and School of Nursing cosponsor the program. Keith G. Meador, M.D., Th.M., M.P.H., is the director of the Health and Ministries Program through which the degree is granted. Candidates can choose among four degree options:

- master in church ministries (mcm) health and nursing ministries track. This program is designed to prepare nurses to serve as healthcare ministers in local congregations.

- master of science in nursing (msn) health and nursing ministries major, a degree that prepares nurses as clinicians and coordinators of health and nursing ministries.

- the joint mcm and msn program. This curriculum is for students seeking a more thorough preparation in both advanced nursing practices and theological studies.

- post-master's certificate in health and nursing ministries. A program for nurses who already hold a master's degree, but who seek further education in the field of congregational-based health ministry.

"Nursing has always embodied an ethic of compassionate presence consistent with the long tradition in Christian ministry of caring for those who suffer," Dr. Meador says of the Duke program. "This joint effort between our Nursing and Divinity Schools makes possible both an intellectual and practical appropriation of the wisdom and practice of theology and medicine."

Degree candidate Karanne Campbell, RN, a veteran public health nurse with experience caring for terminally ill patients, is enthusiastic about the master's program. "This is the most exciting thing I've ever done in my life," she says.

✦━━━━━✦

The Duke program is a clear-cut example of the growing cooperation between the spiritual and the scientific, between theology and medicine.

Once more, such collaboration will become increasingly necessary as the relentless demographic pressure we face exerts an increasing strain on our already badly stressed healthcare system. Well-organized forces of compassion —parish nurses, faith-based organizations and community volunteers, and private healthcare institutions—will have to emerge and combine their resources to meet the needs of our inexorably swelling elderly population.

If this compassionate cooperation does not become a practical reality in coming decades, then there will be hard times ahead for all.

In such difficult times, people have long sought guidance in the wisdom of their elders. Without question, philanthropist Sir John Templeton, 91, is among our wisest and most experienced leaders in the realm of spirituality and its connection to the secular world. Born in rural Tennessee in 1912, Sir John graduated from Yale University and attended Oxford as a Rhodes scholar in the 1930s. During his uniquely successful investment career, he pioneered the development of value-based, globally diversified mutual funds, including the Templeton Growth Fund and the Templeton World Fund. Queen Elizabeth II knighted him in 1972 for his philanthropic efforts.

Sir John Templeton has spent much of his life investigating many aspects of spirituality, including the convergence between faith and science. Beyond the Templeton Foundation's awards to develop medical school curricula on spiritual education and awards to journalists covering religion, the Foundation endows major grants for research investigating the relationship between science and spirituality.

The annual Templeton Prize for Progress in Religion stemmed from Sir John's conviction that honors equivalent to the Nobel prizes should be awarded to innovators in religious thought and action. Mother Teresa of Calcutta received the first prize in 1973. Since then, a number of innovative leaders of all the world's major religions have been Templeton Prize laureates.

Sir John believes that Earth's civilizations are firmly grounded on faith. "We are indebted to our forefathers who recorded in books their spiritual discoveries and revelations," he says. "Alive today are other persons to whom God is revealing further holy truths."

Some of those people are ordained clergy. Some are healthcare professionals. Others are volunteers humbly serving their neighbors.

Speaking from the perspective of wisdom he has gained in his long study of the world's religions, Sir John Templeton addresses people in whom spirituality is the motivator to community service. "An attitude of gratitude creates blessings. Help yourself by helping others; you have the most powerful weapons on Earth — love and prayer."

In this book, we have examined what many consider the most serious challenge our society faces: the relentless demographic pressure that our aging population will exert on America's private and public healthcare system in coming decades. After 2011, more than 40 million members of the Baby Boom generation will be age 65. But that number will double in the subsequent twenty to thirty years. Healthcare costs will rise inexorably as this elderly population swells. As we have noted, Medicare expenditures will double from the 1999 budget of $213 billion per year to over $450 billion annually by 2011. During that period, America's total public and private healthcare will also more than double from $1.2 trillion to $2.8 trillion per year.

We have presented here the extremely grave nature of the problems our country will inevitably confront when demographic and economic realities collide. As tens of millions of Baby Boomers pass through middle age and become elderly in the next two decades, many private healthcare providers — including companies offering supplemental health and long-term care insurance, retirement and assisted-living communities, and nursing homes — will be driven out of business. Once flourishing health maintenance organizations (HMOs) will find increasingly limited Medicare reimbursement inadequate to meet the realities of the marketplace. The federal revenue outlay to provide some form of prescription drug benefits to scores of millions of Medicare recipients might well become an unsupportable burden on our national budget.

During these crucial coming decades, as UCLA gerontologist Edward Schneider has somberly warned, chronic afflictions among the elderly — cardiovascular disease, cancer, diabetes, kidney failure, and respiratory illness, to cite the most threatening — could menace the well-being of millions. These often disabling conditions might well put a crushing financial burden on our healthcare system — *unless* we as a people take concrete actions now to move toward disease prevention and health promotion, so that today's middle-aged people can make the transition to their elderly years in better health than their parents' generation.

But until recently, public policy planners have not considered one of the most promising resources available to meet the challenges our aging society present. The vast reserve of compassion, organizational skill, and community leadership currently present in our spiritual and religious institutions has the potential to meet many of our pressing healthcare needs.

Congregational programs such as wellness ministries and parish nurses stress health promotion and disease prevention nationwide. They have made dramatic progress in combating obesity and diabetes and in reducing smoking and risky sexual behavior in their communities. These efforts are rapidly expanding.

Flourishing volunteer housing efforts such as Habitat for Humanity and Rebuilding Together (Christmas in April) allow tens of thousands of low-income disabled and elderly people to live decent lives in their own homes—increasing their physical and emotional well-being and avoiding expensive care in residential facilities.

Shepherd's Centers of America and Faith in Action volunteers are invaluable in promoting this independent living through private/government/congregational partnerships such as Meals on Wheels, Friendly Callers, Caring Wheels, and Handy Hands. All these programs are also expanding each year.

Dedicated chaplains and lay liturgical volunteers play a crucial role in assuring the spiritual and emotional well-being of millions of elderly now residing in retirement homes and assisted-living facilities. It is essential that this work expand with our graying generations.

Religiously motivated charities appear to be among the most successful and cost-effective means of effecting beneficial social change.

Private philanthropies such as the Robert Wood Johnson Foundation, the Pew Charitable Trusts, the Anne E. Casey Foundation, the Retirement Research Foundation, the Brookdale Foundation, and the John Templeton Foundation have joined with religious institutions to meet community healthcare needs.

Beyond these encouraging trends and this inspiring progress, there is an equally hopeful pattern emerging. The long-skeptical medical community can no longer ignore the persuasive body of evidence linking religious faith and practice with good health.

Healthcare professionals, members of the clergy, public policymakers, and average private citizens have also gained a growing understanding of the traditional connection between faith and the healing arts, between religion and the caring community. The unnecessary—and recent—barrier between spirituality and medicine has begun to fall. Members of the healing professions have become progressively more inclined to accept the contributions to health and well-being that their colleagues in faith communities have made and will continue to make. Many medical schools, for example, now offer courses on the role of spirituality in healing.

Volunteers from faith communities are working in virtually all of our hospitals and assisted-living facilities. And countless thousands of independently living elderly people owe that independence to the dedication of spiritually motivated volunteers.

Are these current trends and efforts sufficient to meet the potentially overwhelming future healthcare challenges we face as a people? Although it is too early to say with certainty, there is reason for optimism.

And there remains tremendous opportunity for each of us to begin now to prepare for the challenges ahead—by becoming more active in health ministries in our local congregations; by training our children to respect, value, and care for older adults in our society (through the example we set); and by working in our neighborhoods, towns, and cities to build links between our hospitals or healthcare systems and our faith communities.

This is the time to act. This is the time to begin investing our energy, our talents, and our faith in the future. Be a person of vision to see the opportunity that exists today. Act now, or soon it may be too late.

Contact Information

THIS IS HOW you can contact some of the volunteer community and national social-service and healthcare organizations discussed in this book.

- **America's Second Harvest.** This group, which works closely with many faith-based communities to end hunger in this country — including hunger among low-income elderly — actively seeks corporate and community contributions and volunteers. For information, contact the group's interactive Web site: **www.secondharvest.org**.

- **Brookdale Foundation's National Group Respite Program.** For more information on services available to people with Alzheimer's disease, their families, and caregivers through the Brookdale Foundation's National Group Respite Program, contact: **www.brookdale foundation.org**.

- **Catholic Charities USA.** Information on the organization's many volunteer and community social-service programs is available at: **www.catholiccharitiesusa.org**, or by contacting Catholic Charities USA, 1731 King Street, Alexandria, VA 22314; Tel.: (703) 549-1390.

- **Central Dallas Ministries.** The large, active Central Dallas Ministries' healthcare program offers the same type of services as Shepherd's Hope of Greater Orlando. For information, contact: Central Dallas Ministries, P.O. Box 71085, Dallas, TX 75371-0385; Tel.: (214) 823-8710.

- **Experience Corps.** Retired people seeking compensated volunteer-type work as teachers' aides may wish to investigate this program. For more information, contact: **www.experiencecorps.org**, or Civic Ventures, 139 Townsend Street, Suite 505, San Francisco, CA 94107; Tel.: (415) 430-0141; e-mail: **info@civicventures.org**.

- **Faith in Action.** The national program of the Robert Wood Johnson Foundation that matches volunteers with disabled or chronically ill persons, many of them homebound elderly. Contact: Faith in Action

National Office, Wake Forest University School of Medicine, Medical Center Blvd., Winston-Salem, NC 27157-1204; call toll free (877) 324-8411; Internet: **www.fiavolunteers.org**.

■ **Habitat for Humanity International.** As we have seen, this volunteer house-building program has provided decent, affordable new homes for thousands of families. Many of the Habitat volunteers come from the program's covenant church affiliates. Contact: **www.habitat.org**.

■ **John Templeton Foundation.** For more information about the academic funding initiatives and awards, contact: **www.templeton.org**.

■ **Lutheran Services in America.** The group provides services for the elderly nationwide. For the organization's interactive Web site, contact: **www.lutheranservices.org**, or call (800) 664-3848.

■ **National Alliance for the Mentally Ill.** For information on the National Alliance for the Mentally Ill, contact: **www.nami.org**, or write NAMI, Colonial Place Three, 2107 Wilson Blvd., Suite 300, Arlington, VA 22201; Tel.: (703) 524-7600; HelpLine: (800) 950-NAMI (6264).

■ **Rebuilding Together (originally Christmas in April).** This national volunteer organization has 252 affiliates serving 955 communities. As discussed earlier, volunteers spend one or two days each April, working in teams drawn from religious congregations and secular groups, to rebuild and repair the homes of the disabled and elderly, as well as homeless shelters and kitchens serving those in need. Contact: **www.rebuildingtogether.org**.

■ **Retirement Research Foundation.** This organization supports research and programs aimed at meeting the social and healthcare needs of our expanding elderly population. Contact: **www.rrf.org**.

■ **Salvation Army.** The organization has a wide variety of interesting volunteer opportunities. For information, contact: **www.thesalvation army.org**.

■ **Shepherd's Centers of America.** Addresses and contact information for Shepherd's Centers of America's nationwide branches are available at their interactive Web site: **www.shepherdcenters.org**, or contact: Shepherd's Centers of America, One West Armour Blvd., Suite 201, Kansas City, MO 64111; Tel.: (816) 960-2022; call toll free (800) 547-7073.

■ **Shepherd's Hope of Greater Orlando, Florida.** Provides healthcare to low-income uninsured people, including people in their early sixties who do not qualify for either Medicaid or Medicare. For information, contact: **www.shepherdshope.org**, or call (407) 876-6699.

■ **U.S. Administration on Aging.** Their Web site provides a number of links to organizations serving the elderly and their families. Contact: **www.aoa.gov**. One of these links is the **Eldercare Locator**, which provides the names, addresses, and telephone numbers of hundreds of local organizations that offer services for seniors in need of homecare or to their caregivers needing respite care. Contact Eldercare Locator toll free, (800) 677-1116, Monday through Friday, 9:00 a.m. to 8:00 p.m. Eastern time, or on the Web at: **www.eldercare.gov**.

■ **Volunteer Match.** This national Internet clearinghouse has links to over 25,000 organizations and 32,000 volunteer opportunities. More than 1,140,000 volunteers have followed its advice: "Get out. Do good." Contact: **www.volunteermatch.org**.

■ **Volunteers in Medicine.** Contact information for the organization's nationwide affiliates is available on the interactive Web site: **www. vimi.org**, or write: Amy R. Hamlin, Executive Director, The Volunteers in Medicine Institute, P.O. Box 24126, Hilton Head, SC 29925-4126; e-mail: vimist@hargray.com; Tel.: (843) 342-5700.

■ **Volunteers of America.** For information on Volunteers of America's nationwide faith-based community outreach network, contact: **www.volunteersofamerica.org**. The organization is a designated intermediary organization connecting the federal government and community social-service nonprofit faith-based groups. For further information, contact: Paul McLendon, Director, Volunteers of America Southeast, Inc., 600 Azalea Road, Mobile, AL 36609; Tel.: (209) 666-4431, or (800) 859-4431, or e-mail: **paulm@voase.org**; or Michael Clemons, Coordinator, Volunteers of America Ohio River Valley, Inc., 1063 Central Avenue, Cincinnati, OH 45202; Tel.: (513) 381-1954.

Appendix B
References

The African American Church

Eng, E., and J. Hatch. "Networking Black Churches and Agencies." *Journal of Prevention in Health Services* (1991).

Foreman, C. H. *The African American Predicament.* Washington, D.C.: Brookings Institution Press, 1999.

Hatch, J., and S. Dethick. "Empowering Black Churches for Health Promotion." *Health Values* (1992): 16.

Hatch, J., N. Moss, and A. Saran. "Community Research: Partnership in Black Communities." *American Journal of Preventive Medicine* (1993): 9.

Rivers, L. E. *Laborers in the Vineyard of the Lord.* Gainesville: University Press of Florida, 2001.

Aging

Address, R., ed. *A Time to Prepare.* New York: UAHC Press, 2002.

———. *That You May Live Long: Caring for Our Aging Parents, Caring for Ourselves.* New York: UAHC Press, 2003.

Bass, S. A., ed. *Older and Active: How Americans over 55 Are Contributing to Society.* New Haven: Yale University Press, 1995.

Bass, S. A., F. G. Caro, and Y. P. Chen, eds. *Achieving a Productive Aging Society.* Westport, Conn.: Auburn House, 1993.

Bianchi, E. C. *Aging as a Spiritual Journey.* New York: Crossroads, 1982.

Clair, J. M., and R. M. Allman, eds. *The Gerontological Prism: Developing Interdisciplinary Bridges.* New York: Baywood Publishing, 2000.

Friedman, M. *Prime Time: How Baby Boomers Will Revolutionize Retirement and Transform America.* New York: Public Affairs, 1999.

Moody, H. R. *Ethics in an Aging Society.* Baltimore: Johns Hopkins University Press, 1992.

———. *The Five Stages of the Soul: Charting the Spiritual Passages That Shape Our Lives.* New York: Doubleday Anchor, 1997.

Nelson, M. E. *Strong Women Stay Young.* New York: Bantam, 1998.

"The Quest to Beat Aging." *Scientific American* (September 2000).

Rowe, J. W., and R. L. Kahn. "The Future of Aging." *Contemporary Long Term Care* (February 1999): 3, 6–44.

———. *Successful Aging.* New York: Pantheon, 1998.

CAREGIVING AND CAREGIVING COMMUNITIES

Address, R., et al. *Becoming a* Kehilat Chesed: *Creating and Sustaining a Caring Congregation.* New York: UAHC Press; 2002.

Bridges, B. J. *Therapeutic Caregiving: A Practical Guide for Persons with Alzheimer's Disease.* Mill Creek, Wash.: BJB Publishers, 1998.

Camp, M., and C. Willis. *You Can't Leave Till You Do the Paperwork.* Philadelphia: Xlibris Corp., 1999.

Carson, V. B., and H. G. Koenig. *Parish Nursing: Stories of Service and Care.* Philadelphia: Templeton Foundation Press, 2002.

Carson, V. B., and H. G. Koenig. *Spiritual Caregiving: Healthcare as a Ministry.* Philadelphia: Templeton Foundation Press, 2004.

Cassell, E. *The Nature of Suffering and the Goals of Medicine.* New York: Oxford University Press, 1991.

Evans, A. *The Healing Church.* Cleveland: United Church Press, 2000.

Frank, A. *At the Will of the Body.* Boston: Houghton Mifflin, 1991.

Haigler, D., K. Mims, and J. Nottingham. *Caring for You: Caring for Me.* Americus, Ga.: Rosalyn Carter Institute, 1998.

Mace, N., and P. Rabins. *The 36-Hour Day: A Family Guide to Caring for Persons with Alzheimer Disease, Related Dementing Illnesses, and Memory Loss in Later Life.* Rev. ed. New York: Warner Books, 2001.

McLeod, R. W. *Caregiving: The Spiritual Journal of Love, Loss and Renewal.* New York: John Wiley & Sons, 1999.

McMillan, D. W., and D. M. Chavis. "Sense of Community: A Definition and Theory." *Journal of Community Psychology* 14 (1986): 6–23.

Morse, J., et al. "Concepts of Caring and Caring as a Concept." *Advances in Nursing Science* 13 (1990): 1–14.

Smith, D. C. *Caregiving: Hospice—Proven Techniques for Healing Body and Soul.* New York: Macmillan, 1997.

Tolstoy, L. *The Death of Ivan Ilyich.* New York: New American Library, 1960.

Turner, R. J., and F. Marino. "Social Support and Social Structure: A Descriptive Epidemiology." *Journal of Health and Social Behavior* 35 (1994): 193–212.

Veatch, R. M. "The Place of Care in Ethical Theory." *Journal of Medicine and Philosophy* 23 (1998): 221–24.

Wethington, E., and R. C. Kessler. "Perceived Support, Received Support and Adjustment to Stressful Life Events." *Journal of Health and Social Behavior* 27 (1986): 78–89.

HABITAT FOR HUMANITY

Fuller, M. *A Simple, Decent Place to Live: The Building of Habitat for Humanity.* Dallas: Word, 1995.

———. *The Theology of the Hammer.* Macon, Ga.: Smyth & Helwys, 1994.

RELIGION AND SPIRITUALITY

Gentzler, R. H. *Designing an Older Adult Ministry.* Nashville: Discipleship Resources, 1999.

Koenig, H. G. *A Gospel for Mature Years.* New York: Haworth Press, 1997.

———. *The Healing Connection.* Rev. ed. Philadelphia: Templeton Foundation Press, 2004.

———. *The Healing Power of Faith.* New York: Simon & Schuster, 1999.

Koenig. H. G., M. McCullough, and D. B. Larson. *Handbook of Religion and Health.* New York: Oxford University Press, 2001.

Moody, H. R. *Five Stages of the Soul.* New York: Random House, 1998.

Templeton, J. *Worldwide Laws of Life.* Philadelphia: Templeton Foundation Press, 1997.

Wilson, J., and T. Janowski. "The Contribution of Religion to Volunteer Work." *Sociology of Religion* 56 (1995): 137–52.

VOLUNTEERISM

Arnish, D. "The Healing Power of Love." *Prevention Magazine* (February 1991).

Hurley, D. "Getting Health from Helping." *Psychology Today* (January 1988).

Koenig, H. G. *Purpose and Power in Retirement: New Opportunities for Meaning and Significance.* Philadelphia: Templeton Foundation Press, 2002.

Lawson, D. M. *Give to Live: How Giving Can Change Your Life.* La Jolla, Calif.: Alti Publishing, 1991.

———. *More Give to Live: How Giving Can Change Your Life.* Powey, Calif.: Alti Publishing, 1999.

———. *Volunteering: 101 Ways You Can Improve the World and Your Life.* Powey, Calif.: Alti Publishing, 1998.

Luks, A. *The Healing Power of Doing Good.* New York: Fawcett/Columbine, 1991.

Index